The Speeches of President Jimmy Carter

Contents

Chapter 1

Inaugural Address

1.1 Jimmy Carter's Inaugural Address

For myself and for our Nation, I want to thank my predecessor for all he has done to heal our land.

In this outward and physical ceremony we attest once again to the inner and spiritual strength of our Nation. As my high school teacher, Miss Julia Coleman, used to say: "We must adjust to changing times and still hold to unchanging principles."

Here before me is the Bible used in the inauguration of our first President, in 1789, and I have just taken the oath of office on the Bible my mother gave me a few years ago, opened to a timeless admonition from the ancient prophet Micah:

"He hath showed thee, O man, what is good; and what doth the Lord require of thee, but to do justly, and to love mercy, and to walk humbly with thy God."

This inauguration ceremony marks a new beginning, a new dedication within our Government, and a new spirit among us all. A President may sense and proclaim that new spirit, but only a people can provide it.

Two centuries ago our Nation's birth was a milestone in the long quest for freedom, but the bold and brilliant dream which excited the founders of this Nation still awaits its consummation. I have no new dream to set forth today, but rather urge a fresh faith in the old dream.

Ours was the first society openly to define itself in terms of both spirituality and of human liberty. It is that unique self-definition which has given us an exceptional appeal, but it also imposes on us a special obligation, to take on those moral duties which, when assumed, seem invariably to be in our own best interests.

You have given me a great responsibility – to stay close to you, to be worthy of you, and to exemplify what you are. Let us create together a new national spirit of unity and trust. Your strength can compensate for my weakness, and your wisdom can help to minimize my mistakes.

Let us learn together and laugh together and work together and pray together, confident that in the end we will triumph together in the right.

The American dream endures. We must once again have full faith in our country – and in one another. I believe America can be better. We can be even stronger than before.

Let our recent mistakes bring a resurgent commitment to the basic principles of our Nation, for we know that if we despise our own government we have no future. We recall in special times when we have stood briefly, but magnificently, united. In those times no prize was beyond our grasp.

But we cannot dwell upon remembered glory. We cannot afford to drift. We reject the prospect of failure or mediocrity or an inferior quality of life for any person. Our Government must at the same time be both competent and compassionate.

We have already found a high degree of personal liberty, and we are now struggling to enhance equality of opportunity. Our commitment to human rights must be absolute, our laws fair, our natural beauty preserved; the powerful must not persecute the weak, and human dignity must be enhanced.

We have learned that "more" is not necessarily "better," that even our great Nation has its recognized limits, and that we can neither answer all questions nor solve all problems. We cannot afford to do everything, nor can we afford to lack boldness as we meet the future. So, together, in a spirit of individual sacrifice for the common good, we must simply do our best.

Our Nation can be strong abroad only if it is strong at home. And we know that the best way to enhance freedom in other lands is to demonstrate here that our democratic system is worthy of emulation.

To be true to ourselves, we must be true to others. We will not behave in foreign places so as to violate our rules and standards here at home, for we know that the trust which our Nation earns is essential to our strength.

The world itself is now dominated by a new spirit. Peoples more numerous and more politically aware are craving and now demanding their place in the sun – not just for the benefit of their own physical condition, but for basic human rights.

The passion for freedom is on the rise. Tapping this new spirit, there can be no nobler nor more ambitious task for America to undertake on this day of a new beginning than to help shape a just and peaceful world that is truly humane.

We are a strong nation, and we will maintain strength so sufficient that it need not be proven in combat – a quiet strength based not merely on the size of an arsenal, but on the nobility of ideas.

We will be ever vigilant and never vulnerable, and we will fight our wars against poverty, ignorance, and injustice – for those are the enemies against which our forces can be honorably marshaled.

We are a purely idealistic Nation, but let no one confuse our idealism with weakness.

Because we are free we can never be indifferent to the fate of freedom elsewhere. Our moral sense dictates a clearcut preference for these societies which share with us an abiding respect for individual human rights. We do not seek to intimidate, but it is clear that a world which others can dominate with impunity would be inhospitable to decency and a threat to the well-being of all people.

The world is still engaged in a massive armaments race designed to ensure continuing equivalent strength among potential adversaries. We pledge perseverance and wisdom in our efforts to limit the world's armaments to those necessary for each nation's own domestic safety. And we will move this year a step toward ultimate goal—the elimination of all nuclear weapons from this Earth. We urge all other people to join us, for success can mean life instead of death.

Within us, the people of the United States, there is evident a serious and purposeful rekindling of confidence. And I join in the hope that when my time as your President has ended, people might say this about our Nation:

That we had remembered the words of Micah and renewed our search for humility, mercy, and justice; that we had torn down the barriers that separated those of different race and region and religion, and where there had been mistrust, built unity, with a respect for diversity; that we had found productive work for those able to perform it; that we had strengthened the American family, which is the basis of our society; that we had ensured respect for the law, and equal treatment under the law, for the weak and the powerful, for the rich and the poor; and that we had enabled our people to be proud of their own Government once again.

I would hope that the nations of the world might say that we had built a lasting peace, built not on weapons of war but on international policies which reflect our own most precious values.

These are not just my goal, and they will not be my accomplishments, but the affirmation of our Nation's continuing moral strength and our belief in an undiminished, ever-expanding American dream.

Chapter 2

State of the Union Addresses

2.1 Jimmy Carter's First State of the Union Address

Two years ago today we had the first caucus in Iowa, and one year ago tomorrow, I walked from here to the White House to take up the duties of President of the United States. I didn't know it then when I walked, but I've been trying to save energy ever since.

I return tonight to fulfill one of those duties of the Constitution: to give to the Congress, and to the Nation, information on the state of the Union.

Militarily, politically, economically, and in spirit, the state of our Union is sound.

We are a great country, a strong country, a vital and dynamic country, and so we will remain.

We are a confident people and a hardworking people, a decent and a compassionate people, and so we will remain.

I want to speak to you tonight about where we are and where we must go, about what we have done and what we must do. And I want to pledge to you my best efforts and ask you to pledge yours.

Each generation of Americans has to face circumstances not of its own choosing, but by which its character is measured and its spirit is tested.

There are times of emergency, when a nation and its leaders must bring their energies to bear on a single urgent task. That was the duty Abraham Lincoln faced when our land was torn apart by conflict in the War Between the States. That was the duty faced by Franklin Roosevelt when he led America out of an economic depression and again when he led America to victory in war.

There are other times when there is no single overwhelming crisis, yet profound national interests are at stake.

At such times the risk of inaction can be equally great. It becomes the task of leaders to call forth the vast and restless energies of our people to build for the future.

That is what Harry Truman did in the years after the Second World War, when we helped Europe and Japan rebuild themselves and secured an international order that has protected freedom from aggression.

We live in such times now, and we face such duties.

We've come through a long period of turmoil and doubt, but we've once again found our moral course, and with a new spirit, we are striving to express our best instincts to the rest of the world.

There is all across our land a growing sense of peace and a sense of common purpose. This sense of unity cannot be expressed in programs or in legislation or in dollars. It's an achievement that belongs to every individual American. This unity ties together, and it towers over all our efforts here in Washington, and it serves as an inspiring beacon for all of us who are elected to serve.

This new atmosphere demands a new spirit, a partnership between those of us who lead and those who elect. The foundations of this partnership are truth, the courage to face hard decisions, concern for one another and the common good over special interests, and a basic faith and trust in the wisdom and strength and judgment of the American people.

For the first time in a generation, we are not haunted by a major international crisis or by domestic turmoil, and we now have a rare and a priceless opportunity to address persistent problems and burdens which come to us as a nation, quietly and steadily getting worse over the years.

As President, I've had to ask you, the Members of Congress, and you, the American people, to come to grips with some of the most difficult and hard questions facing our society.

We must make a maximum effort, because if we do not aim for the best, we are very likely to achieve little. I see no benefit to the country if we delay, because the problems will only get worse.

We need patience and good will, but we really need to realize that there is a limit to the role and the function of government. Government cannot solve our problems, it can't set our goals, it cannot define our vision. Government cannot eliminate poverty or provide a bountiful economy or reduce inflation or save our cities or cure illiteracy or provide energy. And government cannot mandate goodness. Only a true partnership between government and the people can ever hope to reach these goals.

Those of us who govern can sometimes inspire, and we can identify needs and marshal resources, but we simply cannot be the managers of everything and everybody.

We here in Washington must move away from crisis management, and we must establish clear goals for the future, immediate and the distant future, which will let us work together and not in conflict. Never again should we neglect a growing crisis like the shortage of energy, where further delay will only lead to more harsh and painful solutions.

Every day we spend more than $120 million for foreign oil. This slows our economic growth, it lowers the value of the dollar overseas, and it aggravates unemployment and inflation here at home.

Now we know what we must do, increase production. We must cut down on waste. And we must use more of those fuels which are plentiful and more permanent. We must be fair to people, and we must not disrupt our Nation's economy and our budget.

Now, that sounds simple. But I recognize the difficulties involved. I know that it is not easy for the Congress to act. But the fact remains that on the energy legislation, we have failed the American people. Almost 5 years after the oil embargo dramatized the problem for us all, we still do not have a national energy program. Not much longer can we tolerate this stalemate. It undermines our national interest both at home and abroad. We must succeed, and I believe we will.

Our main task at home this year, with energy a central element, is the Nation's economy. We must continue the recovery and further cut unemployment and inflation.

Last year was a good one for the United States. We reached all of our major economic goals for 1977. Four million new jobs were created, an alltime record, and the number of unemployed dropped by more than a million. Unemployment right now is the lowest it has been since 1974, and not since World War II has such a high percentage of American people been employed.

The rate of inflation went down. There was a good growth in business profits and investments, the source of more jobs for our workers, and a higher standard of living for all our people. After taxes and inflation, there was a healthy increase in workers' wages.

And this year, our country will have the first $2 trillion economy in the history of the world.

Now, we are proud of this progress the first year, but we must do even better in the future.

We still have serious problems on which all of us must work together. Our trade deficit is too large. Inflation is still too high, and too many Americans still do not have a job.

Now, I didn't have any simple answers for all these problems. But we have developed an economic policy that is working, because it's simple, balanced, and fair. It's based on four principles: First, the economy must keep on expanding to produce new jobs and better income, which our people need. The fruits of growth must be widely shared. More jobs must be made available to those who have been bypassed until now. And the tax system must be made fairer and simpler.

Secondly, private business and not the Government must lead the expansion in the future.

Third, we must lower the rate of inflation and keep it down. Inflation slows down economic growth, and it's the most cruel to the poor and also to the elderly and others who live on fixed incomes.

And fourth, we must contribute to the strength of the world economy.

I will announce detailed proposals for improving our tax system later this week. We can make our tax laws fairer, we can make them simpler and easier to understand, and at the same time, we can, and we will, reduce the tax burden on American citizens by $25 billion.

The tax reforms and the tax reductions go together. Only with the long overdue reforms will the full tax cut be advisable.

Almost $17 billion in income tax cuts will go to individuals. Ninety-six percent of all American taxpayers will see their taxes go down. For a typical family of four, this means an annual saving of more than $250 a year, or a tax reduction of about 20 percent. A further $2 billion cut in excise taxes will give more relief and also contribute directly to lowering the rate of inflation.

And we will also provide strong additional incentives for business investment and growth through substantial cuts in the corporate tax rates and improvement in the investment tax credit.

Now, these tax proposals will increase opportunity everywhere in the Nation. But additional jobs for the disadvantaged deserve special attention.

We've already passed laws to assure equal access to the voting booth and to restaurants and to schools, to housing, and laws to permit access to jobs. But job opportunity, the chance to earn a decent living, is also a basic human right, which we cannot and will not ignore.

A major priority for our Nation is the final elimination of the barriers that restrict the opportunities available to women and also to black people and Hispanics and other minorities. We've come a long way toward that goal. But there is still much to do. What we inherited from the past must not be permitted to shackle us in the future.

I'll be asking you for a substantial increase in funds for public jobs for our young people, and I also am recommending that the Congress continue the public service employment programs at more than twice the level of a year ago. When welfare reform is completed, we will have more than a million additional jobs so that those on welfare who are able to work can work.

However, again, we know that in our free society, private business is still the best source of new jobs. Therefore, I will propose a new program to encourage businesses to hire young and disadvantaged Americans. These young people only need skills and a chance in order to take their place in our economic system. Let's give them the chance they need. A major step in the right direction would be the early passage of a greatly improved Humphrey-Hawkins bill.

My budget for 1979 addresses these national needs, but it is lean and tight. I have cut waste wherever possible.

I am proposing an increase of less than 2 percent after adjusting for inflation, the smallest increase in the Federal budget in 4 years.

Lately, Federal spending has taken a steadily increasing portion of what Americans produce. Our new budget reverses that trend, and later I hope to bring the Government's toll down even further. And with your help, we'll do that.

In time of high employment and a strong economy, deficit spending should not be a feature of our budget. As the economy continues to gain strength and as our unemployment rates continue to fall, revenues will grow. With careful planning, efficient management, and proper restraint on spending, we can move rapidly toward a balanced budget, and we will.

Next year the budget deficit will be only slightly less than this year. But one-third of the deficit is due to the necessary tax cuts that I've proposed. This year the right choice is to reduce the burden on taxpayers and provide more jobs for our people.

The third element in our program is a renewed attack on inflation. We've learned the hard way that high unemployment will not prevent or cure inflation. Government can help us by stimulating private investment and by maintaining a responsible economic policy. Through a new top-level review process, we will do a better job of reducing Government regulation that drives up costs and drives up prices.

But again, Government alone cannot bring down the rate of inflation. When a level of high inflation is expected to continue, then companies raise prices to protect their profit margins against prospective increases in wages and other costs, while workers demand higher wages as protection against expected price increases. It's like an escalation in the arms race, and understandably, no one wants to disarm alone.

Now, no one firm or a group of workers can halt this process. It's an effort that we must all make together. I'm therefore asking government, business, labor, and other groups to join in a voluntary program to moderate inflation by holding wage and price increases in each sector of the economy during 1978 below the average increases of the last 2 years.

I do not believe in wage and price controls. A sincere commitment to voluntary constraint provides a way, perhaps the only way, to fight inflation without Government interference.

As I came into the Capitol tonight, I saw the farmers, my fellow farmers, standing out in the snow. I'm familiar with their problem, and I know from Congress' action that you are too. When I was running Carters Warehouse, we had spread on our own farms 5-10-15 fertilizer for about $40 a ton. The last time I was home, the price was about $100 a ton. The cost of nitrogen has gone up 150 percent, and the price of products that farmers sell has either stayed the same or gone down a little.

Now, this past year in 1977, you, the Congress, and I together passed a new agricultural act. It went into effect October 1. It'll have its first impact on the 1978 crops. It will help a great deal. It'll add $6 1/2 billion or more to help the farmers with their price supports and target prices.

Last year we had the highest level of exports of farm products in the history of our country, $24 billion. We expect to have more this year. We'll be working together. But I think it's incumbent on us to monitor very carefully the farm situation and continue to work harmoniously with the farmers of our country. What's best for the farmers, the farm families, in the long run is also best for the consumers of our country.

Economic success at home is also the key to success in our international economic policy. An effective energy program, strong investment and productivity, and controlled inflation will provide [improve] our trade balance and balance it, and it will help to protect the integrity of the dollar overseas.

By working closely with our friends abroad, we can promote the economic health of the whole world, with fair and balanced agreements lowering the barriers to trade.

Despite the inevitable pressures that build up when the world economy suffers from high unemployment, we must firmly resist the demands for self-defeating protectionism. But free trade must also be fair trade. And I am determined to protect American industry and American workers against foreign trade practices which are unfair or illegal.

In a separate written message to Congress, I've outlined other domestic initiatives, such as welfare reform, consumer protection, basic education skills, urban policy, reform of our labor laws, and national health care later on this year. I will not repeat these tonight. But there are several other points that I would like to make directly to you.

During these past years, Americans have seen our Government grow far from us.

For some citizens, the Government has almost become like a foreign country, so strange and distant that we've often had to deal with it through trained ambassadors who have sometimes become too powerful and too influential, lawyers, accountants, and lobbyists. This cannot go on.

We must have what Abraham Lincoln wanted, a government for the people.

We've made progress toward that kind of government. You've given me the authority I requested to reorganize the Federal bureaucracy. And I am using that authority.

We've already begun a series of reorganization plans which will be completed over a period of 3 years. We have also proposed abolishing almost 500 Federal advisory and other commissions and boards. But I know that the American people are still sick and tired of Federal paperwork and redtape. Bit by bit we are chopping down the thicket of unnecessary Federal regulations by which Government too often interferes in our personal lives and our personal business. We've cut the public's Federal paperwork load by more than 12 percent in less than a year. And we are not through cutting.

We've made a good start on turning the gobbledygook of Federal regulations into plain English that people can understand. But we know that we still have a long way to go.

We've brought together parts of 11 Government agencies to create a new Department of Energy. And now it's time to take another major step by creating a separate Department of Education.

But even the best organized Government will only be as effective as the people who carry out its policies. For this reason, I consider civil service reform to be absolutely vital. Worked out with the civil servants themselves, this reorganization plan will restore the merit principle to a system which has grown into a bureaucratic maze. It will provide greater management flexibility and better rewards for better performance without compromising job security.

Then and only then can we have a government that is efficient, open, and truly worthy of our people's understanding and respect. I have promised that we will have such a government, and I intend to keep that promise.

In our foreign policy, the separation of people from government has been in the past a source of weakness and error. In a democratic system like ours, foreign policy decisions must be able to stand the test of public examination and public debate. If we make a mistake in this administration, it will be on the side of frankness and openness with the American people.

In our modern world, when the deaths of literally millions of people can result from a few terrifying seconds of destruction, the path of national strength and security is identical to the path of peace.

Tonight, I am happy to report that because we are strong, our Nation is at peace with the world.

We are a confident nation. We've restored a moral basis for our foreign policy. The very heart of our identity as a nation is our firm commitment to human rights.

We stand for human rights because we believe that government has as a purpose to promote the well-being of its citizens. This is true in our domestic policy; it's also true in our foreign policy. The world must know that in support of human rights, the United States will stand firm.

We expect no quick or easy results, but there has been significant movement toward greater freedom and humanity in several parts of the world.

Thousands of political prisoners have been freed. The leaders of the world, even our ideological adversaries, now see that their attitude toward fundamental human rights affects their standing in the international community, and it affects their relations with the United States.

To serve the interests of every American, our foreign policy has three major goals.

The first and prime concern is and will remain the security of our country.

Security is based on our national will, and security is based on the strength of our Armed Forces. We have the will, and militarily we are very strong.

Security also comes through the strength of our alliances. We have reconfirmed our commitment to the defense of Europe, and this year we will demonstrate that commitment by further modernizing and strengthening our military capabilities there.

Security can also be enhanced by agreements with potential adversaries which reduce the threat of nuclear disaster while maintaining our own relative strategic capability.

In areas of peaceful competition with the Soviet Union, we will continue to more than hold our own.

At the same time, we are negotiating with quiet confidence, without haste, with careful determination, to ease the tensions between us and to ensure greater stability and security.

The strategic arms limitation talks have been long and difficult. We want a mutual limit on both the quality and the quantity of the giant nuclear arsenals of both nations, and then we want actual reductions in strategic arms as a major step toward the ultimate elimination of nuclear weapons from the face of the Earth.

If these talks result in an agreement this year, and I trust they will, I pledge to you that the agreement will maintain and enhance the stability of the world's strategic balance and the security of the United States.

For 30 years, concerted but unsuccessful efforts have been made to ban the testing of atomic explosives, both military weapons and peaceful nuclear devices.

We are hard at work with Great Britain and the Soviet Union on an agreement which will stop testing and will protect our national security and provide for adequate verification of compliance. We are now making, I believe, good progress toward this comprehensive ban on nuclear explosions.

We are also working vigorously to halt the proliferation of nuclear weapons among the nations of the world which do not now have them and to reduce the deadly global traffic in conventional arms sales. Our stand for peace is suspect if we are also the principal arms merchant of the world. So, we've decided to cut down our arms transfers abroad on a year-by-year basis and to work with other major arms exporters to encourage their similar constraint.

Every American has a stake in our second major goal, a world at peace. In a nuclear age, each of us is threatened when peace is not secured everywhere. We are trying to promote harmony in those parts of the world where major differences exist among other nations and threaten international peace.

In the Middle East, we are contributing our good offices to maintain the momentum of the current negotiations and to keep open the lines of communication among the Middle Eastern leaders. The whole world has a great stake in the success of these efforts. This is a precious opportunity for a historic settlement of a longstanding conflict, an opportunity which may never come again in our lifetime.

Our role has been difficult and sometimes thankless and controversial. But it has been constructive and it has been necessary, and it will continue.

Our third major foreign policy goal is one that touches the life of every American citizen every day, world economic growth and stability.

This requires strong economic performance by the industrialized democracies like ourselves and progress in resolving the global energy crisis. Last fall, with the help of others, we succeeded in our vigorous efforts to maintain the stability of the price of oil. But as many foreign leaders have emphasized to me personally and, I am sure, to you, the greatest future contribution that America can make to the world economy would be an effective energy conservation program here at home. We will not hesitate to take the actions needed to protect the integrity of the American dollar.

We are trying to develop a more just international system. And in this spirit, we are supporting the struggle for human development in Africa, in Asia, and in Latin America.

Finally, the world is watching to see how we act on one of our most important and controversial items of business, approval of the Panama Canal treaties. The treaties now before the Senate are the result of the work of four administrations, two Democratic, two Republican.

They guarantee that the canal will be open always for unrestricted use by the ships of the world. Our ships have the right to go to the head of the line for priority of passage in times of emergency or need. We retain the permanent right to defend the canal with our own military forces, if necessary, to guarantee its openness and its neutrality.

The treaties are to the clear advantage of ourselves, the Panamanians, and the other users of the canal. Ratifying the Panama Canal treaties will demonstrate our good faith to the world, discourage the spread of hostile ideologies in this hemisphere, and directly contribute to the economic well-being and the security of the United States.

I have to say that that's very welcome applause.

There were two moments on my recent journey which, for me, confirmed the final aims of our foreign policy and what it always must be.

One was in a little village in India, where I met a people as passionately attached to their rights and liberties as we are, but whose children have a far smaller chance for good health or food or education or human fulfillment than a child born in this country.

The other moment was in Warsaw, capital of a nation twice devastated by war in this century. There, people have rebuilt the city which war's destruction took from them. But what was new only emphasized clearly what was lost.

What I saw in those two places crystalized for me the purposes of our own Nation's policy: to ensure economic justice, to advance human rights, to resolve conflicts without violence, and to proclaim in our great democracy our constant faith in the liberty and dignity of human beings everywhere.

We Americans have a great deal of work to do together. In the end, how well we do that work will depend on the spirit in which we approach it. We must seek fresh answers, unhindered by the stale prescriptions of the past.

It has been said that our best years are behind us. But I say again that America's best is still ahead. We have emerged from bitter experiences chastened but proud, confident once again, ready to face challenges once again, and united once again.

We come together tonight at a solemn time. Last week the Senate lost a good and honest man, Lee Metcalf of Montana.

And today, the flag of the United States flew at half-mast from this Capitol and from American installations and ships all over the world, in mourning for Senator Hubert Humphrey.

Because he exemplified so well the joy and the zest of living, his death reminds us not so much of our own mortality, but of the possibilities offered to us by life. He always looked to the future with a special American kind of confidence, of hope and enthusiasm. And the best way that we can honor him is by following his example.

Our task, to use the words of Senator Humphrey, is "reconciliation, rebuilding, and rebirth."

Reconciliation of private needs and interests into a higher purpose.

Rebuilding the old dreams of justice and liberty, and country and community.

Rebirth of our faith in the common good.

Each of us here tonight, and all who are listening in your homes, must rededicate ourselves to serving the common good. We are a community, a beloved community, all of us. Our individual fates are linked, our futures intertwined. And if we act in that knowledge and in that spirit, together, as the Bible says, we can move mountains.

Thank you very much.

2.2 Jimmy Carter's Second State of the Union Address

Mr. President, Mr. Speaker, Members of the 96th Congress, and my fellow citizens:

Tonight I want to examine in a broad sense the state of our American Union-how we are building a new foundation for a peaceful and a prosperous world.

Our children who will be born this year will come of age in the 21st century. What kind of society, what kind of world are we building for them? Will we ourselves be at peace? Will our children enjoy a better quality of life? Will a strong and united America still be a force for freedom and prosperity around the world?

Tonight, there is every sign that the state of our Union is sound.

Our economy offers greater prosperity for more of our people than ever before. Real per capita income and real business profits have risen substantially in the last 2 years. Farm exports are setting an all-time record each year, and farm income last year, net farm income, was up more than 25 percent.

Our liberties are secure. Our military defenses are strong and growing stronger. And more importantly, tonight, America-our beloved country—is at peace.

Our earliest national commitments, modified and reshaped by succeeding generations, have served us well. But the problems that we face today are different from those that confronted earlier generations of Americans. They are more subtle, more complex, and more interrelated. At home, we are recognizing ever more clearly that government alone cannot solve these problems. And abroad, few of them can be solved by the United States alone. But Americans as a united people, working with our allies and friends, have never been afraid to face problems and to solve problems, either here or abroad.

The challenge to us is to build a new and firmer foundation for the future—for a sound economy, for a more effective government, for more political trust, and for a stable peace—so that the America our children inherit will be even stronger and even better than it is today.

We cannot resort to simplistic or extreme solutions which substitute myths for common sense.

In our economy, it is a myth that we must choose endlessly between inflation and recession. Together, we build the foundation for a strong economy, with lower inflation, without contriving either a recession with its high unemployment or unworkable, mandatory government controls.

In our government, it is a myth that we must choose between compassion and competence. Together, we build the foundation for a government that works—and works for people.

In our relations with our potential adversaries, it is a myth that we must choose between confrontation and capitulation. Together, we build the foundation for a stable world of both diversity and peace.

Together, we've already begun to build the foundation for confidence in our economic system. During the last 2 years, in bringing our economy out of the deepest recession since the 1930's, we've created 7,100,000 new jobs. The unemployment rate has gone down 25 percent. And now we must redouble our fight against the persistent inflation that has wracked our country for more than a decade. That's our important domestic issue, and we must do it together.

We know that inflation is a burden for all Americans, but it's a disaster for the poor, the sick, and the old. No American family should be forced to choose among food, warmth, health care, or decent housing because the cost of any of these basic necessities has climbed out of reach.

Three months ago, I outlined to the Nation a balanced anti-inflation program that couples responsible government restraint with responsible wage and price restraint. It's based upon my knowledge that there is a more powerful force than government compulsion—the force created by the cooperative efforts of millions of Americans working toward a common goal.

Business and labor have been increasingly supportive. It's imperative that we in government do our part. We must stop excessive government growth, and we must control government spending habits.

I've sent to this Congress a stringent but a fair budget, one that, since I ran for President in 1976, will have cut the Federal deficit in half. And as a percentage of our gross national product, the deficit will have dropped by almost 75 percent.

This Congress had a good record last year, and I now ask the 96th Congress to continue this partnership in holding the line on excess Federal spending. It will not be easy. But we must be strong, and we must be persistent.

This budget is a clear message that, with the help of you and the American people, I am determined, as President, to bring inflation under control.

The 1980 budget provides enough spending restraint to begin unwinding inflation, but enough support for our country to keep American workers productive and to encourage the investments that provide new jobs. We will continue to mobilize our Nation's resources to reduce our trade deficit substantially this year and to maintain the strength of the American dollar.

We've demonstrated in this restrained budget that we can build on the gains of the past 2 years to provide additional support to educate disadvantaged children, to care for the elderly, to provide nutrition and legal services for the poor, and to strengthen the economic base of our urban communities and, also, our rural areas.

This year, we will take our first steps to develop a national health plan.

We must never accept a permanent group of unemployed Americans, with no hope and no stake in building our society. For those left out of the economy because of discrimination, a lack of skills, or poverty, we must maintain high levels of training, and we must continue to provide jobs.

A responsible budget is not our only weapon to control inflation. We must act now to protect all Americans from health care costs that are rising $1 million per hour, 24 hours a day, doubling every 5 years. We must take control of the largest contributor to that inflation—skyrocketing hospital costs.

There will be no clearer test of the commitment of this Congress to the anti-inflation fight than the legislation that I will submit again this year to hold down inflation in hospital care.

Over the next 5 years, my proposals will save Americans a total of $60 billion, of which $25 billion will be savings to the American taxpayer in the Federal budget itself. The American people have waited long enough. This year we must act on hospital cost containment.

We must also fight inflation by improvements and better enforcement of our antitrust laws and by reducing government obstacles to competition in the private sector.

We must begin to scrutinize the overall effect of regulation in our economy. Through deregulation of the airline industry we've increased profits, cut prices for all Americans, and begun—for one of the few times in the history of our Nation-to actually dismantle a major Federal bureaucracy. This year, we must begin the effort to reform our regulatory processes for the railroad, bus, and the trucking industries.

America has the greatest economic system in the world. Let's reduce government interference and give it a chance to work.

I call on Congress to take other anti-inflation action—to expand our exports to protect American jobs threatened by unfair trade, to conserve energy, to increase production and to speed development of solar power, and to reassess our Nation's technological superiority. American workers who enlist in the fight against inflation deserve not just our gratitude, but they deserve the protection of the real wage insurance proposal that I have already made to the Congress.

To be successful, we must change our attitudes as well as our policies. We cannot afford to live beyond our means. We cannot afford to create programs that we can neither manage nor finance, or to waste our natural resources, and we cannot tolerate mismanagement and fraud. Above all, we must meet the challenges of inflation as a united people.

With the support of the American people, government in recent decades has helped to dismantle racial barriers, has provided assistance for the jobless and the retired, has fed the hungry, has protected the safety, health, and bargaining rights of American workers, and has helped to preserve our natural heritage.

But it's not enough to have created a lot of government programs. Now we must make the good programs more effective and improve or weed out those which are wasteful or unnecessary.

With the support of the Congress, we've begun to reorganize and to get control of the bureaucracy. We are reforming the civil service system, so that we can recognize and reward those who do a good job and correct or remove those who do not.

This year, we must extend major reorganization efforts to education, to economic development, and to the management of our natural resources. We need to enact a sunshine [sunset] law that when government programs have outlived their value, they will automatically be terminated.

There's no such thing as an effective and a noncontroversial reorganization and reform. But we know that honest, effective government is essential to restore public faith in our public action.

None of us can be satisfied when twothirds of the American citizens chose not to vote last year in a national election. Too many Americans feel powerless against the influence of private lobbying groups and the unbelievable flood of private campaign money which threatens our electoral process.

This year, we must regain the public's faith by requiring limited financial funds from public funds for congressional election campaigns. House bill 1 provides for this public financing of campaigns. And I look forward with a great deal of anticipation to signing it at an early date.

A strong economy and an effective government will restore confidence in America. But the path of the future must be charted in peace. We must continue to build a new and a firm foundation for a stable world community.

We are building that new foundation from a position of national strength—the strength of our own defenses, the strength of our friendships with other nations, and of our oldest American ideals.

America's military power is a major force for security and stability in the world. We must maintain our strategic capability and continue the progress of the last 2 years with our NATO Allies, with whom we have increased our readiness, modernized our equipment, and strengthened our defense forces in Europe. I urge you to support the strong defense budget which I have proposed to the Congress.

But our national security in this complicated age requires more than just military might. In less than a lifetime, world population has more than doubled, colonial empires have disappeared, and a hundred new nations have been born. Mass communications, literacy, and migration to the world's cities have all awakened new yearnings for economic justice and human rights among people everywhere.

This demand for justice and human rights is a wave of the future. In such a world, the choice is not which super power will dominate the world. None can and none will. The choice instead is between a world of anarchy and destruction, or a world of cooperation and peace.

In such a world, we seek not to stifle inevitable change, but to influence its course in helpful and constructive ways that enhance our values, our national interests, and the cause of peace.

Towering over this volatile, changing world, like a thundercloud on a summer day, looms the awesome power of nuclear weapons.

We will continue to help shape the forces of change, to anticipate emerging problems of nuclear proliferation and conventional arms sales, and to use our great strength and influence to settle international conflicts in other parts of the world before they erupt and spread.

We have no desire to be the world's policeman. But America does want to be the world's peacemaker.

We are building the foundation for truly global cooperation, not only with Western and industrialized nations but with the developing countries as well. Our ties with Japan and our European allies are stronger than ever, and so are our friendly relations with the people of Latin America, Africa, and the Western Pacific and Asia.

We've won new respect in this hemisphere with the Panama Canal treaties. We've gained new trust with the developing world through our opposition to racism, our commitment to human rights, and our support for majority rule in Africa.

The multilateral trade negotiations are now reaching a successful conclusion, and congressional approval is essential to the economic well-being of our own country and of the world. This will be one of our top priorities in 1979.

We are entering a hopeful era in our relations with one-fourth of the world's people who live in China. The presence of Vice Premier Deng Xiaoping next week will help to inaugurate that new era. And with prompt congressional action on authorizing legislation, we will continue our commitment to a prosperous, peaceful, and secure life for the people of Taiwan.

I'm grateful that in the past year, as in the year before, no American has died in combat anywhere in the world. And in Iran, Nicaragua, Cyprus, Namibia, and Rhodesia, our country is working for peaceful solutions to dangerous conflicts.

In the Middle East, under the most difficult circumstances, we have sought to help ancient enemies lay aside deep-seated differences that have produced four bitter wars in our lifetime.

Our firm commitment to Israel's survival and security is rooted in our deepest convictions and in our knowledge of the strategic importance to our own Nation of a stable Middle East. To promote peace and reconciliation in the region, we must retain the trust and the confidence both of Israel and also of the Arab nations that are sincerely searching for peace.

I am determined, as President, to use the full, beneficial influence of our country so that the precious opportunity for lasting peace between Israel and Egypt will not be lost. The new foundation of international cooperation that we seek excludes no nation. Cooperation with the Soviet Union serves the cause of peace, for in this nuclear age, world peace must include peace between the super powers—and it must mean the control of nuclear arms.

Ten years ago, the United States and the Soviet Union made the historic decision to open the strategic arms limitations talks, or SALT. The purpose of SALT, then as now, is not to gain a unilateral advantage for either nation, but to protect the security of both nations, to reverse the costly and dangerous momentum of the nuclear arms race, to preserve a stable balance of nuclear forces, and to demonstrate to a concerned world that we are determined to help preserve the peace.

The first SALT agreement was concluded in 1972. And since then, during 6 years of negotiation by both Republican and Democratic leaders, nearly all issues of SALT II have been resolved. If the Soviet Union continues to negotiate in good faith, a responsible SALT agreement will be reached.

It's important that the American people understand the nature of the SALT process.

SALT II is not based on sentiment; it's based on self-interest—of the United States and of the Soviet Union. Both nations share a powerful common interest in reducing the threat of a nuclear war. I will sign no agreement which does not enhance our national security.

SALT II does not rely on trust; it will be verifiable. We have very sophisticated, proven means, including our satellites, to determine for ourselves whether or not the Soviet Union is meeting its treaty obligations. I will sign no agreement which cannot he verified.

The American nuclear deterrent will remain strong after SALT II. For example, just one of our relatively invulnerable Poseidon submarines—comprising less than 2 percent of our total nuclear force of submarines, aircraft, and landbased missiles—carries enough warheads to destroy every large- and medium-sized city in the Soviet Union. Our deterrent is overwhelming, and I will sign no agreement unless our deterrent force will remain overwhelming.

A SALT agreement, of course, cannot substitute for wise diplomacy or a strong defense, nor will it end the danger of nuclear war. But it will certainly reduce that danger. It will strengthen our efforts to ban nuclear tests and to stop the spread of atomic weapons to other nations. And it can begin the process of negotiating new agreements which will further limit nuclear arms.

The path of arms control, backed by a strong defense—the path our Nation and every President has walked for 30 years-can lead to a world of law and of international negotiation and consultation in which all peoples might live in peace. In this year 1979, nothing is more important than that the Congress and the people of the United States resolve to continue with me on that path of nuclear arms control and world peace. This is paramount.

I've outlined some of the changes that have transformed the world and which are continuing as we meet here tonight. But we in America need not fear change. The values on which our Nation was founded—individual liberty, self-determination, the potential for human fulfillment in freedom—all of these endure. We find these democratic principles praised, even in books smuggled out of totalitarian nations and on wallposters in lands which we thought were closed to our influence. Our country has regained its special place of leadership in the worldwide struggle for human rights. And that is a commitment that we must keep at home, as well as abroad.

The civil rights revolution freed all Americans, black and white, but its full promise still remains unrealized. I will continue to work with all my strength for equal opportunity for all Americans-and for affirmative action for those who carry the extra burden of past denial of equal opportunity.

We remain committed to improving our labor laws to better protect the rights of American workers. And our Nation must make it clear that the legal rights of women as citizens are guaranteed under the laws of our land by ratifying the equal rights amendment.

As long as I'm President, at home and around the world America's examples and America's influence will be marshaled to advance the cause of human rights.

To establish those values, two centuries ago a bold generation of Americans risked their property, their position, and life itself. We are their heirs, and they are sending us a message across the centuries. The words they made so vivid are now growing faintly indistinct, because they are not heard often enough. They are words like "justice," "equality," "unity," "truth," "sacrifice," "liberty," "faith," and "love."

These words remind us that the duty of our generation of Americans is to renew our Nation's faith—not focused just against foreign threats but against the threats of selfishness, cynicism, and apathy.

The new foundation I've discussed tonight can help us build a nation and a world where every child is nurtured and can look to the future with hope, where the resources now wasted on war can be turned towards meeting human needs, where all people have enough to eat, a decent home, and protection against disease.

It can help us build a nation and a world where all people are free to seek the truth and to add to human understanding, so that all of us may live our lives in peace.

Tonight, I ask you, the Members of the Congress, to join me in building that new foundation—a better foundation-for our beloved country and our world.

Thank you very much.

2.3   Jimmy Carter's Third State of the Union Address

This last few months has not been an easy time for any of us. As we meet tonight, it has never been more clear that the state of our Union depends on the state of the world. And tonight, as throughout our own generation, freedom and peace in the world depend on the state of our Union.

The 1980's have been born in turmoil, strife, and change. This is a time of challenge to our interests and our values and it's a time that tests our wisdom and our skills.

At this time in Iran, 50 Americans are still held captive, innocent victims of terrorism and anarchy. Also at this moment, massive Soviet troops are attempting to subjugate the fiercely independent and deeply religious people of Afghanistan. These two acts—one of international terrorism and one of military aggression—present a serious challenge to the United States of America and indeed to all the nations of the world. Together, we will meet these threats to peace.

I'm determined that the United States will remain the strongest of all nations, but our power will never be used to initiate a threat to the security of any nation or to the rights of any human being. We seek to be and to remain secure—a nation at peace in a stable world. But to be secure we must face the world as it is.

Three basic developments have helped to shape our challenges: the steady growth and increased projection of Soviet military power beyond its own borders; the overwhelming dependence of the Western democracies on oil supplies from the Middle East; and the press of social and religious and economic and political change in the many nations of the developing world, exemplified by the revolution in Iran.

Each of these factors is important in its own right. Each interacts with the others. All must be faced together, squarely and courageously. We will face these challenges, and we will meet them with the best that is in us. And we will not fail.

In response to the abhorrent act in Iran, our Nation has never been aroused and unified so greatly in peacetime. Our position is clear. The United States will not yield to blackmail.

We continue to pursue these specific goals: first, to protect the present and long-range interests of the United States; secondly, to preserve the lives of the American hostages and to secure, as quickly as possible, their safe release, if possible, to avoid bloodshed which might further endanger the lives of our fellow citizens; to enlist the help of other nations in condemning this act of violence, which is shocking and violates the moral and the legal standards of a civilized world; and also to convince and to persuade the Iranian leaders that the real danger to their nation lies in the north, in the Soviet Union and from the Soviet troops now in Afghanistan, and that the unwarranted Iranian quarrel with the United States hampers their response to this far greater danger to them.

If the American hostages are harmed, a severe price will be paid. We will never rest until every one of the American hostages are released.

But now we face a broader and more fundamental challenge in this region because of the recent military action of the Soviet Union.

Now, as during the last 3 1/2 decades, the relationship between our country, the United States of America, and the Soviet Union is the most critical factor in determining whether the world will live at peace or be engulfed in global conflict.

Since the end of the Second World War, America has led other nations in meeting the challenge of mounting Soviet power. This has not been a simple or a static relationship. Between us there has been cooperation, there has been competition, and at times there has been confrontation.

In the 1940's we took the lead in creating the Atlantic Alliance in response to the Soviet Union's suppression and then consolidation of its East European empire and the resulting threat of the Warsaw Pact to Western Europe.

In the 1950's we helped to contain further Soviet challenges in Korea and in the Middle East, and we rearmed to assure the continuation of that containment.

In the 1960's we met the Soviet challenges in Berlin, and we faced the Cuban missile crisis. And we sought to engage the Soviet Union in the important task of moving beyond the cold war and away from confrontation.

And in the 1970's three American Presidents negotiated with the Soviet leaders in attempts to halt the growth of the nuclear arms race. We sought to establish rules of behavior that would reduce the risks of conflict, and we searched for areas of cooperation that could make our relations reciprocal and productive, not only for the sake of our two nations but for the security and peace of the entire world.

In all these actions, we have maintained two commitments: to be ready to meet any challenge by Soviet military power, and to develop ways to resolve disputes and to keep the peace.

Preventing nuclear war is the foremost responsibility of the two superpowers. That's why we've negotiated the strategic arms limitation treaties—SALT I and SALT II. Especially now, in a time of great tension, observing the mutual constraints imposed by the terms of these treaties will be in the best interest of both countries and will help to preserve world peace. I will consult very closely with the Congress on this matter as we strive to control nuclear weapons. That effort to control nuclear weapons will not be abandoned.

We superpowers also have the responsibility to exercise restraint in the use of our great military force. The integrity and the independence of weaker nations must not be threatened. They must know that in our presence they are secure.

But now the Soviet Union has taken a radical and an aggressive new step. It's using its great military power against a relatively defenseless nation. The implications of the Soviet invasion of Afghanistan could pose the most serious threat to the peace since the Second World War.

The vast majority of nations on Earth have condemned this latest Soviet attempt to extend its colonial domination of others and have demanded the immediate withdrawal of Soviet troops. The Moslem world is especially and justifiably outraged by this aggression against an Islamic people. No action of a world power has ever been so quickly and so overwhelmingly condemned. But verbal condemnation is not enough. The Soviet Union must pay a concrete price for their aggression.

While this invasion continues, we and the other nations of the world cannot conduct business as usual with the Soviet Union. That's why the United States has imposed stiff economic penalties on the Soviet Union. I will not issue any permits for Soviet ships to fish in the coastal waters of the United States. I've cut Soviet access to high-technology equipment and to agricultural products. I've limited other commerce with the Soviet Union, and I've asked our allies and friends to join with us in restraining their own trade with the Soviets and not to replace our own embargoed items. And I have notified the Olympic Committee that with Soviet invading forces in Afghanistan, neither the American people nor I will support sending an Olympic team to Moscow.

The Soviet Union is going to have to answer some basic questions: Will it help promote a more stable international environment in which its own legitimate, peaceful concerns can be pursued? Or will it continue to expand its military power far beyond its genuine security needs, and use that power for colonial conquest? The Soviet Union must realize that its decision to use military force in Afghanistan will be costly to every political and economic relationship it values.

The region which is now threatened by Soviet troops in Afghanistan is of great strategic importance: It contains more than two-thirds of the world's exportable oil. The Soviet effort to dominate Afghanistan has brought Soviet military forces to within 300 miles of the Indian Ocean and close to the Straits of Hormuz, a waterway through which most of the world's oil must flow. The Soviet Union is now attempting to consolidate a strategic position, therefore, that poses a grave threat to the free movement of Middle East oil.

This situation demands careful thought, steady nerves, and resolute action, not only for this year but for many years to come. It demands collective efforts to meet this new threat to security in the Persian Gulf and in Southwest Asia. It demands the participation of all those who rely on oil from the Middle East and who are concerned with global peace and stability. And it demands consultation and close cooperation with countries in the area which might be threatened.

Meeting this challenge will take national will, diplomatic and political wisdom, economic sacrifice, and, of course, military capability. We must call on the best that is in us to preserve the security of this crucial region.

Let our position be absolutely clear: An attempt by any outside force to gain control of the Persian Gulf region will be regarded as an assault on the vital interests of the United States of America, and such an assault will be repelled by any means necessary, including military force.

During the past 3 years, you have joined with me to improve our own security and the prospects for peace, not only in the vital oil-producing area of the Persian Gulf region but around the world. We've increased annually our real commitment for defense, and we will sustain this increase of effort throughout the Five Year Defense Program. It's imperative that Congress approve this strong defense budget for 1981, encompassing a 5-percent real growth in authorizations, without any reduction.

We are also improving our capability to deploy U.S. military forces rapidly to distant areas. We've helped to strengthen NATO and our other alliances, and recently we and other NATO members have decided to develop and to deploy modernized, intermediate-range nuclear forces to meet an unwarranted and increased threat from the nuclear weapons of the Soviet Union.

We are working with our allies to prevent conflict in the Middle East. The peace treaty between Egypt and Israel is a notable achievement which represents a strategic asset for America and which also enhances prospects for regional and world peace. We are now engaged in further negotiations to provide full autonomy for the people of the West Bank and Gaza, to resolve the Palestinian issue in all its aspects, and to preserve the peace and security of Israel. Let no one doubt our commitment to the security of Israel. In a few days we will observe an historic event when Israel makes another major withdrawal from the Sinai and when Ambassadors will be exchanged between Israel and Egypt.

We've also expanded our own sphere of friendship. Our deep commitment to human rights and to meeting human needs has improved our relationship with much of the Third World. Our decision to normalize relations with the People's Republic of China will help to preserve peace and stability in Asia and in the Western Pacific.

We've increased and strengthened our naval presence in the Indian Ocean, and we are now making arrangements for key naval and air facilities to be used by our forces in the region of northeast Africa and the Persian Gulf.

We've reconfirmed our 1959 agreement to help Pakistan preserve its independence and its integrity. The United States will take action consistent with our own laws to assist Pakistan in resisting any outside aggression. And I'm asking the Congress specifically to reaffirm this agreement. I'm also working, along with the leaders of other nations, to provide additional military and economic aid for Pakistan. That request will come to you in just a few days.

Finally, we are prepared to work with other countries in the region to share a cooperative security framework that respects differing values and political beliefs, yet which enhances the independence, security, and prosperity of all.

All these efforts combined emphasize our dedication to defend and preserve the vital interests of the region and of the nation which we represent and those of our allies—in Europe and the Pacific, and also in the parts of the world which have such great strategic importance to us, stretching especially through the Middle East and Southwest Asia. With your help, I will pursue these efforts with vigor and with determination. You and I will act as necessary to protect and to preserve our Nation's security.

The men and women of America's Armed Forces are on duty tonight in many parts of the world. I'm proud of the job they are doing, and I know you share that pride. I believe that our volunteer forces are adequate for current defense needs, and I hope that it will not become necessary to impose a draft. However, we must be prepared for that possibility. For this reason, I have determined that the Selective Service System must now be revitalized. I will send legislation and budget proposals to the Congress next month so that we can begin registration and then meet future mobilization needs rapidly if they arise.

We also need clear and quick passage of a new charter to define the legal authority and accountability of our intelligence agencies. We will guarantee that abuses do not recur, but we must tighten our controls on sensitive intelligence information, and we need to remove unwarranted restraints on America's ability to collect intelligence.

The decade ahead will be a time of rapid change, as nations everywhere seek to deal with new problems and age-old tensions. But America need have no fear. We can thrive in a world of change if we remain true to our values and actively engaged in promoting world peace. We will continue to work as we have for peace in the Middle East and southern Africa. We will continue to build our ties with developing nations, respecting and helping to strengthen their national independence which they have struggled so hard to achieve. And we will continue to support the growth of democracy and the protection of human rights.

In repressive regimes, popular frustrations often have no outlet except through violence. But when peoples and their governments can approach their problems together through open, democratic methods, the basis for stability and peace is far more solid and far more enduring. That is why our support for human rights in other countries is in our own national interest as well as part of our own national character.

Peace—a peace that preserves freedom—remains America's first goal. In the coming years, as a mighty nation we will continue to pursue peace. But to be strong abroad we must be strong at home. And in order to be strong, we must continue to face up to the difficult issues that confront us as a nation today.

The crises in Iran and Afghanistan have dramatized a very important lesson: Our excessive dependence on foreign oil is a clear and present danger to our Nation's security. The need has never been more urgent. At long last, we must have a clear, comprehensive energy policy for the United States.

As you well know, I have been working with the Congress in a concentrated and persistent way over the past 3 years to meet this need. We have made progress together. But Congress must act promptly now to complete final action on this vital energy legislation. Our Nation will then have a major conservation effort, important initiatives to develop solar power, realistic pricing based on the true value of oil, strong incentives for the production of coal and other fossil fuels in the United States, and our Nation's most massive peacetime investment in the development of synthetic fuels.

The American people are making progress in energy conservation. Last year we reduced overall petroleum consumption by 8 percent and gasoline consumption by 5 percent below what it was the year before. Now we must do more.

After consultation with the Governors, we will set gasoline conservation goals for each of the 50 States, and I will make them mandatory if these goals are not met.

I've established an import ceiling for 1980 of 8.2 million barrels a day—well below the level of foreign oil purchases in 1977. I expect our imports to be much lower than this, but the ceiling will be enforced by an oil import fee if necessary. I'm prepared to lower these imports still further if the other oil-consuming countries will join us in a fair and mutual reduction. If we have a serious shortage, I will not hesitate to impose mandatory gasoline rationing immediately.

The single biggest factor in the inflation rate last year, the increase in the inflation rate last year, was from one cause: the skyrocketing prices of OPEC oil. We must take whatever actions are necessary to reduce our dependence on foreign oil—and at the same time reduce inflation.

As individuals and as families, few of us can produce energy by ourselves. But all of us can conserve energy—every one of us, every day of our lives. Tonight I call on you—in fact, all the people of America—to help our Nation. Conserve energy. Eliminate waste. Make 1980 indeed a year of energy conservation.

Of course, we must take other actions to strengthen our Nation's economy.

First, we will continue to reduce the deficit and then to balance the Federal budget.

Second, as we continue to work with business to hold down prices, we'll build also on the historic national accord with organized labor to restrain pay increases in a fair fight against inflation.

Third, we will continue our successful efforts to cut paperwork and to dismantle unnecessary Government regulation.

Fourth, we will continue our progress in providing jobs for America, concentrating on a major new program to provide training and work for our young people, especially minority youth. It has been said that "a mind is a terrible thing to waste." We will give our young people new hope for jobs and a better life in the 1980's.

And fifth, we must use the decade of the 1980's to attack the basic structural weaknesses and problems in our economy through measures to increase productivity, savings, and investment.

With these energy and economic policies, we will make America even stronger at home in this decade—just as our foreign and defense policies will make us stronger and safer throughout the world. We will never abandon our struggle for a just and a decent society here at home. That's the heart of America—and it's the source of our ability to inspire other people to defend their own rights abroad.

Our material resources, great as they are, are limited. Our problems are too complex for simple slogans or for quick solutions. We cannot solve them without effort and sacrifice. Walter Lippmann once reminded us, "You took the good things for granted. Now you must earn them again. For every right that you cherish, you have a duty which you must fulfill. For every good which you wish to preserve, you will have to sacrifice your comfort and your ease. There is nothing for nothing any longer."

Our challenges are formidable. But there's a new spirit of unity and resolve in our country. We move into the 1980's with confidence and hope and a bright vision of the America we want: an America strong and free, an America at peace, an America with equal rights for all citizens— and for women, guaranteed in the United States Constitution—an America with jobs and good health and good education for every citizen, an America with a clean and bountiful life in our cities and on our farms, an America that helps to feed the world, an America secure in filling its own energy needs, an America of justice, tolerance, and compassion. For this vision to come true, we must sacrifice, but this national commitment will be an exciting enterprise that will unify our people.

Together as one people, let us work to build our strength at home, and together as one indivisible union, let us seek peace and security throughout the world.

Together let us make of this time of challenge and danger a decade of national resolve and of brave achievement.

Thank you very much.

2.4   Jimmy Carter's Fourth State of the Union Address

To the Congress of the United States:

The State of the Union is sound. Our economy is recovering from a recession. A national energy plan is in place and our dependence on foreign oil is decreasing. We have been at peace for four uninterrupted years.

But, our Nation has serious problems. Inflation and unemployment are unacceptably high. The world oil market is increasingly tight. There are trouble spots throughout the world, and 52 American hostages are being held in Iran against international law and against every precept of human affairs.

However, I firmly believe that, as a result of the progress made in so many domestic and international areas over the past four years, our Nation is stronger, wealthier, more compassionate and freer than it was four years ago. I am proud of that fact. And I believe the Congress should be proud as well, for so much of what has been accomplished over the past four years has been due to the hard work, insights and cooperation of Congress. I applaud the Congress for its efforts and its achievements.

In this State of the Union Message I want to recount the achievements and progress of the last four years and to offer recommendations to the Congress for this year. While my term as President will end before the 97th Congress begins its work in earnest, I hope that my recommendations will serve as a guide for the direction this country should take so we build on the record of the past four years.

RECORD OF PROGRESS

When I took office, our Nation faced a number of serious domestic and international problems:

—no national energy policy existed, and our dependence on foreign oil was rapidly increasing;
—public trust in the integrity and openness of the government was low;
—the Federal government was operating inefficiently in administering essential programs and policies;
—major social problems were being ignored or poorly addressed by the Federal government;
—our defense posture was declining as a result of a defense budget which was continuously shrinking in real terms;
—the strength of the NATO Alliance needed to be bolstered;
—tensions between Israel and Egypt threatened another Middle East war; and
—America's resolve to oppose human rights violations was under serious question.

Over the past 48 months, clear progress has been made in solving the challenges we found in January of 1977:

almost all of our comprehensive energy program have been enacted, and the Department of Energy has been established to administer the program; confidence in the government's integrity has been restored, and respect for the government's openness and fairness has been renewed;

the government has been made more effective and efficient: the Civil Service system was completely reformed for the first time this century;

14 reorganization initiatives have been proposed to the Congress, approved, and implemented;

two new Cabinet departments have been created to consolidate and streamline the government's handling of energy and education problems;

inspectors general have been placed in each Cabinet department to combat fraud, waste and other abuses;

the regulatory process has been reformed through creation of the Regulatory Council, implementation of Executive Order 12044 and its requirement for cost-impact analyses, elimination of unnecessary regulation, and passage of the Regulatory Flexibility Act;

procedures have been established to assure citizen participation in government;

and the airline, trucking, rail and communications industries are being deregulated;

critical social problems, many long ignored by the Federal government, have been addressed directly;

an urban policy was developed and implemented to reverse the decline in our urban areas;

the Social Security System was refinanced to put it on a sound financial basis;

the Humphrey-Hawkins Full Employment Act was enacted;

Federal assistance for education was expanded by more than 75 percent;

the minimum wage was increased to levels needed to ease the effects of inflation;

affirmative action has been pursued aggressively; more blacks, Hispanics and women have been appointed to senior government positions and to judgeships than at any other time in our history;

the ERA ratification deadline was extended to aid the ratification effort;

and minority business procurement by the Federal government has more than doubled;

the Nation's first sectoral policies were put in place, for the auto and steel industries, with my Administration demonstrating the value of cooperation between the government, business and labor;

reversing previous trends, real defense spending has increased every year since 1977;

the real increase in FY 1980 defense spending is well above 3 percent and I expect FY 1981 defense spending to be even higher; looking ahead, the defense program I am proposing is premised on a real increase in defense spending over the next five years of 20 percent or more;

the NATO Alliance has proven its unity in responding to the situations in Eastern Europe and Southwest Asia and in agreeing on the issues to be addressed in the review of the Helsinki Final Act currently underway in Madrid;

the peace process in the Middle East established at Camp David and by the Peace Treaty between Egypt and Israel is being buttressed on two fronts: steady progress in the normalization of Egyptian-Israeli relations in many fields, and the commitment of both Egypt and Israel, with United States' assistance, to see through to successful conclusion the autonomy negotiations for the West Bank and Gaza;

the Panama Canal Treaties have been put into effect, which has helped to improve relations with Latin America; we have continued this Nation's strong commitment to the pursuit of human rights throughout the world, evenhandedly and objectively;

our commitment to a worldwide human rights policy has remained firm;

and many other countries have given high priority to it;

our resolve to oppose aggression, such as the illegal invasion of the Soviet Union into Afghanistan, has been supported by tough action.

I. ENSURING ECONOMIC STRENGTH ECONOMY

During the last decade our Nation has withstood a series of economic shocks unprecedented in peacetime. The most dramatic of these has been the explosive increases of OPEC oil prices. But we have also faced world commodity shortages, natural disasters, agricultural shortages and major challenges to world peace and security. Our ability to deal with these shocks has been impaired because of a decrease in the growth of productivity and the persistence of underlying inflationary forces built up over the past 15 years.

Nevertheless, the economy has proved to be remarkably resilient. Real output has grown at an average rate of 3 percent per year since I took office, and employment has grown by 10 percent. We have added about 8 million productive private sector jobs to the economy. However, unacceptably high inflation— the most difficult economic problem I have faced— persists.

This inflation— which threatens the growth, productivity, and stability of our economy— requires that we restrain the growth of the budget to the maximum extent consistent with national security and human compassion. I have done so in my earlier budgets, and in my FY '82 budget. However, while restraint is essential to any appropriate economic policy, high inflation cannot be attributed solely to government spending. The growth in budget outlays has been more the result of economic factors than the cause of them.

We are now in the early stages of economic recovery following a short recession. Typically, a post-recessionary period has been marked by vigorous economic growth aided by anti-recessionary policy measures such as large tax cuts or big, stimulation spending programs. I have declined to recommend such actions to stimulate economic activity, because the persistent inflationary pressures that beset our economy today dictate a restrained fiscal policy.

Accordingly, I am asking the Congress to postpone until January 1, 1982, the personal tax reductions I had earlier proposed to take effect on January 1 of this year.

However, my 1982 budget proposes significant tax changes to increase the sources of financing for business investment. While emphasizing the need for continued fiscal restraint, this budget takes the first major step in a long-term tax reduction program designed to increase capital formation. The failure of our Nation's capital stock to grow at a rate that keeps pace with its labor force has clearly been one cause of our productivity slowdown. Higher investment rates are also critically needed to meet our Nation's energy needs, and to replace energy-inefficient plants and equipment with new energy-saving physical plants. The level of investment that is called for will not occur in the absence of policies to encourage it.

Therefore, my budget proposes a major liberalization of tax allowances for depreciation, as well as simplified depreciation accounting, increasing the allowable rates by about 40 percent. I am also proposing improvements in the investment tax credit, making it refundable, to meet the investment needs of firms with no current earnings.

These two proposals, along with carefully-phased tax reductions for individuals, will improve both economic efficiency and tax equity. I urge the Congress to enact legislation along the lines and timetable I have proposed.

THE 1982 BUDGET

The FY 1982 budget I have sent to the Congress continues our four-year policy of prudence and restraint. While the budget deficits during my term are higher than I would have liked, their size is determined for the most part by economic conditions. And in spite of these conditions, the relative size of the deficit continues to decline. In 1976, before I took office, the budget deficit equalled 4 percent of gross national product. It had been cut to 2.3 percent in the 1980 fiscal year just ended. My 1982 budget contains a deficit estimated to be less than 1 percent of our gross national product.

The rate of growth in Federal spending has been held to a minimum. Nevertheless, outlays are still rising more rapidly than many had anticipated, the result of many powerful forces in our society:

We face a threat to our security, as events in Afghanistan, the Middle East, and Eastern Europe make clear. We have a steadily aging population and, as a result, the biggest single increase in the Federal budget is the rising cost of retire-ment programs, particularly social security. We face other important domestic needs: to continue responsibility for the disadvantaged; to provide the capital needed by our cities and our transportation systems; to protect our environment; to revitalize American industry; and to increase the export of American goods and services so essential to the creation of jobs and a trade surplus.

Yet the Federal Government itself may not always be the proper source of such assistance. For example, it must not usurp functions if they can be more appropriately decided upon, managed, and financed by the private sector or by State and local governments. My Administration has always sought to consider the proper focus of responsibility for the most efficient resolution of problems.

We have also recognized the need to simplify the system of grants to State and local governments. I have again proposed several grant consolidations in the 1982 budget, including a new proposal that would consolidate several highway programs.

The pressures for growth in Federal use of national resources are great. My Administration has initiated many new approaches to cope with these pressures. We started a multi-year budget system, and we began a system for controlling Federal credit programs. Yet in spite of increasing needs to limit spending growth, we have consistently adhered to these strong budget principles:

Our Nation's armed forces must always stand sufficiently strong to deter aggression and to assure our security. An effective national energy plan is essential to increase domestic production of oil and gas, to encourage conservation of our scarce energy resources, to stimulate conversion to more abundant fuels, and to reduce our trade deficit. The essential human needs for our citizens must be given the highest priority. The Federal Government must lead the way in investment in the Nation's technological future. The Federal Government has an obligation to nurture and protect our environment— the common resource, birthright, and sustenance of the American people.

My 1982 budget continues to support these principles. It also proposes responsible tax reductions to encourage a more productive economy, and adequate funding of our highest priority programs within an overall policy of constraint.

Fiscal restraint must be continued in the years ahead. Budgets must be tight enough to convince those who set wages and prices that the Federal Government is serious about fighting inflation but not so tight as to choke off all growth.

Careful budget policy should be supplemented by other measures designed to reduce inflation at lower cost in lost output and employment. These other steps include measures to increase investment— such as the tax proposals included in my 1982 budget— and measures to increase competition and productivity in our economy. Voluntary incomes policies can also directly influence wages and prices in the direction of moderation and thereby bring inflation down faster and at lower cost to the economy. Through a tax-based incomes policy (TIP) we could provide tax incentives for firms and workers to moderate their wage and price increases. In the coming years, control of Federal expenditures can make possible periodic tax reductions. The Congress should therefore begin now to evaluate the potentialities of a TIP program so that when the next round of tax reductions is appropriate a TIP program will be seriously considered.

EMPLOYMENT

During the last four years we have given top priority to meeting the needs of workers and providing additional job opportunities to those who seek work. Since the end of 1976:

almost 9 million new jobs have been added to the nation's economy total employment has reached 97 million. More jobs than ever before are held by women, minorities and young people. Employment over the past four years has increased by: 17% for adult women 11% for blacks, and 30% for Hispanics employment of black teenagers increased by more than 5% , reversing the decline that occurred in the previous eight years.

Major initiatives launched by this Administration helped bring about these accomplishments and have provided a solid foundation for employment and training policy in the 1980's. In 1977, as part of the comprehensive economic stimulus program:

425,000 public service jobs were created A $1 billion youth employment initiative funded 200,000 jobs the doubling of the Job Corps to 44,000 slots began and 1 million summer youth jobs were approved— a 25 percent increase.

In 1978:

the Humphrey-Hawkins Full Employment Act became law the $400 million Private Sector Initiatives Program was begun a targeted jobs tax credit for disadvantaged youth and others with special employment barriers was enacted the Comprehensive Employment and Training Act was reauthorized for four years.

In 1979:

a $6 billion welfare reform proposal was introduced with funding for 400,000 public service jobs welfare reform demonstration projects were launched in communities around the country the Vice President initiated a nationwide review of youth unemployment in this country.

In 1980:

the findings of the Vice President's Task Force revealed the major education and employment deficits that exist for poor and minority youngsters. As a result a $2 billion youth education and jobs initiative was introduced to provide unemployed youth with the basic education and work experience they need to compete in the labor market of the 1980's. As part of the economic revitalization program several steps were proposed to aid workers in high unemployment communities:

an additional 13 weeks of unemployment benefits for the long term unemployed. $600 million to train the disadvantaged and unemployed for new private sector jobs. positive adjustment demonstrations to aid workers in declining industries. The important Title VII Private Sector Initiatives Program was reauthorized for an additional two years.

In addition to making significant progress in helping the disadvantaged and unemployed, important gains were realized for all workers:

an historic national accord with organized labor made it possible for the views of working men and women to be heard as the nation's economic and domestic policies were formulated. the Mine Safety and Health Act brought about improved working conditions for the nation's 500,000 miners. substantial reforms of Occupational Safety and Health Administration were accomplished to help reduce unnecessary burdens on business and to focus on major health and safety problems. the minimum wage was increased over a four year period from $2.30 to $3.35 an hour. the Black Lung Benefit Reform Act was signed into law. attempts to weaken Davis-Bacon Act were defeated.

While substantial gains have been made in the last four years, continued efforts are required to ensure that this progress is continued:

government must continue to make labor a full partner in the policy decisions that affect the interests of working men and women. a broad, bipartisan effort to combat youth unemployment must be sustained compassionate reform of the nation's welfare system should be continued with employment opportunities provided for those able to work. workers in declining industries should be provided new skills and help in finding employment

TRADE

Over the past year, the U.S. trade picture improved as a result of solid export gains in both manufactured and agricultural products. Agricultural exports reached a new record of over $40 billion, while manufactured exports have grown by 24 percent to a record $144 billion. In these areas the United States recorded significant surpluses of $24 billion and $19 billion respectively. While our oil imports remained a major drain on our foreign exchange earnings, that drain was somewhat moderated by a 19 percent decline in the volume of oil imports.

U.S. trade negotiators made significant progress over the past year in assuring effective implementation of the agreements negotiated during the Tokyo Round of Multilateral Trade Negotiations. Agreements reached with the Japanese government, for example, will assure that the United States will be able to expand its exports to the Japanese market in such key areas as telecommunications equipment, tobacco, and lumber. Efforts by U.S. trade negotiators also helped to persuade a number of key developing countries to accept many of the non-tariff codes negotiated during the Multilateral Trade Negotiations. This will assure that these countries will increasingly assume obligations under the international trading system.

A difficult world economic environment posed a challenge for the management of trade relations. U.S. trade negotiators were called upon to manage serious sectoral problems in such areas as steel, and helped to assure that U.S. chemical exports will have continued access to the European market.

Close consultations with the private sector in the United States have enabled U.S. trade negotiators to pinpoint obstacles to U.S. trade in services, and to build a basis for future negotiations. Services have been an increasingly important source of export earnings for the United States, and the United States must assure continued and increased access to foreign markets.

The trade position of the United States has improved. But vigorous efforts are needed in a number of areas to assure continued market access for U.S. exports, particularly agricultural and high technology products, in which the United States continues to have a strong competitive edge. Continued efforts are also needed to remove many domestic disincentives, which now hamper U.S. export growth. And we must ensure that countries do not manipulate investment, or impose investment performance requirements which distort trade and cost us jobs in this country.

In short, we must continue to seek free— but fair— trade. That is the policy my Administration has pursued from the beginning, even in areas where foreign competition has clearly affected our domestic industry. In the steel industry, for instance, we have put Trigger Price Mechanism into place to help prevent the dumping of steel. That action has strengthened the domestic steel industry. In the automobile industry, we have worked— without resort to import quotas— to strengthen the industry's ability to modernize and compete effectively.

SMALL BUSINESS

I have often said that there is nothing small about small business in America. These firms account for nearly one-half our gross national product; over half of new technology; and much more than half of the jobs created by industry.

Because this sector of the economy is the very lifeblood of our National economy, we have done much together to improve the competitive climate for smaller firms. These concerted efforts have been an integral part of my program to revitalize the economy.

They include my campaign to shrink substantially the cash and time consuming red tape burden imposed on business. They include my personally-directed policy of ambitiously increasing the Federal contracting dollars going to small firms, especially those owned by women and minorities. And they include my proposals to reinvigorate existing small businesses and assist the creation of new ones through tax reform; financing assistance; market expansion; and support of product innovation.

Many of my initiatives to facilitate the creation and growth of small businesses were made in response to the White House Conference on Small Business, which I convened. My Administration began the implementation of most of the ideas produced last year by that citizen's advisory body; others need to be addressed. I have proposed the reconvening of the Conference next year to review progress; reassess priorities; and set new goals. In the interim I hope that the incoming Administration and the new Congress will work with the committee I have established to keep these business development ideas alive and help implement Conference recommendations.

MINORITY BUSINESS

One of the most successful developments of my Administration has been the growth and strengthening of minority business. This is the first Administration to put the issue on the policy agenda as a matter of major importance. To implement the results of our early efforts in this field I submitted legislation to Congress designed to further the development of minority business.

We have reorganized the Office of Minority Business into the Minority Business Development Administration in the Department of Commerce. MBDA has already proven to be a major factor in assisting minority businesses to achieve equitable competitive positions in the marketplace.

The Federal government's procurement from minority-owned firms has nearly tripled since I took office. Federal deposits in minority-owned banks have more than doubled and minority ownership of radio and television stations has nearly doubled. The SBA administered 8(a) Pilot Program for procurement with the Army proved to be successful and I recently expanded the number of agencies involved to include NASA and the Departments of Energy and Transportation.

I firmly believe the critical path to full freedom and equality for America's minorities rests with the ability of minority communities to participate competitively in the free enterprise system. I believe the government has a fundamental responsibility to assist in the development of minority business and I hope the progress made in the last four years will continue.

II. CREATING ENERGY SECURITY

Since I took office, my highest legislative priorities have involved the reorientation and redirection of U.S. energy activities and for the first time, to establish a coordinated national energy policy. The struggle to achieve that policy has been long and difficult, but the accomplishments of the past four years make clear that our country is finally serious about the problems caused by our overdependence on foreign oil. Our progress should not be lost. We must rely on and encourage multiple forms of energy production— coal, crude oil, natural gas, solar, nuclear, synthetics— and energy conservation. The framework put in place over the last four years will enable us to do this.

NATIONAL ENERGY POLICY

As a result of actions my Administration and the Congress have taken over the past four years, our country finally has a national energy policy:

Under my program of phased decontrol, domestic crude oil price controls will end September 30, 1981. As a result exploratory drilling activities have reached an all-time high; Prices for new natural gas are being decontrolled under the Natural Gas Policy Act— and natural gas production is now at an all time high; the supply shortages of several years ago have been eliminated; The windfall profits tax on crude oil has been enacted providing $227 billion over ten years for assistance to low-income households, increased mass transit funding, and a massive investment in the production and development of alternative energy sources; The Synthetic Fuels Corporation has been established to help private companies build the facilities to produce energy from synthetic fuels; Solar energy funding has been quadrupled, solar energy tax credits enacted, and a Solar Energy and Energy Conservation Bank has been established; A route has been chosen to bring natural gas from the North Slope of Alaska to the lower 48 states; Coal production and consumption incentives have been increased, and coal production is now at its highest level in history; A gasoline rationing plan has been approved by Congress for possible use in the event of a severe energy supply shortage or interruption; Gasohol production has been dramatically increased, with a program being put in place to produce 500 million gallons of alcohol fuel by the end of this year— an amount that could enable gasohol to meet the demand for 10 percent of all unleaded gasoline; New energy conservation incentives have been provided for individuals, businesses and communities and conservation has increased dramatically. The U.S. has reduced oil imports by 25 percent— or 2 million barrels per day— over the past four years.

INCREASED DEVELOPMENT OF DOMESTIC ENERGY SOURCES

Although it is essential that the Nation reduce its dependence on imported fossil fuels and complete the transition to reliance on domestic renewable sources of energy, it is also important that this transition be accomplished in an orderly, economic, and environmentally sound manner. To this end, the Administration has launched several initiatives.

Leasing of oil and natural gas on federal lands, particularly the outer continental shelf, has been accelerated at the same time as the Administration has reformed leasing procedures through the 1978 amendments to the Outer Continental Shelf Lands Act. In 1979 the Interior Department held six OCS lease sales, the greatest number ever, which resulted in federal receipts of $6.5 billion, another record. The five-year OCS Leasing schedule was completed, requiring 36 sales over the next five years.

Since 1971 no general federal coal lease sales were suspended. Over the past four years the Administration has completely revised the federal coal leasing program to bring it into compliance with the requirements of 1976 Federal Land Planning and Management Act and other statutory provisions. The program is designed to balance the competing interests that affect resource development on public lands and to ensure that adequate supplies of coal will be available to meet national needs. As a result, the first general competitive federal coal lease sale in ten years will be held this month.

In July 1980, I signed into law the Energy Security Act of 1980 which established the Synthetic Fuels Corporation. The Corporation is designed to spur the development of commercial technologies for production of synthetic fuels, such as liquid and gaseous fuels from coal and the production of oil from oil shale. The Act provides the Corporation with an initial $22 billion to accomplish these objectives. The principal purpose of the legislation is to ensure that the nation will have available in the late 1980's the option to undertake commercial development of synthetic fuels if that becomes necessary. The Energy Security Act also provides significant incentives for the development of gasohol and biomass fuels, thereby enhancing the nation's supply of alternative energy sources.

COMMITMENT TO A SUSTAINABLE ENERGY FUTURE

The Administration's 1977 National Energy Plan marked an historic departure from the policies of previous Administrations. The plan stressed the importance of both energy production and conservation to achieving our ultimate national goal of relying primarily on secure sources of energy. The National Energy Plan made energy conservation a cornerstone of our national energy policy.

In 1978, I initiated the Administration's Solar Domestic Policy Review. This represented the first step towards widespread introduction of renewable energy sources into the Nation's economy. As a result of the Review, I issued the 1979 Solar Message to Congress, the first such message in the Nation's history. The Message outlined the Administration's solar program and established an ambitious national goal for the year 2000 of obtaining 20 percent of this Nation's energy from solar and renewable sources. The thrust of the federal solar program is to help industry develop solar energy sources by emphasizing basic research and development of solar technologies which are not currently economic, such as photovoltaics, which generate energy directly from the sun. At the same time, through tax incentives, education, and the Solar Energy and Energy Conservation Bank, the solar program seeks to encourage state and local governments, industry, and our citizens to expand their use of solar and renewable resource technologies currently available.

As a result of these policies and programs, the energy efficiency of the American economy has improved markedly and investments in renewable energy sources have grown significantly. It now takes 3 1/2 percent less energy to produce a constant dollar of GNP than it did in January 1977. This increase in efficiency represents a savings of over 1.3 million barrels per day of oil equivalent, about the level of total oil production now occurring in Alaska. Over the same period,

Federal support for conservation and solar energy has increased by more than 3000 percent, to $3.3 billion in FY 1981, including the tax credits for solar energy and energy conservation investments— these credits are expected to amount to $1.2 billion in FY 1981 and $1.5 billion in FY 1982.

COMMITMENT TO NUCLEAR SAFETY AND SECURITY

Since January 1977, significant progress has been achieved in resolving three critical problems resulting from the use of nuclear energy: radioactive waste management, nuclear safety and weapons proliferation.

In 1977, the Administration announced its nuclear nonproliferation policy and initiated the International Fuel Cycle Evaluation. In 1978, Congress passed the Nuclear Nonproliferation Act, an historic piece of legislation.

In February 1980, the Administration transmitted its nuclear waste management policy to the Congress. This policy was a major advance over all previous efforts. The principal aspects of that policy are: acknowledging the seriousness of the problem and the numerous technical and institutional issues; adopting a technically and environmentally conservative approach to the first permanent repository; and providing the states with significant involvement in nuclear waste disposal decisions by creating the State Planning Council. While much of the plan can be and is being implemented administratively, some new authorities are needed. The Congress should give early priority to enacting provisions for away-from-reactor storage and the State Planning Council.

The accident at Three Mile Island made the nation acutely aware of the safety risks posed by nuclear power plants. In response, the President established the Kemeny Commission to review the accident and make recommendations. Virtually all of the Commission's substantive recommendations were adopted by the Administration and are now being implemented by the Nuclear Regulatory Commission. The Congress adopted the President's proposed plan for the Nuclear Regulatory Commission and the Nuclear Safety Oversight Committee was established to ensure that the Administration's decisions were implemented.

Nuclear safety will remain a vital concern in the years ahead. We must continue to press ahead for the safe, secure disposal of radioactive wastes, and prevention of nuclear proliferation.

While significant growth in foreign demand for U.S. steam coal is foreseen, congestion must be removed at major U.S. coal exporting ports such as Hampton Roads, Virginia, and Baltimore, Maryland. My Administration has worked through the Interagency Coal Task Force Study to promote cooperation and coordination of resources between shippers, railroads, vessel broker/ operators and port operators, and to determine the most appropriate Federal role in expanding and modernizing coal export facilities, including dredging deeper channels at selected ports. As a result of the Task Force's efforts, administrative steps have been taken by the Corps of Engineers to reduce significantly the amount of time required for planning and economic review of port dredging proposals. The Administration has also recommended that the Congress enact legislation to give the President generic authority to recommend appropriations for channel dredging activities. Private industry will, of course, play the major role in developing the United States' coal export facilities, but the government must continue to work to facilitate transportation to foreign markets.

III. ENHANCING BASIC HUMAN AND SOCIAL NEEDS

For too long prior to my Administration, many of our Nation's basic human and social needs were being ignored or handled insensitively by the Federal government. Over the last four years, we have significantly increased funding for many of the vital programs in these areas; developed new programs where needs were unaddressed; targeted Federal support to those individuals and areas most in need of our assistance; and removed barriers that have unnecessarily kept many disadvantaged citizens from obtaining aid for their most basic needs.

Our record has produced clear progress in the effort to solve some of the country's fundamental human and social problems. My Administration and the Congress, working together, have demonstrated that government must and can meet our citizens' basic human and social needs in a responsible and compassionate way.

But there is an unfinished agenda still before the Congress. If we are to meet our obligations to help all Americans realize the dreams of sound health care, decent housing, effective social services, a good education, and a meaningful job, important legislation still must be enacted. National Health Insurance, Welfare Reform, Child Health Assessment Program, are before the Congress and I urge their passage.

HEALTH NATIONAL HEALTH PLAN

During my Administration, I proposed to Congress a National Health Plan which will enable the country to reach the goal of comprehensive, universal health care coverage. The legislation I submitted lays the foundation for this comprehensive plan and addresses the most serious problems of health financing and delivery. It is realistic and enactable. It does not overpromise or overspend, and, as a result, can be the solution to the thirty years of Congressional battles on national health insurance. My Plan includes the following key features:

nearly 15 million additional poor would receive fully-subsidized comprehensive coverage; pre-natal and delivery services are provided for all pregnant women and coverage is provided for all acute care for infants in their first year of life; the elderly and disabled would have a limit of $1,250 placed on annual out-of-pocket medical expenses and would no longer face limits on hospital coverage; all full-time employees and their families would receive insurance against at least major medical expenses under mandated employer coverage; Medicare and Medicaid would be combined and expanded into an umbrella Federal program, Healthcare, for increased program efficiency, accountability and uniformity

and

strong cost controls and health system reforms would be implemented, including greater incentives for Health Maintenance Organizations.

I urge the new Congress to compare my Plan with the alternatives— programs which either do too little to improve the health care needs of Americans most in need or programs which would impose substantial financial burdens on the American taxpayers. I hope the Congress will see the need for and the benefits of my Plan and work toward prompt enactment. We cannot afford further delay in this vital area.

HEALTH CARE COST CONTROL

Inflation in health care costs remains unacceptably high. Throughout my Administration, legislation to reduce health care cost inflation was one of my highest priorities, but was not passed by the Congress. Therefore, my FY 1982 budget proposes sharing the responsibility for health care cost control with the private sector, through voluntary hospital cost guidelines and intensified monitoring. In the longer term, the health care reimbursement system must be reformed. We must move away from inflationary cost-based reimbursement and fee-for-service, and toward a system of prospective reimbursement, under which health care providers would operate within predetermined budgets. This reimbursement reform is essential to ultimately control inflation in health care costs, and will be a significant challenge to the new Congress.

HEALTH PROMOTION AND DISEASE PREVENTION

During my Administration, the Surgeon General released "Healthy People," a landmark report on health promotion and disease prevention. The report signals the growing consensus that the Nation's health strategy must be refocused in the 1980's to emphasize the prevention of disease. Specifically, the report lays out measurable and achieveable goals in the reduction of mortality which can be reached by 1990.

I urge the new Congress to endorse the principles of "Healthy People," and to adopt the recommendations to achieve its goals. This will necessitate adoption of a broader concept of health care, to include such areas as environmental health, workplace health and safety, commercial product safety, traffic safety, and health education, promotion and information.

MATERNAL AND CHILD HEALTH

Ensuring a healthy start in life for children remains not only a high priority of my Administration, but also one of the most cost effective forms of health care.

When I took office, immunization levels for preventable childhood diseases had fallen to 70%. As a result of a concerted nationwide effort during my Administration, I am pleased to report that now at least 90% of children under 15, and virtually all school-age children are immunized. In addition, reported cases of measles and mumps are at their lowest levels ever.

Under the National Health Plan I have proposed, there would be no cost-sharing for prenatal and delivery services for all pregnant women and for acute care provided to infants in their first year of life. These preventive services have extremely high returns in terms of improved newborn and long-term child health.

Under the Child Health Assurance Program (CHAP) legislation which I submitted to the Congress, and which passed the House, an additional two million low-income children under 18 would become eligible for Medicaid benefits, which would include special health assessments. CHAP would also improve the continuity of care for the nearly 14 million children now eligible for Medicaid. An additional 100,000 low-income pregnant women would become eligible for prenatal care under the proposal. I strongly urge the new Congress to enact CHAP and thereby provide millions of needy children with essential health services. The legislation has had strong bipartisan support, which should continue as the details of the bill are completed.

I also urge the new Congress to provide strong support for two highly successful ongoing programs: the special supplemental food program for women, infants and children (WIC) and Family Planning. The food supplements under WIC have been shown to effectively prevent ill health and thereby reduce later medical costs. The Family Planning program has been effective at reducing unwanted pregnancies among low-income women and adolescents.

EXPANSION OF SERVICES TO THE POOR AND UNDERSERVED

During my Administration, health services to the poor and underserved have been dramatically increased. The number of National Health Service Corps (NHSC) assignees providing services in medically underserved communities has grown from 500 in 1977 to nearly 3,000 in 1981. The population served by the NHSC has more than tripled since 1977. The number of Community Health Centers providing services in high priority underserved areas has doubled during my Administration, and will serve an estimated six million people in 1981. I strongly urge the new Congress to support these highly successful programs.

MENTAL HEALTH

One of the most significant health achievements during my Administration was the recent passage of the Mental Health Systems Act, which grew out of recommendations of my Commission on Mental Health. I join many others in my gratitude to the First Lady for her tireless and effective contribution to the passage of this important legislation.

The Act is designed to inaugurate a new era of Federal and State partnership in the planning and provision of mental health services. In addition, the Act specifically provides for prevention and support services to the chronically mentally ill to prevent unnecessary institutionalization and for the development of community-based mental health services. I urge the new Congress to provide adequate support for the full and timely implementation of this Act.

HEALTH PROTECTION

With my active support, the Congress recently passed "Medigap" legislation, which provides for voluntary certification of health insurance policies supplemental to Medicare, to curb widespread abuses in this area.

In the area of toxic agent control, legislation which I submitted to the Congress recently passed. This will provide for a "super-fund" to cover hazardous waste cleanup costs.

In the area of accidental injury control, we have established automobile safety standards and increased enforcement activities with respect to the 55 MPH speed limit. By the end of the decade these actions are expected to save over 13,000 lives and 100,000 serious injuries each year.

I urge the new Congress to continue strong support for all these activities.

FOOD AND NUTRITION

Building on the comprehensive reform of the Food Stamp Program that I proposed and Congress passed in 1977, my Administration and the Congress worked together in 1979 and 1980 to enact several other important changes in the Program. These changes will further simplify administration and reduce fraud and error, will make the program more responsive to the needs of the elderly and disabled, and will increase the cap on allowable program expenditures. The Food Stamp Act will expire at the end of fiscal 1981. It is essential that the new Administration and the Congress continue this program to ensure complete eradication of the debilitating malnutrition witnessed and documented among thousands of children in the 1960's.

DRUG ABUSE PREVENTION

At the beginning of my Administration there were over a half million heroin addicts in the United States. Our continued emphasis on reducing the supply of heroin, as well as providing treatment and rehabilitation to its victims, has reduced the heroin addict population, reduced the number of heroin overdose deaths by 80%, and reduced the number of heroin related injuries by 50%. We have also seen and encouraged a national movement of parents and citizens committed to reversing the very serious and disturbing trends of adolescent drug abuse.

Drug abuse in many forms will continue to detract, however, from the quality of life of many Americans. To prevent that, I see four great challenges in the years ahead. First, we must deal aggressively with the supplies of illegal drugs at their source, through joint crop destruction programs with foreign nations and increased law enforcement and border interdiction. Second, we must look to citizens and parents across the country to help educate the increasing numbers of American youth who are experimenting with drugs to the dangers of drug abuse. Education is a key factor in reducing drug abuse. Third, we must focus our efforts on drug and alcohol abuse in the workplace for not only does this abuse contribute to low productivity but it also destroys the satisfaction and sense of purpose all Americans can gain from the work experience. Fourth, we need a change in attitude, from an attitude which condones the casual use of drugs to one that recognizes the appropriate use of drugs for medical purposes and condemns the inappropriate and harmful abuse of drugs. I hope the Congress and the new Administration will take action to meet each of these challenges.

Education

The American people have always recognized that education is one of the soundest investments they can make. The dividends are reflected in every dimension of our national life— from the strength of our economy and national security to the vitality of our music, art, and literature. Among the accomplishments that have given me the most satisfaction over the last four years are the contributions that my Administration has been able to make to the well-being of students and educators throughout the country.

This Administration has collaborated successfully with the Congress on landmark education legislation. Working with the Congressional leadership, my Administration spotlighted the importance of education by creating a new Department of Education. The Department has given education a stronger voice at the Federal level, while at the same time reserving the actual control and operation of education to states, localities, and private institutions. The Department has successfully combined nearly 150 Federal education programs into a cohesive, streamlined organization that is more responsive to the needs of educators and students. The Department has made strides to cut red tape and paperwork and thereby to make the flow of Federal dollars to school districts and institutions of higher education more efficient. It is crucial that the Department be kept intact and strengthened.

Our collaboration with the Congress has resulted in numerous other important legislative accomplishments for education. A little over two years ago, I signed into law on the same day two major bills— one benefiting elementary and secondary education and the other, postsecondary education. The Education Amendments of 1978 embodied nearly all of my Administration's proposals for improvements in the Elementary and Secondary Education Act, including important new programs to improve students' achievement in the basic skills and to aid school districts with exceptionally high concentrations of children from low-income families. The Middle Income Student Assistance Act, legislation jointly sponsored by this Administration and the Congressional leadership, expanded eligibility for need-based Basic Educational Opportunity Grants to approximately one-third of the students enrolled in post-secondary education and made many more students eligible for the first time for other types of grants, work-study, and loans.

Just three and a half months ago, my Administration and the Congress successfully concluded over two years of work on a major reauthorization bill that further expands benefits to postsecondary education. Reflected in the Education Amendments of 1980 are major Administration recommendations for improvements in the Higher Education Act— including proposals for better loan access for students; a new parent loan program; simplified application procedures for student financial aid; a strengthened Federal commitment to developing colleges, particularly the historically Black institutions; a new authorization for equipment and facilities modernization funding for the nation's major research universities; and revitalized international education programs.

Supplementing these legislative accomplishments have been important administrative actions aimed at reducing paperwork and simplifying regulations associated with Federal education programs. We also launched major initiatives to reduce the backlog of defaulted student loans and otherwise to curb fraud, abuse, and waste in education programs.

To insure that the education enterprise is ready to meet the scientific and technological changes of the future, we undertook a major study of the status of science and engineering education throughout the nation. I hope that the findings from this report will serve as a springboard for needed reforms at all levels of education.

I am proud that this Administration has been able to provide the financial means to realize many of our legislative and administrative goals. Compared to the previous administration's last budget, I have requested the largest overall increase in Federal funding for education in our nation's history. My budget requests have been particularly sensitive to the needs of special populations like minorities, women, the educationally and economically disadvantaged, the handicapped, and students with limited English-speaking ability. At the same time, I have requested significant increases for many programs designed to enhance the quality of American education, including programs relating to important areas as diverse as international education, research libraries, museums, and teacher centers.

Last year, I proposed to the Congress a major legislative initiative that would direct $2 billion into education and job training programs designed to alleviate youth unemployment through improved linkages between the schools and the work place. This legislation generated bipartisan support; but unfortunately, action on it was not completed in the final, rushed days of the 96th Congress. I urge the new Congress— as it undertakes broad efforts to strengthen the economy as well as more specific tasks like reauthorizing the Vocational Education Act— to make the needs of our nation's unemployed youth a top priority for action. Only by combining a basic skills education program together with work training and employment incentives can we make substantial progress in eliminating one of the most severe social problems in our nation— youth unemployment, particularly among minorities. I am proud of the progress already made through passage of the Youth Employment and Demonstration Project Act of 1977 and the substantial increase in our investment in youth employment programs. The new legislation would cap these efforts.

INCOME SECURITY SOCIAL SECURITY

One of the highest priorities of my Administration has been to continue the tradition of effectiveness and efficiency widely associated with the social security program, and to assure present and future beneficiaries that they will receive their benefits as expected. The earned benefits that are paid monthly to retired and disabled American workers and their families provide a significant measure of economic protection to millions of people who might otherwise face retirement or possible disability with fear. I have enacted changes to improve the benefits of many social security beneficiaries during my years as President.

The last four years have presented a special set of concerns over the financial stability of the social security system. Shortly after taking office I proposed and Congress enacted legislation to protect the stability of the old age and survivors trust fund and prevent the imminent exhaustion of the disability insurance trust fund, and to correct a flaw in the benefit formula that was threatening the long run health of the entire social security system. The actions taken by the Congress at my request helped stabilize the system. That legislation was later complemented by the Disability Insurance Amendments of 1980 which further bolstered the disability insurance program, and reduced certain inequities among beneficiaries.

My commitment to the essential retirement and disability protection provided to 35 million people each month has been demonstrated by the fact that without interruption those beneficiaries have continued to receive their social security benefits, including annual cost of living increases. Changing and unpredictable economic circumstances require that we continue to monitor the financial stability of the social security system. To correct anticipated short-term strains on the system, I proposed last year that the three funds be allowed to borrow from one another, and I urge the Congress again this year to adopt such interfund borrowing. To further strengthen the social security system and provide a greater degree of assurance to beneficiaries, given projected future economic uncertainties, additional action should be taken. Among the additional financing options available are borrowing from the general fund, financing half of the hospital insurance fund with general revenues, and increasing the payroll tax rate. The latter option is particularly unpalatable given the significant increase in the tax rate already mandated in law.

This Administration continues to oppose cuts in basic social security benefits and taxing social security benefits. The Administration continues to support annual indexing of social security benefits.

WELFARE REFORM

In 1979 I proposed a welfare reform package which offers solutions to some of the most urgent problems in our welfare system. This proposal is embodied in two bills, The Work and Training Opportunities Act and The Social Welfare Reform Amendments Act. The House passed the second of these two proposals. Within the framework of our present welfare system, my reform proposals offer achievable means to increase self-sufficiency through work rather than welfare, more adequate assistance to people unable to work, the removal of inequities in coverage under current programs, and fiscal relief needed by States and localities.

Our current welfare system is long overdue for serious reform; the system is wasteful and not fully effective. The legislation I have proposed will help eliminate inequities by establishing a national minimum benefit, and by directly relating benefit levels to the poverty threshold. It will reduce program complexity, which leads to inefficiency and waste, by simplifying and coordinating administration among different programs.

I urge the Congress to take action in this area along the lines I have recommended.

CHILD WELFARE

My Administration has worked closely with the Congress on legislation which is designed to improve greatly the child welfare services and foster care programs and to create a Federal system of adoption assistance. These improvements will be achieved with the recent enactment of H.R. 3434, the Adoption Assistance and Child Welfare Act of 1980. The well-being of children in need of homes and their permanent placement have been a primary concern of my Administration. This legislation will ensure that children are not lost in the foster care system, but instead will be returned to their families where possible or placed in permanent adoptive homes.

LOW-INCOME ENERGY ASSISTANCE

In 1979 I proposed a program to provide an annual total of $1.6 billion to low-income households which are hardest hit by rising energy bills. With the cooperation of Congress, we were able to move quickly to provide assistance to eligible households in time to meet their winter heating bills.

In response to the extreme heat conditions affecting many parts of the country during 1980, I directed the Community Services Administration to make available over $27 million to assist low-income individuals, especially the elderly, facing life threatening circumstances due to extreme heat.

Congress amended and reauthorized the low-income energy assistance program for fiscal year 1981, and provided $1.85 billion to meet anticipated increasing need. The need for a program to help low-income households with rising energy expenses will not abate in the near future. The low-income energy assistance program should be reauthorized to meet those needs.

HOUSING

For the past 14 months, high interest rates have had a severe impact on the nation's housing market. Yet the current pressures and uncertainties should not obscure the achievements of the past four years.

Working with the Congress, the regulatory agencies, and the financial community, my Administration has brought about an expanded and steadier flow of funds into home mortgages. Deregulation of the interest rates payable by depository institutions, the evolution of variable and renegotiated rate mortgages, development of high yielding savings certificates, and expansion of the secondary mortgage market have all increased housing's ability to attract capital and have assured that mortgage money would not be cut off when interest rates rose. These actions will diminish the cyclicality of the housing industry. Further, we have secured legislation updating the Federal Government's emergency authority to provide support for the housing industry through the Brooke-Cranston program, and creating a new Section 235 housing stimulus program. These tools will enable the Federal Government to deal quickly and effectively with serious distress in this critical industry.

We have also worked to expand homeownership opportunities for Americans. By using innovative financing mechanisms, such as the graduated payment mortgage, we have increased the access of middle income families to housing credit. By revitalizing the Section 235 program, we have enabled nearly 100,000 moderate income households to purchase new homes. By reducing paperwork and regulation in Federal programs, and by working with State and local governments to ease the regulatory burden, we have helped to hold down housing costs and produce affordable housing.

As a result of these governmentwide efforts, 5 1/2 million more American families bought homes in the past four years than in any equivalent period in history. And more than 7 million homes have begun construction during my Administration, 1 million more than in the previous four years.

We have devoted particular effort to meeting the housing needs of low and moderate income families. In the past four years, more than 1 million subsidized units have been made available for occupancy by lower income Americans and more than 600,000 assisted units have gone into construction. In addition, we have undertaken a series of measures to revitalize and preserve the nation's 2 million units of public and assisted housing.

For Fiscal Year 1982, I am proposing to continue our commitment to lower income housing. I am requesting funds to support 260,000 units of Section 8 and public housing, maintaining these programs at the level provided by Congress in Fiscal 1981.

While we have made progress in the past four years, in the future there are reasons for concern. Home price inflation and high interest rates threaten to put homeownership out of reach for first-time homebuyers. Lower income households, the elderly and those dependent upon rental housing face rising rents, low levels of rental housing construction by historic standards, and the threat of displacement due to conversion to condominiums and other factors. Housing will face strong competition for investment capital from the industrial sector generally and the energy industries, in particular.

To address these issues, I appointed a Presidential Task Force and Advisory Group last October. While this effort will not proceed due to the election result, I hope the incoming Administration will proceed with a similar venture.

The most important action government can take to meet America's housing needs is to restore stability to the economy and bring down the rate of inflation. Inflation has driven up home prices, operating costs and interest rates. Market uncertainty about inflation has contributed to the instability in interest rates, which has been an added burden to home-builders and homebuyers alike. By making a long-term commitment to provide a framework for greater investment, sustained economic growth, and price stability, my Administration has begun the work of creating a healthy environment for housing.

TRANSPORTATION

With the passage of the Airline Deregulation Act of 1978, the Motor Carrier Act of 1980, and the Harley O. Staggers Rail Act of 1980, my Administration, working with the Congress, has initiated a new era of reduced regulation of transportation industries. Deregulation will lead to increased productivity and operating efficiencies in the industries involved, and stimulate price and service competition, to the benefit of consumers generally. I urge the new Administration to continue our efforts on behalf of deregulation legislation for the intercity passenger bus industry as well.

In the coming decade, the most significant challenge facing the nation in transportation services will be to improve a deteriorating physical infrastructure of roadways, railroads, waterways and mass transit systems, in order to conserve costly energy supplies while promoting effective transportation services.

HIGHWAYS

Our vast network of highways, which account for 90 percent of travel and 80 percent by value of freight traffic goods movement, is deteriorating. If current trends continue, a major proportion of the Interstate pavement will have deteriorated by the end of the 1980's.

Arresting the deterioration of the nation's system of highways is a high priority objective for the 1980's. We must reorient the Federal mission from major new construction projects to the stewardship of the existing Interstate Highway System. Interstate gaps should be judged on the connections they make and on their compatibility with community needs.

During this decade, highway investments will be needed to increase productivity, particularly in the elimination of bottlenecks, provide more efficient connections to ports and seek low-cost solutions to traffic demand.

My Administration has therefore recommended redefining completion of the Interstate system, consolidating over 27 categorical assistance programs into nine, and initiating a major repair and rehabilitation program for segments of the Interstate system. This effort should help maintain the condition and performance of the Nation's highways, particularly the Interstate and primary system; provide a realistic means to complete the Interstate system by 1990; ensure better program delivery through consolidation, and assist urban revitalization. In addition, the Congress must address the urgent funding problems of the highway trust fund, and the need to generate greater revenues.

MASS TRANSIT

In the past decade the nation's public transit systems' ridership increased at an annual average of 1.1% each year in the 1970's (6.9% in 1979). Continued increases in the cost of fuel are expected to make transit a growing part of the nation's transportation system.

As a result, my Administration projected a ten year, $43 billion program to increase mass transit capacity by 50 percent, and promote more energy efficient vehicle uses in the next decade. The first part of this proposal was the five year, $24.7 billion Urban Mass Transportation Administration reauthorization legislation I sent to the Congress in March, 1980. I urge the 97th Congress to quickly enact this or similar legislation in 1981.

My Administration was also the first to have proposed and signed into law a non-urban formula grant program to assist rural areas and small communities with public transportation programs to end their dependence on the automobile, promote energy conservation and efficiency, and provide transportation services to impoverished rural communities.

A principal need of the 1980's will be maintaining mobility for all segments of the population in the face of severely increasing transportation costs and uncertainty of fuel supplies. We must improve the flexibility of our transportation system and offer greater choice and diversity in transportation services. While the private automobile will continue to be the principal means of transportation for many Americans, public transportation can become an increasingly attractive alternative. We, therefore, want to explore a variety of paratransit modes, various types of buses, modern rapid transit, regional rail systems and light rail systems.

Highway planning and transit planning must be integrated and related to State, regional, district and neighborhood planning efforts now in place or emerging. Low density development and land use threaten the fiscal capacity of many communities to support needed services and infrastructure.

ELDERLY AND HANDICAPPED

TRANSPORTATION

Transportation policies in the 1980's must pay increasing attention to the needs of the elderly and handicapped. By 1990, the number of people over 65 will have grown from today's 19 million to 27 million. During the same period, the number of handicapped— people who have difficulty using transit as well as autos, including the elderly— is expected to increase from 9 to 11 million, making up 4.5 percent of the population.

We must not retreat from a policy that affords a significant and growing portion of our population accessible public transportation while recognizing that the handicapped are a diverse group and will need flexible, door-to-door service where regular public transportation will not do the job.

RAILROADS

In addition, the Federal government must reassess the appropriate Federal role of support for passenger and freight rail services such as Amtrak and Conrail. Our goal through federal assistance should be to maintain and enhance adequate rail service, where it is not otherwise available to needy communities. But Federal subsidies must be closely scrutinized to be sure they are a stimulus to, and not a replacement for, private investment and initiative. Federal assistance cannot mean permanent subsidies for unprofitable operations.

WATERWAYS AND RURAL TRANSPORTATION

There is a growing need in rural and small communities for improved transportation services. Rail freight service to many communities has declined as railroads abandon unproductive branch lines. At the same time, rural roads are often inadequate to handle large, heavily-loaded trucks. The increased demand for "harvest to harbor" service has also placed an increased burden on rural transportation systems, while bottlenecks along the Mississippi River delay grain shipments to the Gulf of Mexico.

We have made some progress:

— To further develop the nation's waterways, my Administration began construction of a new 1,200 foot lock at the site of Lock and Dam 26 on the Mississippi River. When opened in 1987, the new lock will have a capacity of 86 million tons per year, an 18 percent increase over the present system. The U.S. Army Corps of Engineers has also undertaken studies to assess the feasibility of expanding the Bonneville Locks. Rehabilitation of John Day Lock was begun in 1980 and should be completed in 1982. My Administration also supports the completion of the Upper Mississippi River Master Plan to determine the feasibility of constructing a second lock at Alton, Illinois. These efforts will help alleviate delays in transporting corn, soybeans and other goods along the Mississippi River to the Gulf of Mexico.

— The Department of Transportation's new Small Community and Rural Transportation Policy will target federal assistance for passenger transportation, roads and highways, truck service, and railroad freight service to rural areas. This policy implements and expands upon the earlier White House Initiative, "Improving Transportation in Rural America," announced in June, 1979, and the President's "Small Community and Rural Development Policy" announced in December, 1979. The Congress should seek ways to balance rail branch line abandonment with the service needs of rural and farm communities, provide financial assistance to rail branch line rehabilitation where appropriate, assist shippers to adjust to rail branch line abandonment where it takes place, and help make it possible for trucking firms to serve light density markets with dependable and efficient trucking services.

MARITIME POLICY

During my Administration I have sought to ensure that the U.S. maritime industry will not have to function at an unfair competitive disadvantage in the international market. As I indicated in my maritime policy statement to the Congress in July, 1979, the American merchant marine is vital to our Nation's welfare, and Federal actions should promote rather than harm it. In pursuit of this objective, I signed into law the Controlled Carrier Act of 1978, authorizing the Federal Maritime Commission to regulate certain rate cutting practices of some state-controlled carriers, and recently signed a bilateral maritime agreement with the People's Republic of China that will expand the access of American ships to 20 specified Chinese ports, and set aside for American-flag ships a substantial share (at least one-third) of the cargo between our countries. This agreement should officially foster expanded U.S. and Chinese shipping services linking the two countries, and will provide further momentum to the growth of Sino-American trade.

There is also a need to modernize and expand the dry bulk segment of our fleet. Our heavy dependence on foreign carriage of U.S.-bulk cargoes deprives the U.S. economy of seafaring and shipbuilding jobs, adds to the balance-of-payments deficit, deprives the Government of substantial tax revenues, and leaves the United States dependent on foreign-flag shipping for a continued supply of raw materials to support the civil economy and war production in time of war.

I therefore sent to the Congress proposed legislation to strengthen this woefully weak segment of the U.S.-flag fleet by removing certain disincentives to U.S. construction of dry bulkers and their operation under U.S. registry. Enactment of this proposed legislation would establish the basis for accelerating the rebuilding of the U.S.-flag dry bulk fleet toward a level commensurate with the position of the United States as the world's leading bulk trading country.

During the past year the Administration has stated its support for legislation that would provide specific Federal assistance for the installation of fuel-efficient engines in existing American ships, and would strengthen this country's shipbuilding mobilization base. Strengthening the fleet is important, but we must also maintain our shipbuilding base for future ship construction.

Provisions in existing laws calling for substantial or exclusive use of American-flag vessels to carry cargoes generated by the Government must be vigorously pursued.

I have therefore supported requirements that 50 percent of oil purchased for the strategic petroleum reserve be transported in U.S.-flag vessels, that the Cargo Preference Act be applied to materials furnished for the U.S. assisted construction of air bases in Israel, and to cargoes transported pursuant to the Chrysler Corporation Loan Guarantee Act. In addition, the deep Seabed Hard Mineral Resources Act requires that at least one ore carrier per mine site be a U.S.-flag vessel.

Much has been done, and much remains to be done. The FY 1982 budget includes a $107 million authorization for Construction Differential Subsidy ("CDS") funds which, added to the unobligated CDS balance of $100 million from 1980, and the recently enacted $135 million 1981 authorization, will provide an average of $171 million in CDS funds in 1981 and 1982.

COAL EXPORT POLICY

While significant growth in foreign demand for U.S. steam coal is foreseen, congestion at major U.S. coal exporting ports such as Hampton Roads, Virginia, and Baltimore, Maryland, could delay and impede exports.

My Administration has worked through the Interagency Coal Task Force Study, which I created, to promote cooperation and coordination of resources between shippers, railroads, vessel broker/ operators and port operators, and to determine the most appropriate Federal role in expanding and modernizing coal export facilities, including dredging deeper channels at selected ports.

Some progress has already been made. In addition to action taken by transshippers to reduce the number of coal classifications used whenever possible, by the Norfolk and Western Railroad to upgrade its computer capability to quickly inventory its coal cars in its yards, and by the Chessie Railroad which is reactivating Pier 15 in Newport News and has established a berth near its Curtis Bay Pier in Baltimore to decrease delays in vessel berthing, public activities will include:

— A $26.5 million plan developed by the State of Pennsylvania and Conrail to increase Conrail's coal handling capacity at Philadelphia;

— A proposal by the State of Virginia to construct a steam coal port on the Craney Island Disposal area in Portsmouth harbor;

— Plans by Mobile, Alabama, which operates the only publicly owned coal terminal in the U.S. to enlarge its capacity at McDuffie Island to 10 million tons ground storage and 100 car unit train unloading capability;

— Development at New Orleans of steam coal facilities that are expected to add over 20 million tons of annual capacity by 1983; and

— The Corps of Engineers, working with other interested Federal agencies, will determine which ports should be dredged, to what depth and on what schedule, in order to accommodate larger coal carrying vessels.

Private industry will, of course, play a major role in developing the United States' coal export facilities. The new Administration should continue to work to eliminate transportation bottlenecks that impede our access to foreign markets.

Special Needs

WOMEN

The past four years have been years of rapid advancement for women. Our focus has been two-fold: to provide American women with a full range of opportunities and to make them a part of the mainstream of every aspect of our national life and leadership.

I have appointed a record number of women to judgeships and to top government posts. Fully 22 percent of all my appointees are women, and I nominated 41 of the 46 women who sit on the Federal bench today. For the first time in our history, women occupy policymaking positions at the highest level of every Federal agency and department and have demonstrated their ability to serve our citizens well.

We have strengthened the rights of employed women by consolidating and strengthening enforcement of sex discrimination laws under the EEOC, by expanding employment rights of pregnant women through the Pregnancy Disability Bill, and by increasing federal employment opportunities for women through civil service reform, and flexi-time and part-time employment.

By executive order, I created the first national program to provide women businessowners with technical assistance, grants, loans, and improved access to federal contracts.

We have been sensitive to the needs of women who are homemakers. I established an Office of Families within HHS and sponsored the White House Conference on Families. We initiated a program targeting CETA funds to help displaced homemakers. The Social Security system was amended to eliminate the widow's penalty and a comprehensive study of discriminatory provisions and possible changes was presented to Congress. Legislation was passed to give divorced spouses of foreign service officers rights to share in pension benefits.

We created an office on domestic violence within HHS to coordinate the 12 agencies that now have domestic violence relief programs, and to distribute information on the problem and the services available to victims.

Despite a stringent budget for FY 1981, the Administration consistently supported the Women's Educational Equity Act and family planning activities, as well as other programs that affect women, such as food stamps, WIC, and social security.

We have been concerned not only about the American woman's opportunities, but ensuring equality for women around the world. In November, 1980, I sent to the Senate the Convention on the Elimination of All Forms of Discrimination Against Women. This United Nations document is the most comprehensive and detailed international agreement which seeks the advancement of women.

On women's issues, I have sought the counsel of men and women in and out of government and from all regions of our country. I established two panels— the President's Advisory Committee for Women and the Interdepartmental Task Force on Women— to advise me on these issues. The mandate for both groups expired on December 31, but they have left behind a comprehensive review of the status of women in our society today. That review provides excellent guidance for the work remaining in our battle against sex discrimination.

Even though we have made progress, much remains on the agenda for women. I remain committed to the Equal Rights Amendment and will continue to work for its passage. It is essential to the goal of bringing America's women fully into the mainstream of American life that the ERA be ratified.

The efforts begun for women in employment, business and education should be continued and strengthened. Money should be available to states to establish programs to help the victims of domestic violence. Congress should pass a national health care plan and a welfare reform program, and these measures should reflect the needs of women.

The talents of women should continue to be used to the fullest inside and outside of government, and efforts should continue to see that they have the widest range of opportunities and options.

HANDICAPPED

I hope that my Administration will be remembered in this area for leading the way toward full civil rights for handicapped Americans. When I took office, no federal agency had yet issued 504 regulations. As I leave office, this first step by every major agency and department in the federal government is almost complete. But it is only a first step. The years ahead will require steadfast dedication by the President to protect and promote these precious rights in the classroom, in the workplace, and in all public facilities so that handicapped individuals may join the American mainstream and contribute to the fullest their resources and talents to our economic and social life.

Just as we supported, in an unprecedented way, the civil rights of disabled persons in schools and in the workplace, other initiatives in health prevention, such as our immunization and nutrition programs for young children and new intense efforts to reverse spinal cord injury, must continue so that the incidence of disability continues to decline.

This year is the U.N.-declared International Year of Disabled Persons. We are organizing activities to celebrate and promote this important commemorative year within the government as well as in cooperation with private sector efforts in this country and around the world. The International Year will give our country the opportunity to recognize the talents and capabilities of our fellow citizens with disabilities. We can also share our rehabilitation and treatment skills with other countries and learn from them as well. I am proud that the United States leads the world in mainstreaming and treating disabled people. However, we have a long way to go before all psychological and physical barriers to disabled people are torn down and they can be full participants in our American way of life. We must pledge our full commitment to this goal during the International Year.

FAMILIES

Because of my concern for American families, my Administration convened last year the first White House Conference on Families which involved seven national hearings, over 506 state and local events, three White House Conferences, and the direct participation of more than 125,000 citizens. The Conference reaffirmed the centrality of families in our lives and nation but documented problems American families face as well. We also established the Office of Families within the Department of Health and Human Services to review government policies and programs that affect families.

I expect the departments and agencies within the executive branch of the Federal government as well as Members of Congress, corporate and business leaders, and State and local officials across the country, to study closely the recommendations of the White House Conference and implement them appropriately. As public policy is developed and implemented by the Federal government, cognizance of the work of the Conference should be taken as a pragmatic and essential step.

The Conference has done a good job of establishing an agenda for action to assure that the policies of the Federal government are more sensitive in their impact on families. I hope the Congress will review and seriously consider the Conference's recommendations.

OLDER AMERICANS

My Administration has taken great strides toward solving the difficult problems faced by older Americans. Early in my term we worked successfully with the Congress to assure adequate revenues for the Social Security Trust Funds. And last year the strength of the Social Security System was strengthened by legislation I proposed to permit borrowing among the separate trust funds. I have also signed into law legislation prohibiting employers from requiring retirement prior to age 70, and removing mandatory retirement for most Federal employees. In addition, my Administration worked very closely with Congress to amend the Older Americans Act in a way that has already improved administration of its housing, social services, food delivery, and employment programs.

This year, I will be submitting to Congress a budget which again demonstrates my commitment to programs for the elderly. It will include, as my previous budgets have, increased funding for nutrition, senior centers and home health care, and will focus added resources on the needs of older Americans.

With the 1981 White House Conference on Aging approaching, I hope the new Administration will make every effort to assure an effective and useful conference. This Conference should enable older Americans to voice their concerns and give us guidance in our continued efforts to ensure the quality of life so richly deserved by our senior citizens.

REFUGEES

We cannot hope to build a just and humane society at home if we ignore the humanitarian claims of refugees, their lives at stake, who have nowhere else to turn. Our country can be proud that hundreds of thousands of people around the world would risk everything they have— including their own lives— to come to our country.

This Administration initiated and implemented the first comprehensive reform of our refugee and immigration policies in over 25 years. We also established the first refugee coordination office in the Department of State under the leadership of a special ambassador and coordinator for refugee affairs and programs. The new legislation and the coordinator's office will bring common sense and consolidation to our Nation's previously fragmented, inconsistent, and in many ways, outdated, refugee and immigration policies.

With the unexpected arrival of thousands of Cubans and Haitians who sought refuge in our country last year, outside of our regular immigration and refugee admissions process, our country and its government were tested in being compassionate and responsive to a major human emergency. Because we had taken steps to reorganize our refugee programs, we met that test successfully. I am proud that the American people responded to this crisis with their traditional good will and hospitality. Also, we would never have been able to handle this unprecedented emergency without the efforts of the private resettlement agencies who have always been there to help refugees in crises.

Immigrants to this country always contribute more toward making our country stronger than they ever take from the system. I am confident that the newest arrivals to our country will carry on this tradition.

While we must remain committed to aiding and assisting those who come to our shores, at the same time we must uphold our immigration and refugee policies and provide adequate enforcement resources. As a result of our enforcement policy, the illegal flow from Cuba has been halted and an orderly process has been initiated to make certain that our refugee and immigration laws are honored.

This year the Select Commission on Immigration and Refugee Policy will complete its work and forward its advice and recommendations. I hope that the recommendations will be carefully considered by the new Administration and the Congress, for it is clear that we must take additional action to keep our immigration policy responsive to emergencies and ever changing times.

VETERANS

This country and its leadership has a continuing and unique obligation to the men and women who served their nation in the armed forces and help maintain or restore peace in the world.

My commitment to veterans, as evidenced by my record, is characterized by a conscientious and consistent emphasis in these general areas:

First, we have worked to honor the Vietnam veteran. During my Administration, and under the leadership of VA Administrator Max Cleland, I was proud to lead our country in an overdue acknowledgement of our Nation's gratitude to the men and women who served their country during the bitter war in Southeast Asia. Their homecoming was deferred and seemed doomed to be ignored. Our country has matured in the last four years and at long last we were able to separate the war from the warrior and honor these veterans. But with our acknowledgement of their service goes an understanding that some Vietnam veterans have unique needs and problems.

My Administration was able to launch a long sought after psychological readjustment and outreach program, unprecedented in its popularity, sensitivity and success. This program must be continued. The Administration has also grappled with the difficult questions posed by some veterans who served in Southeast Asia and were exposed to potentially harmful substances, including the herbicide known as Agent Orange. We have launched scientific inquiries that should answer many veterans' questions about their health and should provide the basis for establishing sound compensation policy. We cannot rest until their concerns are dealt with in a sensitive, expeditious and compassionate fashion.

Second, we have focused the VA health care system in the needs of the service-connected disabled veteran. We initiated and are implementing the first reform of the VA vocational rehabilitation system since its inception in 1943. Also, my Administration was the first to seek a cost-of-living increase for the recipients of VA compensation every year. My last budget also makes such a request. The Administration also launched the Disabled Veterans Outreach Program in the Department of Labor which has successfully placed disabled veterans in jobs. Services provided by the VA health care system will be further targeted to the special needs of disabled veterans during the coming year.

Third, the VA health care system, the largest in the free world, has maintained its independence and high quality during my Administration. We have made the system more efficient and have therefore treated more veterans than ever before by concentrating on out-patient care and through modern management improvements. As the median age of the American veteran population increases, we must concentrate on further changes within the VA system to keep it independent and to serve as a model to the nation and to the world as a center for research, treatment and rehabilitation.

Government Assistance

GENERAL AID TO STATE AND LOCAL

GOVERNMENTS

Since taking office, I have been strongly committed to strengthening the fiscal and economic condition of our Nation's

State and local governments. I have accomplished this goal by encouraging economic development of local communities, and by supporting the General Revenue Sharing and other essential grant-in-aid programs.

GRANTS-IN-AID TO STATES AND LOCALITIES

During my Administration, total grants-in-aid to State and local governments have increased by more than 40 percent, from $68 billion in Fiscal Year 1977 to $96 billion in Fiscal Year 1981. This significant increase in aid has allowed States and localities to maintain services that are essential to their citizens without imposing onerous tax burdens. It also has allowed us to establish an unprecedented partnership between the leaders of the Federal government and State and local government elected officials.

GENERAL REVENUE SHARING

Last year Congress enacted legislation that extends the General Revenue Sharing program for three more years. This program is the cornerstone of our efforts to maintain the fiscal health of our Nation's local government. It will provide $4.6 billion in each of the next three years to cities, counties and towns. This program is essential to the continued ability of our local governments to provide essential police, fire and sanitation services.

This legislation renewing GRS will be the cornerstone of Federal-State-local government relations in the 1980's. This policy will emphasize the need for all levels of government to cooperate in order to meet the needs of the most fiscally strained cities and counties, and also will emphasize the important role that GRS can play in forging this partnership. I am grateful that Congress moved quickly to assure that our Nation's localities can begin the 1980's in sound fiscal condition.

COUNTER-CYCLICAL ASSISTANCE

Last year, I proposed that Congress enact a $1 billion counter-cyclical fiscal assistance program to protect States and localities from unexpected changes in the national economy. This program unfortunately was not enacted by the [full] Congress. I, therefore, have not included funding for counter-cyclical aid in my Fiscal Year 1982 budget. Nevertheless, I urge Congress to enact a permanent stand-by counter-cyclical program, so that States and cities can be protected during the next economic downturn.

URBAN POLICY

Three years ago, I proposed the Nation's first comprehensive urban policy. That policy involved more than one hundred improvements in existing Federal programs, four new Executive Orders and nineteen pieces of urban-oriented legislation. With Congress' cooperation, sixteen of these bills have now been signed into law.

ECONOMIC DEVELOPMENT

One of the principal goals of my domestic policy has been to strengthen the private sector economic base of our Nation's economically troubled urban and rural areas. With Congress' cooperation, we have substantially expanded the Federal government's economic development programs and provided new tax incentives for private investment in urban and rural communities. These programs have helped many communities to attract new private sector jobs and investments and to retain the jobs and investments that already are in place.

When I took office, the Federal government was spending less than $300 million annually on economic development programs, and only $60 million of those funds in our Nation's urban areas. Since that time, we have created the Urban Development Action Grant (UDAG) program and substantially expanded the economic development programs in the Commerce Department. My FY 1982 budget requests more than $1.5 billion for economic development grants, loans and interest subsidies and almost $1.5 billion for loan guarantees. Approximately 60 percent of these funds will be spent in our Nation's urban areas. In addition, we have extended the 10 percent investment credit to include rehabilitation of existing industrial facilities as well as new construction.

I continue to believe that the development of private sector investment and jobs is the key to revitalizing our Nation's economically depressed urban and rural areas. To ensure that the necessary economic development goes forward, the Congress must continue to provide strong support for the UDAG program and the programs for the Economic Development Administration. Those programs provide a foundation for the economic development of our Nation in the 1980's.

COMMUNITY DEVELOPMENT

The partnership among Federal, State and local governments to revitalize our Nation's communities has been a high priority of my Administration. When I took office, I proposed a substantial expansion of the Community Development Block Grant (CDBG) program and the enactment of a new $400 million Urban Development Action Grant (UDAG) program.

Both of these programs have provided essential community and economic development assistance to our Nation's cities and counties.

Last year, Congress reauthorized both the CDBG and UDAG programs. The CDBG program was reauthorized for three more years with annual funding increases of $150 million, and the UDAG program was extended for three years at the current funding level of $675 million annually. My 1982 budget requests full funding for both of these programs. These actions should help our Nation's cities and counties to continue the progress they have made in the last three years.

NEIGHBORHOODS

During my Administration we have taken numerous positive steps to achieve a full partnership of neighborhood organizations and government at all levels. We have successfully fought against red lining and housing discrimination. We created innovative Self Help funding and technical resource transfer mechanisms. We have created unique methods of access for neighborhood organizations to have a participating role in Federal and State government decision-making. Neighborhood based organizations are the threshold of the American community.

The Federal government will need to develop more innovative and practical ways for neighborhood based organizations to successfully participate in the identification and solution of local and neighborhood concerns. Full partnership will only be achieved with the knowing participation of leaders of government, business, education and unions. Neither state nor Federal solutions imposed from on high will suffice. Neighborhoods are the fabric and soul of this great land. Neighborhoods define the weave that has been used to create a permanent fabric. The Federal government must take every opportunity to provide access and influence to the individuals and organizations affected at the neighborhood level.

Rural Policy

Since the beginning of my Administration, I have been committed to improving the effectiveness with which the Federal government deals with the problems and needs of a rapidly changing rural America. The rapid growth of some rural areas has placed a heavy strain on communities and their resources. There are also persistent problems of poverty and economic stagnation in other parts of rural America. Some rural areas continue to lose population, as they have for the past several decades.

In December, 1979, I announced the Small Community and Rural Development Policy. It was the culmination of several years' work and was designed to address the varying needs of our rural population. In 1980, my Administration worked with the Congress to pass the Rural Development Policy Act of 1980, which when fully implemented will allow us to meet the needs of rural people and their communities more effectively and more efficiently.

As a result of the policy and the accompanying legislation, we have:

— Created the position of Under Secretary of Agriculture for Small Community and Rural Development to provide overall leadership.

— Established a White House Working Group to assist in the implementation of the policy.

— Worked with more than 40 governors to form State rural development councils to work in partnership with the White House Working Group, and the Federal agencies, to better deliver State and Federal programs to rural areas.

— Directed the White House Working Group to annually review existing and proposed policies, programs, and budget levels to determine their adequacy in meeting rural needs and the fulfilling of the policy's objectives and principles.

This effort on the part of my Administration and the Congress has resulted in a landmark policy. For the first time, rural affairs has received the prominence it has always deserved. It is a policy that can truly help alleviate the diverse and differing problems rural America will face in the 1980's.

With the help and dedication of a great many people around the country who are concerned with rural affairs, we have constructed a mechanism for dealing effectively with rural problems. There is now a great opportunity to successfully combine Federal efforts with the efforts of rural community leaders and residents. It is my hope this spirit of cooperation and record of accomplishment will be continued in the coming years.

CONSUMERS

In September, 1979, I signed an Executive Order designed to strengthen and coordinate Federal consumer programs and to establish procedures to improve and facilitate consumer participation in government decision-making. Forty Federal agencies have adopted programs to comply with the requirements of the Order. These programs will improve complaint handling, provide better information to consumers, enhance opportunities for public participation in government proceedings, and assure that the consumer point of view is considered in all programs, policies, and regulations.

While substantial progress has been made in assuring a consumer presence in Federal agencies, work must continue to meet fully the goals of the Executive Order. Close monitoring of agency compliance with the requirements of the Order is necessary. Continued evaluation to assure that the programs are effective and making maximum use of available resources is also essential. As a complement to these initiatives, efforts to provide financial assistance in regulatory proceedings to citizen groups, small businesses, and others whose participation is limited by their economic circumstances must continue to be pursued.

It is essential that consumer representatives in government pay particular attention to the needs and interests of low-income consumers and minorities. The Office of Consumer Affairs' publication, "People Power: What Communities Are Doing to Counter Inflation," catalogues some of the ways that government and the private sector can assist the less powerful in our society to help themselves. New ways should be found to help foster this new people's movement which is founded on the principle of self-reliance.

Science and Technology

Science and technology contribute immeasurably to the lives of all Americans. Our high standard of living is largely the product of the technology that surrounds us in the home or factory. Our good health is due in large part to our ever increasing scientific understanding. Our national security is assured by the application pate science and technology will bring.

The Federal government has a special role to play in science and technology. Although the fruits of scientific achievements surround us, it is often difficult to predict the benefits that will arise from a given scientific venture. And these benefits, even if predictable, do not usually lead to ownership rights. Accordingly, the Government has a special obligation to support science as an investment in our future.

My Administration has sought to reverse a decade-long decline in funding. Despite the need for fiscal restraint, real support of basic research has grown nearly 11% during my term in office. And, my Administration has sought to increase the support of long-term research in the variety of mission agencies. In this way, we can harness the American genius for innovation to meet the economic, energy, health, and security challenges that confront our nation.

— International Relations and National Security. Science and technology are becoming increasingly important elements of our national security and foreign policies. This is especially so in the current age of sophisticated defense systems and of growing dependence among all countries on modern technology for all aspects of their economic strength. For these reasons, scientific and technological considerations have been integral elements of the Administration's decision-making on such national security and foreign policy issues as the modernization of our strategic weaponry, arms control, technology transfer, the growing bilateral relationship with China, and our relations with the developing world.

Four themes have shaped U.S. policy in international scientific and technological cooperation: pursuit of new international initiatives to advance our own research and development objectives; development and strengthening of scientific exchange to bridge politically ideological, and cultural divisions between this country and other countries; formulation of programs and institutional relations to help developing countries use science and technology beneficially; and cooperation with other nations to manage technologies with local impact. At my direction, my Science and Technology Adviser has actively pursued international programs in support of these four themes. We have given special attention to scientific and technical relations with China, to new forms of scientific and technical cooperation with Japan, to cooperation with Mexico, other Latin American and Caribbean countries and several states in Black America, and to the proposed Institute for Scientific and Technological Cooperation.

In particular our cooperation with developing countries reflects the importance that each of them has placed on the relationship between economic growth and scientific and technological capability. It also reflects their view that the great strength of the U.S. in science and technology makes close relations with the U.S. technical community an especially productive means of enhancing this capability. Scientific and technological assistance is a key linkage between the U.S. and the developing world, a linkage that has been under-utilized in the past and one which we must continue to work to strengthen.

— Space Policy. The Administration has established a framework for a strong and evolving space program for the 1980's.

The Administration's space policy reaffirmed the separation of military space systems and the open civil space program, and at the same time, provided new guidance on technology transfer between the civil and military programs. The civil space program centers on three basic tenets: First, our space policy will reflect a balanced strategy of applications, science, and technology development. Second, activities will be pursued when they can be uniquely or more efficiently accomplished in space. Third, a premature commitment to a high challenge, space-engineering initiative of the complexity of Apollo is inappropriate. As the Shuttle development phases down, however, there will be added flexibility to consider new space applications, space science and new space exploration activities.

— Technology Development. The Shuttle dominates our technology development effort and correctly so. It represents one of the most sophisticated technological challenges ever undertaken, and as a result, has encountered technical problems. Nonetheless, the first manned orbital flight is now scheduled for March, 1981. I have been pleased to support strongly the necessary funds for the Shuttle throughout my Administration.

— Space Applications. Since 1972, the U.S. has conducted experimental civil remote sensing through Landsat satellites, thereby realizing many successful applications. Recognizing this fact, I directed the implementation of an operational civil land satellite remote sensing system, with the operational management responsibility in Commerce's National Oceanic and Atmospheric Administration. In addition, because ocean observations from space can meet common civil and military data requirements, a National Oceanic Satellite System has been proposed as a major FY 1981 new start.

— Space Science Exploration. The goals of this Administration's policy in space science have been to: (1) continue a vigorous program of planetary exploration to understand the origin and evolution of the solar system; (2) utilize the space telescope and free-flying satellites to usher in a new era of astronomy; (3) develop a better understanding of the sun and its interaction with the terrestrial environment; and (4) utilize the Shuttle and Spacelab to conduct basic research that complements earth-based life science investigations.

DISTRICT OF COLUMBIA

Washington, D.C., is home to both the Federal Government and to more than half a million American citizens. I have worked to improve the relationship between the Federal establishment and the Government of the District of Columbia in order to further the goals and spirit of home rule. The City controls more of its own destiny than was the case four years ago. Yet, despite the close cooperation between my Administration and that of Mayor Barry, we have not yet seen the necessary number of states ratify the Constitutional Amendment granting full voting representation in the Congress to the citizens of this city. It is my hope that this inequity will be rectified. The country and the people who inhabit Washington deserve no less.

THE ARTS

The arts are a precious national resource.

Federal support for the arts has been enhanced during my Administration by expanding government funding and services to arts institutions, individual artists, scholars, and teachers through the National Endowment for the Arts. We have broadened its scope and reach to a more diverse population. We have also reactivated the Federal Council on the Arts and Humanities.

It is my hope that during the coming years the new Administration and the Congress will:

— Continue support of institutions promoting development and understanding of the arts;

— Encourage business participants in a comprehensive effort to achieve a truly mixed economy of support for the arts;

— Explore a variety of mechanisms to nurture the creative talent of our citizens and build audiences for their work;

— Support strong, active National Endowments for the Arts;

— Seek greater recognition for the rich cultural tradition of the nation's minorities;

— Provide grants for the arts in low-income neighborhoods.

THE HUMANITIES

In recently reauthorizing Federal appropriations for the National Endowment for the Humanities, the Congress has once again reaffirmed that "the encouragement and support of national progress and scholarship in the humanities . . . while primarily a matter for private and local initiative, is also an appropriate matter of concern to the Federal Government" and that "a high civilization must not limit its efforts to science and technology alone but must give full value and support to the other great branches of man's scholarly and cultural activity in order to achieve a better understanding of the past, a better analysis of the present, and a better view of the future."

I believe we are in agreement that the humanities illuminate the values underlying important personal, social, and national questions raised in our society by its multiple links to and increasing dependence on technology, and by the diverse heritage of our many regions and ethnic groups. The humanities cast light on the broad issue of the role in a society of men and women of imagination and energy— those individuals who through their own example define "the spirit of the age," and in so doing move nations. Our Government's support for the humanities, within the framework laid down by the Congress, is a recognition of their essential nourishment of the life of the mind and vital enrichment of our national life.

I will be proposing an increase in funding this year sufficient to enable the Endowment to maintain the same level of support offered our citizens in Fiscal Year 1981.

In the allocation of this funding, special emphasis will be given to:

— Humanities education in the nation's schools, in response to the great needs that have arisen in this area;

— Scholarly research designed to increase our understanding of the cultures, traditions, and historical forces at work in other nations and in our own;

— Drawing attention to the physical disintegration of the raw material of our cultural heritage— books, manuscripts, periodicals, and other documents— and to the development of techniques to prevent the destruction and to preserve those materials; and

— The dissemination of quality programming in the humanities to increasingly large American audiences through the use of radio and television.

The dominant effort in the Endowment's expenditures will be a commitment to strengthen and promulgate scholarly excellence and achievement in work in the humanities in our schools, colleges, universities, libraries, museums and other cultural institutions, as well as in the work of individual scholars or collaborative groups engaged in advanced research in the humanities.

In making its grants the Endowment will increase its emphasis on techniques which stimulate support for the humanities from non-Federal sources, in order to reinforce our tradition of private philanthropy in this field, and to insure and expand the financial viability of our cultural institutions and life.

INSULAR AREAS

I have been firmly committed to self-determination for Puerto Rico, the Virgin Islands, Guam, American Samoa and the Northern Mariana Islands, and have vigorously supported the realization of whatever political status aspirations are democratically chosen by their peoples. This principle was the keystone of the comprehensive territorial policy I sent the Congress last year. I am pleased that most of the legislative elements of that policy were endorsed by the 96th Congress.

The unique cultures, fragile economies, and locations of our Caribbean and Pacific Islands are distinct assets to the United States which require the sensitive application of policy. The United States Government should pursue initiatives begun by my Administration and the Congress to stimulate insular economic development; enhance treatment under Federal programs eliminating current inequities; provide vitally needed special assistance and coordinate and rationalize policies. These measures will result in greater self-sufficiency and balanced growth. In particular, I hope that the new Congress will support funding for fiscal management, comprehensive planning and other technical assistance for the territories, as well as create the commission I have proposed to review the applicability of all Federal laws to the insular areas and make recommendations for appropriate modification.

IV. REMOVING GOVERNMENTAL WASTE AND INEFFICIENCY

One of my major commitments has been to restore public faith in our Federal government by cutting out waste and inefficiency. In the past four years, we have made dramatic advances toward this goal, many of them previously considered impossible to achieve. Where government rules and operations were unnecessary, they have been eliminated, as with airline, rail, trucking and financial deregulation. Where government functions are needed, they have been streamlined, through such landmark measures as the Civil Service Reform Act of 1978. I hope that the new administration and the Congress will keep up the momentum we have established for effective and responsible change in this area of crucial public concern.

CIVIL SERVICE REFORM

In March 1978, I submitted the Civil Service Reform Act to Congress. I called it the centerpiece of my efforts to reform and reorganize the government. With bipartisan support from Congress, the bill passed, and I am pleased to say that implementation is running well ahead of the statutory schedule. Throughout the service, we are putting into place the means to assure that reward and retention are based on performance and not simply on length of time on the job. In the first real test of the Reform Act, 98 percent of the eligible top-level managers joined the Senior Executive Service, choosing to relinquish job protections for the challenge and potential reward of this new corps of top executives. Though the Act does not require several of its key elements to be in operation for another year, some Federal agencies already have established merit pay systems for GS-13-15 managers, and most agencies are well on their way to establishing new performance standards for all their employees. All have paid out, or are now in the process of paying out, performance bonuses earned by outstanding members of the Senior Executive Service. Dismissals have increased by 10 percent, and dismissals specifically for inadequate job performance have risen 1500 percent, since the Act was adopted. Finally, we have established a fully independent Merit Systems Protection Board and Special Counsel to protect the rights of whistle-blowers and other Federal employees faced with threats to their rights.

In 1981, civil service reform faces critical challenges, all agencies must have fully functioning performance appraisal systems for all employees, and merit pay systems for compensating the government's 130,000 GS-13-15 managers. Performance bonuses for members of the Senior Executive Service will surely receive scrutiny. If this attention is balanced and constructive, it can only enhance the chances for ultimate success of our bipartisan commitment to the revolutionary and crucial "pay for performance" concept.

REGULATORY REFORM

During the past four years we have made tremendous progress in regulatory reform. We have discarded old economic regulations that prevented competition and raised consumer costs, and we have imposed strong management principles on the regulatory programs the country needs, cutting paperwork and other wasteful burdens. The challenge for the future is to continue the progress in both areas without crippling vital health and safety programs.

Our economic deregulation program has achieved major successes in five areas:

Airlines: The Airline Deregulation Act is generating healthy competition, saving billions in fares, and making the airlines more efficient. The Act provides that in 1985 the CAB itself will go out of existence.

Trucking: The trucking deregulation bill opens the industry to competition and allows truckers wide latitude on the routes they drive and the goods they haul. The bill also phases out most of the old law's immunity for setting rates. The Congressional Budget Office estimates these reforms will save as much as $8 billion per year and cut as much as half a percentage point from the inflation rate.

Railroads: Overregulation has stifled railroad management initiative, service, and competitive pricing. The new legislation gives the railroads the freedom they need to rebuild a strong, efficient railroad industry.

Financial Institutions: With the help of the Congress, over the past four years we have achieved two major pieces of financial reform legislation, legislation which has provided the basis for the most far-reaching changes in the financial services industry since the 1930's. The International Banking Act of 1978 was designed to reduce the advantages that foreign banks operating in the United States possessed in comparison to domestic banks. The Depository Institutions Deregulation and Monetary Control Act, adopted last March, provides for the phased elimination of a variety of anti-competitive barriers to financial institutions and freedom to offer services to and attract the savings of consumers, especially small savers.

Recently, I submitted to the Congress my Administration's recommendations for the phased liberalization of restrictions on geographic expansion by commercial banks. Last year the Administration and financial regulatory agencies proposed legislation to permit the interstate acquisition of failing depository institutions. In view of the difficult outlook for some depository institutions I strongly urge the Congress to take prompt favorable action on the failing bank legislation.

Telecommunications: While Congress did not pass legislation in this area, the Federal Communications Commission has taken dramatic action to open all aspects of communications to competition and to eliminate regulations in the areas where competition made them obsolete. The public is benefitting from an explosion of competition and new services.

While these initiatives represent dramatic progress in economic deregulation, continued work is needed. I urge Congress to act on communications legislation and to consider other proposed deregulation measures, such as legislation on the bus industry. In addition, the regulatory commissions must maintain their commitment to competition as the best regulator of all.

The other part of my reform program covers the regulations that are needed to protect the health, safety, and welfare of our citizens. For these regulations, my Administration has created a management program to cut costs without sacrificing goals. Under my Executive Order 12044, we required agencies to analyze the costs of their major new rules and consider alternative approaches, such as performance standards and voluntary codes, that may make rules less costly and more flexible. We created the Regulatory Analysis Review Group in the White House to analyze the most costly proposed new rules and find ways to improve them. The Regulatory Council was established to provide the first Government-wide listing of upcoming rules and eliminate overlapping and conflicting regulations. Agencies have launched "sunset" programs to weed out outmoded old regulations. We have acted to encourage public participation in regulatory decision-making.

These steps have already saved billions of dollars in regulatory costs and slashed thousands of outmoded regulations. We are moving steadily toward a regulatory system that provides needed protections fairly, predictably, and at minimum cost.

I urge Congress to continue on this steady path and resist the simplistic solutions that have been proposed as alternatives. Proposals like legislative veto and increased judicial review will add another layer to the regulatory process, making it more cumbersome and inefficient. The right approach to reform is to improve the individual statutes, where they need change, and to ensure that the regulatory agencies implement those statutes sensibly.

PAPERWORK REDUCTION

The Federal Government imposes a huge paperwork burden on business, local government, and the private sector. Many of these forms are needed for vital government functions, but others are duplicative, overly complex or obsolete.

During my Administration we cut the paperwork burden by 15 percent, and we created procedures to continue this progress. The new Paperwork Reduction Act centralizes, in OMB, oversight of all agencies' information requirements and strengthens OMB's authority to eliminate needless forms. The "paperwork budget" process, which I established by executive order, applies the discipline of the budget process to the hours of reporting time imposed on the public, forcing agencies to scrutinize all their forms each year. With effective implementation, these steps should allow further, substantial paperwork cuts in the years ahead.

TIGHTENING STANDARDS FOR GOVERNMENTAL EFFICIENCY AND INTEGRITY

To develop a foundation to carry out energy policy, we consolidated scattered energy programs and launched the Synthetic Fuels Corporation; to give education the priority it deserves and at the same time reduce HHS to more manageable size, I gave education a seat at the Cabinet table, to create a stronger system for attacking waste and fraud, I reorganized audit and investigative functions by putting an Inspector General in major agencies. Since I took office, we have submitted 14 reorganization initiatives and had them all approved by Congress. We have saved hundreds of millions of dollars through the adoption of businesslike cash management principles and set strict standards for personal financial disclosure and conflict of interest avoidance by high Federal officials.

To streamline the structure of the government, we have secured approval of 14 reorganization initiatives, improving the efficiency of the most important sectors of the government, including energy, education, and civil rights enforcement. We have eliminated more than 300 advisory committees as well as other agencies, boards and commissions which were obsolete or ineffective. Independent Inspectors General have been appointed in major agencies to attack fraud and waste. More than a billion dollars of questionable transactions have been identified through their audit activities.

The adoption of business-like cash management and debt collection initiatives will save over $1 billion, by streamlining the processing of receipts, by controlling disbursements more carefully, and by reducing idle cash balances. Finally this Administration has set strict standards for personal financial disclosure and conflict of interest avoidance by high Federal officials, to elevate the level of public trust in the government.

V. PROTECTING BASIC RIGHTS AND LIBERTIES

I am extremely proud of the advances we have made in ensuring equality and protecting the basic freedoms of all Americans.

—The Equal Employment Opportunity Commission (EEOC) and the Office of Federal Contract Compliance (OFCCP) have been reorganized and strengthened and a permanent civil rights unit has been established in OMB.

— To avoid fragmented, inconsistent and duplicative enforcement of civil rights laws, three agencies have been given coordinative and standard-setting responsibilities in discrete areas: EEOC for all employment-related activities, HUD for all those relating to housing, and the Department of Justice for all other areas.

— With the enactment of the Right to Financial Privacy Act and a bill limiting police search of newsrooms, we have begun to establish a sound, comprehensive, privacy program.

Ratification of the Equal Rights Amendment must be aggressively pursued. Only one year remains in which to obtain ratification by three additional states.

The Congress must give early attention to a number of important bills which remain. These bills would:

— strengthen the laws against discrimination in housing. Until it is enacted, the 1968 Civil Rights Act's promise of equal access to housing will remain unfulfilled;

— establish a charter for the FBI and the intelligence agencies. The failure to define in law the duties and responsibilities of these agencies has made possible some of the abuses which have occurred in recent years;

— establish privacy safeguards for medical research, bank, insurance, and credit records; and provide special protection for election fund transfer systems.

EQUAL RIGHTS AMENDMENT

I remain committed as strongly as possible to the ratification of the Equal Rights Amendment.

As a result of our efforts in 1978, the Equal Rights Amendment's deadline for ratification was extended for three years. We have now one year and three States left. We cannot afford any delay in marshalling our resources and efforts to obtain the ratification of those three additional States.

Although the Congress has no official role in the ratification process at this point, you do have the ability to affect public opinion and the support of State Legislators for the Amendment. I urge Members from States which have not yet ratified the Equal Rights Amendment to use their influence to secure ratification. I will continue my own efforts to help ensure ratification of the Equal Rights Amendment.

MARTIN LUTHER KING, JR.

Dr. Martin Luther King, Jr. led this Nation's effort to provide all its citizens with civil rights and equal opportunities. His commitment to human rights, peace and non-violence stands as a monument to his humanity and courage. As one of our Nation's most outstanding leaders, it is appropriate that his birthday be commemorated as a national holiday. I hope the Congress will enact legislation this year that will achieve this goal.

FAIR HOUSING

The Fair Housing Act Amendments of 1980 passed the House of Representatives by an overwhelming bipartisan majority only to die in the Senate at the close of the 96th Congress. The leaders of both parties have pledged to make the enactment of fair housing legislation a top priority of the incoming Congress. The need is pressing and a strengthened federal enforcement effort must be the primary method of resolution.

CRIMINAL CODE

The Federal criminal laws are often archaic, frequently contradictory and imprecise, and clearly in need of revision and codification. The new Administration should continue the work which has been begun to develop a Federal criminal code which simplifies and clarifies our criminal laws, while maintaining our basic civil liberties and protections.

PRIVACY

As our public and private institutions collect more and more information and as communications and computer technologies advance, we must act to protect the personal privacy of our citizens.

In the past four years we acted on the report of the Privacy Commission and established a national privacy policy. We worked with Congress to pass legislation restricting wiretaps and law enforcement access to bank records and to reporters' files. We reduced the number of personal files held by the government and restricted the transfer of personal information among Federal agencies. We also worked with the Organization for Economic Cooperation and Development to establish international guidelines to protect the privacy of personal information that is transferred across borders.

VI. PROTECTING AND DEVELOPING OUR NATURAL RESOURCES

Two of our Nation's most precious natural resources are our environment and our vast agricultural capacity. From the beginning of my Administration, I have worked with the Congress to enhance and protect, as well as develop our natural resources. In the environmental areas, I have been especially concerned about the importance of balancing the need for resource development with preserving a clean environment, and have taken numerous actions to foster this goal. In the agricultural area, I have taken the steps needed to improve farm incomes and to increase our agricultural production to record levels. That progress must be continued in the 1980's.

ENVIRONMENT

Preserving the quality of our environment has been among the most important objectives of my Administration and of the Congress. As a result of these shared commitments and the dedicated efforts of many members of the Congress and my Administration, we have achieved several historic accomplishments.

PROTECTION OF ALASKA LANDS

Passage of the Alaska National Interest Lands Conservation Act was one of the most important conservation actions of this century. At stake was the fate of millions of acres of beautiful land, outstanding and unique wildlife populations, native cultures, and the opportunity to ensure that future generations of Americans would be able to enjoy the benefits of these nationally significant resources. As a result of the leadership, commitment, and persistence of my Administration and the Congressional leadership, the Alaska Lands Bill was signed into law last December.

The Act adds 97 million acres of new parks and refuges, more than doubling the size of our National Park and National Wildlife Refuge Systems. The bill triples the size of our national wilderness system, increasing its size by 56 million acres. And by adding 25 free-flowing river segments to the Wild and Scenic River System, the bill almost doubles the river mileage in that system. The Alaska Lands Act reaffirms our commitment to the environment and strikes a balance between protecting areas of great beauty and allowing development of Alaska's oil, gas, mineral, and timber resources.

PROTECTION OF NATURAL RESOURCES

In addition to the Alaska Lands Act, over the past four years we have been able to expand significantly the national wilderness and parks systems. In 1978, the Congress passed the historical Omnibus Parks Act, which made 12 additions to the National Park System. The Act also established the first two national trails since the National Trails System Act was passed in 1968. Then, in 1980, as a result of my 1979 Environmental Message, the Federal land management agencies have established almost 300 new National Recreational Trails. With the completion of the RARE II process, which eliminated the uncertainty surrounding the status of millions of acres of land, we called for over 15 million acres of new wilderness in the nation's National Forest, in 1980 the Congress established about 4.5 million acres of wilderness in the lower 48 states. In addition, the Administration recommended legislation to protect Lake Tahoe, and through an Executive Order has already established a mechanism to help ensure the Lake's protection. Finally, in 1980 the Administration established the Channel Islands Marine Sanctuary.

Administration actions over the past four years stressed the importance of providing Federal support only for water resource projects that are economically and environmentally sound. This policy should have a major and lasting influence on the federal government's role in water resource development and management. The Administration's actions to recommend to the Congress only economically and environmentally sound water resource projects for funding resulted not only in our opposing uneconomic projects but also, in 1979, in the first Administration proposal of new project starts in 4 years.

One of the most significant water policy actions of the past four years was the Administration's June 6, 1978 Water Policy Reform Message to the Congress. This Message established a new national water resources policy with the following objectives:

— to give priority emphasis to water conservation;

— to consider environmental requirements and values more fully and along with economic factors in the planning and management of water projects and programs;

— to enhance cooperation between state and federal agencies in water resources planning and management.

In addition, the Executive Office of the President established 11 policy decision criteria to evaluate the proposed federal water projects, the Water Resources Council developed and adopted a new set of Principles and Standards for water projects which is binding on all federal construction agencies, and improved regulations were developed to implement the National Historic Preservation Act and the Fish and Wildlife Coordination Act. As a result, water resource projects must be determined to be economically sound before the Administration will recommend authorization or appropriation. Over the years ahead, this policy will help to reduce wasteful federal spending by targeting federal funds to the highest priority water resource projects.

In the pursuit of this policy, however, we cannot lose projects. In the part that sound water resource projects play in providing irrigation, power, and flood control. We must also recognize the special needs of particular regions of the country in evaluating the need for additional projects.

ADDRESSING GLOBAL RESOURCE AND ENVIRONMENTAL PROBLEMS

The Global 2000 Report to the President, prepared in response to my 1977 Environment Message, is the first of its kind. Never before has our government, or any government, taken such a comprehensive, long-range look at the interrelated global issues of resources, population, and environment.

The Report's conclusions are important. They point to a rapid increase in population and human needs through the year 2000 while at the same time a decline in the earth's capacity to meet those needs, unless nations of the world act decisively to alter current trends.

The United States has contributed actively to a series of U.N. conferences on the environment, population, and resources, and is preparing for the 1981 Conference on New and Renewable Sources of Energy. Following my 1977 Environmental Message, the Administration development assistance programs have added emphasis to natural resource management and environmental protection. My 1979 Environmental Message called attention to the alarming loss of world forests, particularly in the tropics. An interagency task force on tropical forests has developed a U.S. government program to encourage conservation and wise management of tropical forests. The Administration is encouraging action by other nations and world organizations to the same purpose. The United States is a world leader in wildlife conservation and the assessment of environmental effects of government actions. The January 5, 1979, Executive Order directing U.S. government agencies to consider the effects of their major actions abroad, is another example of this leadership.

COMMITMENT TO CONTROL OF POLLUTION AND HAZARDOUS CHEMICALS

Over the past four years, there has been steady progress towards cleaner air and water, sustained by the commitment of Congress and the Administration to these important national objectives. In addition, the Administration has developed several new pollution compliance approaches such as alternative and innovative waste water treatment projects, the "bubble" concept, the "offset" policy, and permit consolidation, all of which are designed to reduce regulatory burdens on the private sector.

One of the most pressing problems to come to light in the past four years has been improper hazardous waste disposal. The Administration has moved on three fronts. First, we proposed the Oil Hazardous Substances and Hazardous Waste Response, Liability and Compensation Act (the Superfund bill) to provide comprehensive authority and $1.6 billion in funds to clean up abandoned hazardous waste disposal sites. In November 1980 the Congress passed a Superfund bill which I signed into law.

Second, the administration established a hazardous waste enforcement strike force to ensure that when available, responsible parties are required to clean up sites posing dangers to public health and to the environment. To date, 50 lawsuits have been brought by the strike force.

Third, regulations implementing subtitle C of the Resource Conservation and Recovery Act were issued. The regulations establish comprehensive controls for hazardous waste and, together with vigorous enforcement, will help to ensure that Love Canal will not be repeated.

THE FUTURE

For the future, we cannot,and we must not, forget that we are charged with the stewardship of an irreplaceable environment and natural heritage. Our children, and our children's children, are dependent upon our maintaining our commitment to preserving and enhancing the quality of our environment. It is my hope that when our descendants look back on the 1980's they will be able to affirm:

— that we kept our commitment to the restoration of environmental quality;

— that we protected the public health from the continuing dangers of toxic chemicals, from pollution, from hazardous and radioactive waste, and that we made our communities safer, healthier and better places to live;

— that we preserved America's wilderness areas and particularly its last great frontier, Alaska, for the benefit of all

Americans in perpetuity;

— that we put this nation on a path to a sustainable energy future, one based increasingly on renewable resources and on energy conservation;

— that we moved to protect America's countryside and coastland from mismanagement and irresponsibility;

— that we redirected the management of the nation's water resources toward water conservation, sound development and environmental protection;

— that we faced squarely such worldwide problems as the destruction of forests, acid rain, carbon dioxide build-up and nuclear proliferation; and

— that we protected the habitat and the existence of our own species on this earth.

AGRICULTURE THE FARM ECONOMY

The farm economy is sound and its future is bright. Agriculture remains a major bulwark of the nation's economy and an even more important factor in the world food system. The demand for America's agricultural abundance, here and abroad, continues to grow. In the near-term, the strength of this demand is expected to press hard against supplies, resulting in continued price strength.

The health and vitality of current-day agriculture represents a significant departure from the situation that existed when I came to office four years ago. In January 1977, the farm economy was in serious trouble. Farm prices and farm income were falling rapidly. Grain prices were at their lowest levels in years and steadily falling. Livestock producers, in their fourth straight year of record losses, were liquidating breeding herds at an unparalleled rate. Dairy farmers were losing money on every hundredweight of milk they produced. Sugar prices were in a nosedive.

Through a combination of improvements in old, established programs and the adoption of new approaches where innovation and change were needed, my Administration turned this situation around. Commodity prices have steadily risen. Farm income turned upward. U.S. farm exports set new records each year, increasing over 80 percent for the four year period. Livestock producers began rebuilding their herds. Dairy farmers began to earn a profit again.

RECENT POLICY INITIATIVES

Several major agricultural policy initiatives have been undertaken over the past year. Some are the culmination of policy proposals made earlier in this Administration; others are measures taken to help farmers offset the impact of rapid inflation in production costs. In combination, they represent a significant strengthening of our nation's food and agricultural policy. These initiatives include:

FOOD SECURITY RESERVE

The Congress authorized formation of a 4 million ton food grain reserve for use in international food assistance. This reserve makes it possible for the United States to stand behind its food aid commitment to food deficit nations, even during periods of short supplies and high prices. This corrects a serious fault in our past food assistance policy.

COMPREHENSIVE CROP INSURANCE

The Congress also authorized a significant new crop insurance program during 1980. This measure provides farmers with an important new program tool for sharing the economic risks that are inherent to agriculture. When fully operational, it will replace a hodgepodge of disaster programs that suffered from numerous shortcomings.

SPECIAL LOAN RATES

Another legislative measure passed late in the 2nd session of the 96th Congress authorizes the Secretary of Agriculture to provide higher loan rates to farmers who enter their grain in the farmer-owned grain reserve. This additional incentive to participate will further strengthen the reserve.

INCREASED LOAN PRICES

In July 1980, I administratively raised loan prices for wheat, feedgrains, and soybeans to help offset the effects of a serious cost-price squeeze. At the same time, the release and call prices for the grain reserve were adjusted upward.

HIGHER TARGET PRICES

The Agricultural Adjustment Act of 1980 raised the target prices for 1980-crop wheat and feed grain crops. This change corrected for shortcomings in the adjustment formula contained in the Food and Agriculture Act of 1977.

FUTURE AGENDA

The food and agricultural policies adopted by this Administration over the past four years, including those described above, will provide a firm foundation for future governmental actions in this field. Expiration of the Food and Agriculture Act of 1977 later this year will require early attention by the Congress. With relatively minor changes, most of the authorities contained in the 1977 Act should be extended in their present form. The farmer-owned grain reserve has proven to be a particularly effective means of stabilizing grain markets and should be preserved in essentially its present form.

Beyond this, it will be important for the Congress to keep a close eye on price-cost developments in the farm sector. As noted above, some of the actions I took last year were for the purpose of providing relief from the cost-price squeeze facing farmers. Should these pressures continue, further actions might be required.

My Administration has devoted particular attention to the issues of world hunger, agricultural land use, and the future structure of American agriculture. I encourage the Congress and the next Administration to review the results of these landmark enquiries and, where deemed appropriate, to act on their recommendations.

Following a careful review of the situation, I recently extended the suspension of grain sales to the Soviet Union. I am satisfied that this action has served its purpose effectively and fairly. However, as long as this suspension must remain in effect, it will be important for the next Administration and the Congress to take whatever actions are necessary to ensure that the burden does not fall unfairly on our Nation's farmers. This has been a key feature of my Administration's policy, and it should be maintained.

VII. FOREIGN POLICY

From the time I assumed office four years ago this month, I have stressed the need for this country to assert a leading role in a world undergoing the most extensive and intensive change in human history.

My policies have been directed in particular at three areas of change:

— the steady growth and increased projection abroad of Soviet military power, power that has grown faster than our own over the past two decades.

— the overwhelming dependence of Western nations, which now increasingly includes the United States, on vital oil supplies from the Middle East.

— the pressures of change in many nations of the developing world, in Iran and uncertainty about the future stability of many developing countries.

As a result of those fundamental facts, we face some of the most serious challenges in the history of this nation. The Soviet invasion of Afghanistan is a threat to global peace, to East-West relations, and to regional stable flow of oil. As the unprecedented relations, an and overwhelming vote in the General Assembly demonstrated, countries across the world, and particularly the nonaligned, regard the Soviet invasion as a threat to their independence and security. Turmoil within the region adjacent to the Persian Gulf poses risks for the security and prosperity of every oil importing nation and thus for the entire global economy. The continuing holding of American hostages in Iran is both an affront to civilized people everywhere, and a serious impediment to meeting the self-evident threat to widely-shared common interests, including those of Iran.

But as we focus our most urgent efforts on pressing problems, we will continue to pursue the benefits that only change can bring. For it always has been the essence of America that we want to move on, we understand that prosperity, progress and most of all peace cannot be had by standing still. A world of nations striving to preserve their independence, and of peoples aspiring for economic development and political freedom, is not a world hostile to the ideals and interests of the United States. We face powerful adversaries, but we have strong friends and dependable allies. We have common interests with the vast majority of the world's nations and peoples.

There have been encouraging developments in recent years, as well as matters requiring continued vigilance and concern:

— Our alliances with the world's most advanced and democratic states from Western Europe through Japan are stronger than ever.

— We have helped to bring about a dramatic improvement in relations between Egypt and Israel and an historic step towards a comprehensive Arab-Israeli settlement.

— Our relations with China are growing closer, providing a major new dimension in our policy in Asia and the world.

— Across southern Africa from Rhodesia to Namibia we are helping with the peaceful transition to majority rule in a context of respect for minority as well as majority rights.

— We have worked domestically and with our allies to respond to an uncertain energy situation by conservation and diversification of energy supplies based on internationally agreed targets.

— We have unambiguously demonstrated our commitment to defend Western interests in Southwest Asia, and we have significantly increased our ability to do so.

— And over the past four years the U.S. has developed an energy program which is comprehensive and ambitious. New institutions have been established such as the Synthetic Fuels Corporation and Solar Bank. Price decontrol for oil and gas is proceeding. American consumers have risen to the challenge, and we have experienced real improvements in consumption patterns.

The central challenge for us today is to our steadfastedness of purpose. We are no longer tempted by isolationism. But we must also learn to deal effectively with the contradictions of the world, the need to cooperate with potential adversaries without euphoria, without undermining our determination to compete with such adversaries and if necessary confront the threats they may pose to our security.

We face a broad range of threats and opportunities. We have and should continue to pursue a broad range of defense, diplomatic and economic capabilities and objectives.

I see six basic goals for America in the world over the 1980's:

— First, we will continue, as we have over the past four years, to build America's military strength and that of our allies and friends. Neither the Soviet Union nor any other nation will have reason to question our will to sustain the strongest and most flexible defense forces.

— Second, we will pursue an active diplomacy in the world, working, together with our friends and allies, to resolve disputes through peaceful means and to make any aggressor pay a heavy price.

— Third, we will strive to resolve pressing international economic problems, particularly energy and inflation, and continue to pursue our still larger objective of global economic growth through expanded trade and development assistance and through the preservation of an open multilateral trading system.

— Fourth, we will continue vigorously to support the process of building democratic institutions and improving human rights protection around the world. We are deeply convinced that the future lies not with dictatorship but democracy.

— Fifth, we remain deeply committed to the process of mutual and verifiable arms control, particularly to the effort to prevent the spread and further development of nuclear weapons. Our decision to defer, but not abandon our efforts to secure ratification of the SALT II Treaty reflects our firm conviction that the United States has a profound national security interest in the constraints on Soviet nuclear forces which only that treaty can provide.

— Sixth, we must continue to look ahead in order to evaluate and respond to resource, environment and population challenges through the end of this century.

One very immediate and pressing objective that is uppermost on our minds and those of the American people is the release of our hostages in Iran.

We have no basic quarrel with the nation, the revolution or the people of Iran. The threat to them comes not from American policy but from Soviet actions in the region. We are prepared to work with the government of Iran to develop a new and mutually beneficial relationship.

But that will not be possible so long as Iran continues to hold Americans hostages, in defiance of the world community and civilized behavior. They must be released unharmed. We have thus far pursued a measured program of peaceful diplomatic and economic steps in an attempt to resolve this issue without resorting to other remedies available to us under international law. This reflects the deep respect of our nation for the rule of law and for the safety of our people being held, and our belief that a great power bears a responsibility to use its strength in a measured and judicious manner. But our patience is not unlimited and our concern for the well-being of our fellow citizens grows each day.

ENHANCING NATIONAL SECURITY, AMERICAN MILITARY STRENGTH

The maintenance of national security is my first concern, as it has been for every president before me.

We must have both the military power and the political will to deter our adversaries and to support our friends and allies.

We must pay whatever price is required to remain the strongest nation in the world. That price has increased as the military power of our major adversary has grown and its readiness to use that power been made all too evident in Afghanistan. The real increases in defense spending, therefore probably will be higher than previously projected; protecting our security may require a larger share of our national wealth in the future.

THE U.S.-SOVIET RELATIONSHIP

We are demonstrating to the Soviet Union across a broad front that it will pay a heavy price for its aggression in terms of our relationship. Throughout the last decades U.S.-Soviet relations have been a mixture of cooperation and competition. The Soviet invasion of Afghanistan and the imposition of a puppet government have highlighted in the starkest terms the darker side of their policies, going well beyond competition and the legitimate pursuit of national interest, and violating all norms of international law and practice.

This attempt to subjugate an independent, non-aligned Islamic people is a callous violation of international law and the United Nations Charter, two fundamentals of international order. Hence, it is also a dangerous threat to world peace. For the first time since the communization of Eastern Europe after World War II, the Soviets have sent combat forces into an area that was not previously under their control, into a non-aligned and sovereign state.

The destruction of the independence of the Afghanistan government and the occupation by the Soviet Union have altered the strategic situation in that part of the world in a very ominous fashion. It has significantly shortened the striking distance to the Indian Ocean and the Persian Gulf for the Soviet Union.

It has also eliminated a buffer between the Soviet Union and Pakistan and presented a new threat to Iran. These two countries are now far more vulnerable to Soviet political intimidation. If that intimidation were to prove effective, the Soviet Union could control an area of vital strategic and economic significance to the survival of Western Europe, the Far East, and ultimately the United States.

It has now been over a year since the Soviet invasion of Afghanistan dealt a major blow to U.S.-Soviet relations and the entire international system. The U.S. response has proven to be serious and far-reaching. It has been increasingly effective, imposing real and sustained costs on the U.S.S.R.'s economy and international image.

Meanwhile, we have encouraged and supported efforts to reach a political settlement in Afghanistan which would lead to a withdrawal of Soviet forces from that country and meet the interests of all concerned. It is Soviet intransigence that has kept those efforts from bearing fruit.

Meanwhile, an overwhelming November resolution of the United Nations General Assembly on Afghanistan has again made clear that the world has not and will not forget Afghanistan. And our response continues to make it clear that Soviet use of force in pursuit of its international objectives is incompatible with the notion of business-as-usual.

BILATERAL COMMUNICATION

U.S.-Soviet relations remain strained by the continued Soviet presence in Afghanistan, by growing Soviet military capabilities, and by the Soviets' apparent willingness to use those capabilities without respect for the most basic norms of international behavior.

But the U.S.-Soviet relationship remains the single most important element in determining whether there will be war or peace. And so, despite serious strains in our relations, we have maintained a dialogue with the Soviet Union over the past year. Through this dialogue, we have ensured against bilateral misunderstandings and miscalculations which might escalate out of control, and have managed to avoid the injection of superpower rivalries into areas of tension like the Iran-Iraq conflict.

POLAND

Now, as was the case a year ago, the prospect of Soviet use of force threatens the international order. The Soviet Union has completed preparations for a possible military intervention against Poland. Although the situation in Poland has shown signs of stabilizing recently, Soviet forces remain in a high state of readiness and they could move into Poland on short notice. We continue to believe that the Polish people should be allowed to work out their internal problems themselves, without outside interference, and we have made clear to the Soviet leadership that any intervention in Poland would have severe and prolonged consequences for East-West detente, and U.S.-Soviet relations in particular.

DEFENSE BUDGET

For many years the Soviets have steadily increased their real defense spending, expanded their strategic forces, strengthened their forces in Europe and Asia, and enhanced their capability for projecting military force around the world directly or through the use of proxies. Afghanistan dramatizes the vastly increased military power of the Soviet Union.

The Soviet Union has built a war machine far beyond any reasonable requirements for their own defense and security. In contrast, our own defense spending declined in real terms every year from 1968 through 1976.

We have reversed this decline in our own effort. Every year since 1976 there has been a real increase in our defense spending, and our lead has encouraged increases by our allies. With the support of the Congress, we must and will make an even greater effort in the years ahead.

The Fiscal Year 1982 budget would increase funding authority for defense to more than $196 billion. This amount, together with a supplemental request for FY 1981 of about $6 billion, will more than meet my Administration's pledge for a sustained growth of 3 percent in real expenditures, and provides for 5 percent in program growth in FY 1982 and beyond.

The trends we mean to correct cannot be remedied overnight; we must be willing to see this program through. To ensure that we do so I am setting a growth rate for defense that we can sustain over the long haul.

The defense program I have proposed for the next five years will require some sacrifice, but sacrifice we can well afford.

The defense program emphasizes four areas:

1.It ensures that our strategic nuclear forces will be equivalent to those of the Soviet Union and that deterrence against nuclear war will be maintained; 2.It upgrades our forces so that the military balance between NATO and the Warsaw Pact will continue to deter the outbreak of war, conventional or nuclear, in Europe; 3.It provides us the ability to come quickly to the aid of friends and allies around the globe; 4.And it ensures that our Navy will continue to be the most powerful on the seas.

STRATEGIC FORCES

We are strengthening each of the three legs of our strategic forces. The cruise missile production which will begin next year will modernize our strategic air deterrent. B-52 capabilities will also be improved. These steps will maintain and enhance the B-52 fleet by improving its ability to deliver weapons against increasingly heavily defended targets.

We are also modernizing our strategic submarine force. Four more POSEIDON submarines backfitted with new, 4,000 mile TRIDENT I missiles began deployments in 1980. Nine TRIDENT submarines have been authorized through 1981, and we propose one more each year.

The new M-X missile program to enhance our land-based intercontinental ballistic missile force continues to make progress. Technical refinements in the basing design over the last year will result in operational benefits, lower costs, and reduced environmental impact. The M-X program continues to be an essential ingredient in our strategic posture, providing survivability, endurance, secure command and control and the capability to threaten targets the Soviets hold dear.

Our new systems will enable U.S. strategic forces to maintain equivalence in the face of the mounting Soviet challenge. We would however need an even greater investment in strategic systems to meet the likely Soviet buildup without SALT.

STRATEGIC DOCTRINE

This Administration's systematic contributions to the necessary evolution of strategic doctrine began in 1977 when I commissioned a comprehensive net assessment. From that base a number of thorough investigations of specific topics continued. I should emphasize that the need for an evolutionary doctrine is driven not by any change in our basic objective, which remains peace and freedom for all mankind. Rather, the need for change is driven by the inexorable buildup of Soviet military power and the increasing propensity of Soviet leaders to use this power in coercion and outright aggression to impose their will on others.

I have codified our evolving strategic doctrine in a number of interrelated and mutually supporting Presidential Directives. Their overarching theme is to provide a doctrinal basis, and the specific program to implement it, that tells the world that no potential adversary of the United States could ever conclude that the fruits of his aggression would be significant or worth the enormous costs of our retaliation.

The Presidential Directives include:

PD-18: An overview of our strategic objectives PD-37: Basic space policy PD-41: Civil Defense PD-53: Survivability and endurance for telecommunications PD-57: Mobilization planning PD-58: Continuity of Government PD-59: Countervailing Strategy for General War

These policies have been devised to deter, first and foremost, Soviet aggression. As such they confront not only Soviet military forces but also Soviet military doctrine. By definition deterrence requires that we shape Soviet assessments about the risks of war, assessments they will make using their doctrine, not ours.

But at the same time we in no way seek to emulate their doctrine. In particular, nothing in our policy contemplates that nuclear warfare could ever be a deliberate instrument for achieving our own goals of peace and freedom. Moreover, our policies are carefully devised to provide the greatest possible incentives and opportunities for future progress in arms control.

Finally, our doctrinal evolution has been undertaken with appropriate consultation with our NATO Allies and others. We are fully consistent with NATO's strategy of flexible response.

FORCES FOR NATO

We are greatly accelerating our ability to reinforce Western Europe with massive ground and air forces in a crisis. We are undertaking a major modernization program for the Army's weapons and equipment, adding armor, firepower, and tactical mobility.

We are prepositioning more heavy equipment in Europe to help us cope with attacks with little warning, and greatly strengthening our airlift and sealift capabilities.

We are also improving our tactical air forces, buying about 1700 new fighter and attack aircraft over the next five years, and increasing the number of Air Force fighter wings by over 10 percent.

We are working closely with our European allies to secure the Host Nation Support necessary to enable us to deploy more quickly a greater ratio of combat forces to the European theater at a lower cost to the United States.

SECURITY ASSISTANCE

As we move to enhance U.S. defense capabilities, we must not lose sight of the need to assist others in maintaining their own security and independence. Events since World War II, most recently in Southwest Asia, have amply demonstrated that U.S. security cannot exist in a vacuum, and that our own prospects for peace are closely tied to those of our friends. The security assistance programs which I am proposing for the coming fiscal year thus directly promote vital U.S. foreign policy and national security aims, and are integral parts of our efforts to improve and upgrade our own military forces.

More specifically, these programs, which are part of our overall foreign aid request, promote U.S. security in two principal ways. First, they assist friendly and allied nations to develop the capability to defend themselves and maintain their own independence. An example during this past year was the timely support provided Thailand to help bolster that country's defenses against the large numbers of Soviet-backed Vietnamese troops ranged along its eastern frontier. In addition, over the years these programs have been important to the continued independence of other friends and allies such as Israel, Greece, Turkey and Korea. Second, security assistance constitutes an essential element in the broad cooperative relationships we have established with many nations which permit either U.S. bases on their territory or access by U.S. forces to their facilities. These programs have been particularly important with regard to the recently-concluded access agreements with various countries in the Persian Gulf and Indian Ocean regions and have been crucial to the protection of our interests throughout Southwest Asia.

RAPID DEPLOYMENT FORCES

We are systematically enhancing our ability to respond rapidly to non-NATO contingencies wherever required by our commitments or when our vital interests are threatened.

The rapid deployment forces we are assembling will be extraordinarily flexible: They could range in size from a few ships or air squadrons to formations as large as 100,000 men, together with their support. Our forces will be prepared for rapid deployment to any region of strategic significance.

Among the specific initiatives we are taking to help us respond to crises outside of Europe are:

the development of a new fleet of large cargo aircraft with intercontinental range; the design and procurement of a force of Maritime Prepositioning Ships that will carry heavy equipment and supplies for three Marine Corps brigades; the procurement of fast sealift ships to move large quantities of men and material quickly from the U.S. to overseas areas of deployment; increasing training and exercise activities to ensure that our forces will be well prepared to deploy and operate in distant areas.

In addition, our European allies have agreed on the importance of providing support to U.S. deployments to Southwest Asia.

NAVAL FORCES

Seapower is indispensable to our global position, in peace and also in war. Our shipbuilding program will sustain a 550-ship Navy in the 1990's and we will continue to build the most capable ships afloat.

The program I have proposed will assure the ability of our Navy to operate in high threat areas, to maintain control of the seas and protect vital lines of communication, both military and economic and to provide the strong maritime component of our rapid deployment forces. This is essential for operations in remote areas of the world, where we cannot predict far in advance the precise location of trouble, or preposition equipment on land.

MILITARY PERSONNEL

No matter how capable or advanced our weapons systems, our military security depends on the abilities, the training and the dedication of the people who serve in our armed forces. I am determined to recruit and to retain under any foreseeable circumstances an ample level of such skilled and experienced military personnel. This Administration has supported for FY 1981 the largest peacetime increase ever in military pay and allowances.

We have enhanced our readiness and combat endurance by improving the Reserve Components. All reservists are assigned to units structured to complement and provide needed depth to our active forces. Some reserve personnel have also now been equipped with new equipment.

MOBILIZATION PLANNING

We have completed our first phase of mobilization planning, the first such Presidentially-directed effort since World War II. The government-wide exercise of our mobilization plans at the end of 1980 showed, first, that planning pays off and, second, that much more needs to be done.

OUR INTELLIGENCE POSTURE

Our national interests are critically dependent on a strong and effective intelligence capability. We will maintain and strengthen the intelligence capabilities needed to assure our national security. Maintenance of and continued improvements in our multi-faceted intelligence effort are essential if we are to cope successfully with the turbulence and uncertainties of today's world.

The intelligence budget I have submitted to the Congress responds to our needs in a responsible way, providing for significant growth over the Fiscal Year 1981 budget. This growth will enable us to develop new technical means of intelligence collection while also assuring that the more traditional methods of intelligence work are also given proper stress. We must continue to integrate both modes of collection in our analyses.

REGIONAL POLICIES

Every President for over three decades has recognized that America's interests are global and that we must pursue a global foreign policy.

Two world wars have made clear our stake in Western Europe and the North Atlantic area. We are also inextricably linked with the Far East, politically, economically, and militarily. In both of these, the United States has a permanent presence and security commitments which would be automatically triggered. We have become increasingly conscious of our growing interests in a third area, the Middle East and the Persian Gulf area.

We have vital stakes in other major regions of the world as well. We have long recognized that in an era of interdependence, our own security and prosperity depend upon a larger common effort with friends and allies throughout the world.

THE ATLANTIC ALLIANCE

In recognition of the threat which the Soviet invasion of Afghanistan posed to Western interests in both Europe and Southwest Asia, NATO foreign and defense ministers have expressed full support for U.S. efforts to develop a capability to respond to a contingency in Southwest Asia and have approved an extensive program to help fill the gap which could be created by the diversion of U.S. forces to that region.

The U.S. has not been alone in seeking to maintain stability in the Southwest Asia area and insure access to the needed resources there. The European nations with the capability to do so are improving their own forces in the region and providing greater economic and political support to the residents of the area. In the face of the potential danger posed by the Iran-Iraq conflict, we have developed coordination among the Western forces in the area of the Persian Gulf in order to be able to safeguard passage in that essential waterway.

Concerning developments in and around Poland the allies have achieved the highest level of cohesion and unity of purpose in making clear the effects on future East-West relations of a precipitous Soviet act there.

The alliance has continued to build on the progress of the past three years in improving its conventional forces through the Long-Term Defense Program. Though economic conditions throughout Europe today are making its achievement difficult, the yearly real increase of 3 percent in defense spending remains a goal actively sought by the alliance.

The NATO alliance also has moved forward during the past year with the implementation of its historic December 1979 decision to modernize its Theater Nuclear Force capabilities through deployment of improved Pershing ballistic missiles and ground-launched cruise missiles in Europe. Our allies continue to cooperate actively with us in this important joint endeavor, whose purpose is to demonstrate convincingly to the Soviet Union the potential costs of a nuclear conflict in Europe. At the same time, we offered convincing evidence of our commitment to arms control in Europe by initiating preliminary consultations with the Soviet Union in Geneva on the subject of negotiated limits on long-range theater nuclear forces. Also, during 1980 we initiated and carried out a withdrawal from our nuclear weapons stockpile in Europe of 1,000 nuclear warheads. This successful drawdown in our nuclear stockpile was a further tangible demonstration of our commitment to the updating of our existing theater nuclear forces in Europe.

In the NATO area, we continued to work closely with other countries in providing resources to help Turkey regain economic health. We regretted that massive political and internal security problems led the Turkish military to take over the government on September 12. The new Turkish authorities are making some progress in resolving those problems, and they have pledged an early return to civilian government. The tradition of the Turkish military gives us cause to take that pledge seriously. We welcomed the reestablishment of Greece's links to the integrated military command structure of the Atlantic Alliance— a move which we had strongly encouraged— as a major step toward strengthening NATO's vital southern flank at a time of international crisis and tension in adjacent areas. Greek reintegration exemplifies the importance which the allies place on cooperating in the common defense and shows that the allies can make the difficult decisions necessary to insure their continued security. We also welcomed the resumption of the intercommunal talks on Cyprus.

THE U.S. AND THE PACIFIC NATIONS

The United States is a Pacific nation, as much as it is an Atlantic nation. Our interests in Asia are as important to us as our interests in Europe. Our trade with Asia is as great as our trade with Europe. During the past four years we have regained a strong, dynamic and flexible posture for the United States in this vital region.

Our major alliances with Japan, Australia and New Zealand are now stronger than they ever have been, and together with the nations of western Europe, we have begun to form the basic political structure for dealing with international crises that affect us all. Japan, Australia and New Zealand have given us strong support in developing a strategy for responding to instability in the Persian Gulf.

Normalization of U.S. relations with China has facilitated China's full entry into the international community and encouraged a constructive Chinese role in the Asia-Pacific region. Our relations with China have been rapidly consolidated over the past year through the conclusion of a series of bilateral agreements. We have established a pattern of frequent and frank consultations between our two governments, exemplified by a series of high-level visits and by regular exchanges at the working level, through which we have been able to identify increasingly broad areas of common interest on which we can cooperate.

United States relations with the Association of Southeast Asian Nations (ASEAN) have also expanded dramatically in the past four years. ASEAN is now the focus for U.S. policy in Southeast Asia, and its cohesion and strength are essential to stability in this critical area and beyond.

Soviet-supported Vietnamese aggression in Indo-china has posed a major challenge to regional stability. In response, we have reiterated our security commitment to Thailand and have provided emergency security assistance for Thai forces facing a Vietnamese military threat along the Thai-Cambodian border. We have worked closely with ASEAN and the U.N. to press for withdrawal of Vietnamese forces from Cambodia and to encourage a political settlement in Cambodia which permits that nation to be governed by leaders of its own choice. We still look forward to the day when Cambodia peacefully can begin the process of rebuilding its social, economic and political institutions, after years of devastation and occupation. And, on humanitarian grounds and in support of our friends in the region, we have worked vigorously with international organizations to arrange relief and resettlement for the exodus of Indo-chinese refugees which threatened to overwhelm these nations.

We have maintained our alliance with Korea and helped assure Korea's security during a difficult period of political transition.

We have amended our military base agreement with the Philippines, ensuring stable access to these bases through 1991. The importance of our Philippine bases to the strategic flexibility of U.S. forces and our access to the Indian Ocean is self-evident.

Finally, we are in the process of concluding a long negotiation establishing Micronesia's status as a freely associated state.

We enter the 1980's with a firm strategic footing in East Asia and the Pacific, based on stable and productive U.S. relations with the majority of countries of the region. We have established a stable level of U.S. involvement in the region, appropriate to our own interests and to the interests of our friends and allies there.

THE MIDDLE EAST AND SOUTHWEST ASIA

The continuing Soviet occupation of Afghanistan and the dislocations caused by the Iraq-Iran war serve as constant reminders of the critical importance for us, and our allies, of a third strategic zone stretching across the Middle East, the Persian Gulf, and much of the Indian subcontinent. This Southwest Asian region has served as a key strategic and commercial link between East and West over the centuries. Today it produces two-thirds of the world's oil exports, providing most of the energy needs of our European allies and Japan. It has experienced almost continuous conflict between nations, internal instabilities in many countries, and regional rivalries, combined with very rapid economic and social change. And now the Soviet Union remains in occupation of one of these nations, ignoring world opinion which has called on it to get out.

We have taken several measures to meet these challenges.

MIDDLE EAST

In the Middle East, our determination to consolidate what has already been achieved in the peace process— and to buttress that accomplishment with further progress toward a comprehensive peace settlement— must remain a central goal of our foreign policy. Pursuant to their peace treaty, Egypt and Israel have made steady progress in the normalization of their relations in a variety of fields, bringing the benefits of peace directly to their people. The new relationship between Egypt and Israel stands as an example of peaceful cooperation in an increasingly fragmented and turbulent region.

Both President Sadat and Prime Minister Begin remain committed to the current negotiations to provide full autonomy to the inhabitants of the West Bank and Gaza. These negotiations have been complex and difficult, but they have already made significant progress, and it is vital that the two sides, with our assistance, see the process through to a successful conclusion. We also recognize the need to broaden the peace process to include other parties to the conflict and believe that a successful autonomy agreement is an essential first step toward this objective.

We have also taken a number of steps to strengthen our bilateral relations with both Israel and Egypt. We share important strategic interests with both of these countries.

We remain committed to Israel's security and are prepared to take concrete steps to support Israel whenever that security is threatened.

PERSIAN GULF

The Persian Gulf has been a vital crossroads for trade between Europe and Asia at many key moments in history. It has become essential in recent years for its supply of oil to the United States, our allies, and our friends. We have taken effective measures to control our own consumption of imported fuel, working in cooperation with the other key industrial / nations of the world. However, there is little doubt that the healthy growth of our American and world economies will depend for many years on continued safe access to the Persian Gulf's oil production. The denial of these oil supplies would threaten not only our own but world security.

The potent new threat from an advancing Soviet Union, against the background of regional instability of which it can take advantage, requires that we reinforce our ability to defend our regional friends and to protect the flow of oil. We are continuing to build on the strong political, economic, social and humanitarian ties which bind this government and the American people to friendly governments and peoples of the Persian Gulf.

We have also embarked on a course to reinforce the trust and confidence our regional friends have in our ability to come to their assistance rapidly with American military force if needed. We have increased our naval presence in the Indian Ocean. We have created a Rapid Deployment Force which can move quickly to the Gulf— or indeed any other area of the world where outside aggression threatens. We have concluded several agreements with countries which are prepared to let us use their airports and naval facilities in an emergency. We have met requests for reasonable amounts of American weaponry from regional countries which are anxious to defend themselves. And we are discussing with a number of our area friends further ways we can help to improve their security and ours, both for the short and the longer term.

SOUTH ASIA

We seek a South Asia comprising sovereign and stable states, free of outside interference, which can strengthen their political institutions according to their own national genius and can develop their economies for the betterment of their people.

The Soviet invasion of Afghanistan has posed a new challenge to this region, and particularly to neighboring Pakistan. We are engaged in a continuing dialogue with the Pakistan government concerning its development and security requirements and the economic burden imposed by Afghan refugees who have fled to Pakistan. We are participating with other aid consortium members in debt rescheduling and will continue to cooperate through the UNHCR in providing refugee assistance. We remain commited to Pakistan's territorial integrity and independence.

Developments in the broad South/Southwest Asian region have also lent a new importance to our relations with India, the largest and strongest power in the area. We share India's interest in a more constructive relationship. Indian policies and perceptions at times differ from our own, and we have established a candid dialogue with this sister democracy which seeks to avoid the misunderstandings which have sometimes complicated our ties.

We attach major importance to strong economic assistance programs to the countries in the area, which include a majority of the poor of the non-Communist world. We believe that these programs will help achieve stability in the area, an objective we share with the countries in the region. Great progress has been achieved by these countries in increasing food production; international cooperation in harnessing the great river resources of South Asia would contribute further to this goal and help to increase energy production.

We continue to give high priority to our non-proliferation goals in the area in the context of our broad global and regional priorities. The decision to continue supply of nuclear fuel to the Indian Tarapur reactors was sensitive to this effort.

AFRICA

The United States has achieved a new level of trust and cooperation with Africa. Our efforts, together with our allies, to achieve peace in southern Africa, our increased efforts to help the poorest countries in Africa to combat poverty, and our expanded efforts to promote trade and investment have led to growing respect for the U.S. and to cooperation in areas of vital interest to the United States.

Africa is a continent of poor nations for the most part. It also contains many of the mineral resources vital for our economy. We have worked with Africa in a spirit of mutual cooperation to help the African nations solve their problems of poverty and to develop stronger ties between our private sector and African economies. Our assistance to Africa has more than doubled in the last four years. Equally important, we set in motion new mechanisms for private investment and trade.

Nigeria is the largest country in Black Africa and the second largest oil supplier to the United States. During this Administration we have greatly expanded and improved our relationship with Nigeria and other West African states whose aspirations for a constitutional democratic order we share and support. This interest was manifested both symbolically and practically by the visit of Vice President Mondale to West Africa in July (1980) and the successful visit to Washington of the President of Nigeria in October.

During Vice President Mondale's visit, a Joint Agricultural Consultative Committee was established, with the U.S. represented entirely by the private sector. This could herald a new role for the American private sector in helping solve the world's serious food shortages. I am pleased to say that our relations with Nigeria are at an all-time high, providing the foundation for an even stronger relationship in the years ahead.

Another tenet of this Administration's approach to African problems has `◆been encouragement and support for regional solutions to Africa's problems. We have supported initiatives by the Organization of African Unity to solve the protracted conflict in the western Sahara, Chad, and the Horn. In Chad, the world is watching with dismay as a country torn by a devastating civil war has become a fertile field for Libya's exploitation, thus demonstrating that threats to peace can come from forces within as well as without Africa.

In southern Africa the United States continues to pursue a policy of encouraging peaceful development toward majority rule. In 1980, Southern Rhodesia became independent as Zimbabwe, a multiracial nation under a system of majority rule. Zimbabwean independence last April was the culmination of a long struggle within the country and diplomatic efforts involving Great Britain, African states neighboring Zimbabwe, and the United States.

The focus of our efforts in pursuit of majority rule in southern Africa has now turned to Namibia. Negotiations are proceeding among concerned parties under the leadership of U.N. Secretary General Waldheim. This should lead to implementation of the U.N. plan for self-determination and independence for Namibia during 1981. If these negotiations are successfully concluded, sixty-five years of uncertainty over the status of the territory, including a seven-year-long war, will be ended.

In response to our active concern with issues of importance to Africans, African states have cooperated with us on issues of importance to our national interests. African states voted overwhelmingly in favor of the U.N. Resolution calling for release of the hostages, and for the U.N. Resolution condemning the Soviet invasion of Afghanistan. Two countries of Africa have signed access agreements with the U.S. allowing us use of naval and air facilities in the Indian Ocean.

Africans have become increasingly vocal on human rights. African leaders have spoken out on the issue of political prisoners, and the OAU is drafting its own Charter on Human Rights. Three countries in Africa— Nigeria, Ghana, and Uganda— have returned to civilian rule during the past year.

U.S. cooperation with Africa on all these matters represents a strong base on which we can build in future years.

Liberia is a country of long-standing ties with the U.S. and the site of considerable U.S. investment and facilities. This past April a coup replaced the government and a period of political and economic uncertainty ensued. The U.S. acted swiftly to meet this situation. We, together with African leaders, urged the release of political prisoners, and many have been released; we provided emergency economic assistance to help avoid economic collapse, and helped to involve the IMF and the banking community to bring about economic stability; and we have worked closely with the new leaders to maintain Liberia's strong ties with the West and to protect America's vital interests.

NORTH AFRICA

In early 1979, following a Libyan-inspired commando attack on a Tunisian provincial city, the U.S. responded promptly to Tunisia's urgent request for assistance, both by airlifting needed military equipment and by making clear our longstanding interest in the security and integrity of this friendly country. The U.S. remains determined to oppose other irresponsible Libyan aspirations. Despairing of a productive dialogue with the Libyan authorities, the U.S. closed down its embassy in Libya and later expelled six Libyan diplomats in Washington in order to deter an intimidation campaign against Libyan citizens in the U.S.

U.S. relations with Algeria have improved, and Algeria has played an indispensable and effective role as intermediary between Iran and the U.S. over the hostage issue.

The strengthening of our arms supply relationship with Morocco has helped to deal with attacks inside its internationally recognized frontiers and to strengthen its confidence in seeking a political settlement of the Western Sahara conflict. While not assuming a mediatory role, the U.S. encouraged all interested parties to turn their energies to a peaceful and sensible compromise resolution of the war in the Sahara and supported efforts by the Organization of African Unity toward that end. As the year drew to a close, the U.S. was encouraged by evolution in the attitudes of all sides, and is hopeful that their differences will be peacefully resolved in the year ahead so that the vast economic potential of North Africa can be developed for the well-being of the people living there.

LATIN AMERICA AND THE CARIBBEAN

The principles of our policies in this hemisphere have been clear and constant over the last four years. We support democracy and respect for human rights. We have struggled with many to help free the region of both repression and terrorism. We have respected ideological diversity and opposed outside intervention in purely internal affairs. We will act, though, in response to a request for assistance by a country threatened by external aggression. We support social and economic development within a democratic framework. We support the peaceful settlement of disputes. We strongly encourage regional cooperation and shared responsibilities within the hemisphere to all these ends, and we have eagerly and regularly sought the advice of the leaders of the region on a wide range of issues.

Last November, I spoke to the General Assembly of the Organization of American States of a cause that has been closest to my heart— human rights. It is an issue that has found its time in the hemisphere. The cause is not mine alone, but an historic movement that will endure.

At Riobamba, Ecuador, last September four Andean Pact countries, Costa Rica, and Panama broke new ground by adopting a "Code of Conduct," that joint action in defense of human rights does not violate the principles of nonintervention in the internal affairs of states in this hemisphere. The Organization of American States has twice condemned the coup that overturned the democratic process in Bolivia and the widespread abuse of human rights by the regime which seized power. The Inter-American Commission on Human Rights has gained world acclaim for its dispassionate reports. It completed two major country studies this year in addition to its annual report. In a resolution adopted without opposition, the OAS General Assembly in November strongly supported the work of the Commission. The American Convention on Human Rights is in force and an Inter-American Court has been created to judge human rights violations. This convention has been pending before the Senate for two years; I hope the United States this year will join the other nations of the hemisphere in ratifying a convention which embodies principles that are our tradition.

The trend in favor of democracy has continued. During this past year, Peru inaugurated a democratically elected government. Brazil continues its process of liberalization. In Central America, Hondurans voted in record numbers in their first national elections in over eight years. In the Caribbean seven elections have returned governments firmly committed to the democratic traditions of the Commonwealth.

Another major contribution to peace in the hemisphere is Latin America's own Treaty for the Prohibition of Nuclear Weapons. On behalf of the United States, I signed Protocol I of this Treaty in May of 1977 and sent it to the Senate for ratification. I urge that it be acted upon promptly by the Senate in order that it be brought into the widest possible effect in the Latin American region.

Regional cooperation for development is gaining from Central America to the Andes, and throughout the Caribbean. The Caribbean Group for Cooperation in Economic Development, which we established with 29 other nations in 1977, has helped channel $750 million in external support for growth in the Caribbean. The recent meeting of the Chiefs of State of the Eastern Caribbean set a new precedent for cooperation in that region. Mexico and Venezuela jointly and Trinidad and Tobago separately have established oil facilities that will provide substantial assistance to their oil importing neighbors. The peace treaty between El Salvador and Honduras will hopefully stimulate Central America to move forward again toward economic integration. Formation of Caribbean/ Central American Action, a private sector organization, has given a major impetus to improving people-to-people bonds and strengthening the role of private enterprise in the development of democratic societies.

The Panama treaties have been in force for over a year. A new partnership has been created with Panama; it is a model for large and small nations. A longstanding issue that divided us from our neighbors has been resolved. The security of the canal has been enhanced. The canal is operating as well as ever, with traffic through it reaching record levels this year. Canal employees, American and Panamanian alike, have remained on the job and have found their living and working conditions virtually unchanged.

In 1980, relations with Mexico continued to improve due in large measure to the effectiveness of the Coordinator for Mexican Affairs and the expanded use of the U.S.-Mexico Consultative Mechanism. By holding periodic meetings of its various working groups, we have been able to prevent mutual concerns from becoming political issues. The Secretary of State visited Mexico City in November, and, along with the Mexican Secretary of Foreign Relations, reviewed the performance of the Consultative Mechanism. The office of the Coordinator has ensured the implementation of my directive to all agencies to accord high priority to Mexican concerns. Trade with Mexico rose by almost 60 percent to nearly $30 billion, making that country our third largest trading partner.

These are all encouraging developments. Other problems remain, however.

The impact of large-scale migration is affecting many countries in the hemisphere. The most serious manifestation was the massive, illegal exodus from Cuba last summer. The Cuban government unilaterally encouraged the disorderly and even deadly migration of 125,000 of its citizens in complete disregard for international law or the immigration laws of its neighbors. Migrations of this nature clearly require concerted action, and we have asked the OAS to explore means of dealing with similar situations which may occur in the future.

We have a long-standing treaty with Colombia on Quita Sueno, Roncador, and Serrano which remains to be ratified by the Senate.

In Central America, the future of Nicaragua is unclear. Recent tensions, the restrictions on the press and political activity, an inordinate Cuban presence in the country and the tragic killing by the security forces of a businessman well known for his democratic orientation, cause us considerable concern. These are not encouraging developments. But those who seek a free society remain in the contest for their nation's destiny. They have asked us to help rebuild their country, and by our assistance, to demonstrate that the democratic nations do not intend to abandon Nicaragua to the Cubans. As long as those who intend to pursue their pluralistic goals play important roles in Nicaragua, it deserves our continuing support.

In El Salvador, we have supported the efforts of the Junta to change the fundamental basis of an inequitable system and to give a stake in a new nation to those millions of people, who for so long, lived without hope or dignity. As the government struggles against those who would restore an old tyranny or impose a new one, the United States will continue to stand behind them.

We have increased our aid to the Caribbean, an area vital to our national security, and we should continue to build close relations based on mutual respect and understanding, and common interests.

As the nations of this hemisphere prepare to move further into the 1980's, I am struck by the depth of underlying commitment that there is to our common principles: non-intervention, peaceful settlement of disputes, cooperation for development, democracy and defense of basic human rights. I leave office satisfied that the political, economic, social and organizational basis for further progress with respect to all these principles have been substantially strengthened in the past four years. I am particularly reassured by the leadership by other nations of the hemisphere in advancing these principles. The success of our common task of improving the circumstances of all peoples and nations in the hemisphere can only be assured by the sharing of responsibility. I look forward to a hemisphere that at the end of this decade has proven itself anew as a leader in the promotion of both national and human dignity.

THE INTERNATIONAL ECONOMY

A growing defense effort and a vigorous foreign policy rest upon a strong economy here in the United States. And the strength of our own economy depends upon our ability to lead and compete in the international marketplace.

ENERGY

Last year, the war between Iraq and Iran led to the loss of nearly 4 million barrels of oil to world markets, the third major oil market disruption in the past seven years. This crisis has vividly demonstrated once again both the value of lessened dependence on oil imports and the continuing instability of the Persian Gulf area.

Under the leadership of the United States, the 21 members of the International Energy Agency took collective action to ensure that the oil shortfall stemming from the Iran-Iraq war would not be aggravated by competition for scarce spot market supplies. We are also working together to see that those nations most seriously affected by the oil disruption— including our key NATO allies Turkey and Portugal— can get the oil they need. At the most recent IEA Ministerial meeting we joined the other members in pledging to take those policy measures necessary to slice our joint oil imports in the first quarter of 1981 by 2.2 million barrels.

Our international cooperation efforts in the energy field are not limited to crisis management. At the Economic Summit meetings in Tokyo and Venice, the heads of government of the seven major industrial democracies agreed to a series of tough energy conservation and production goals. We are working together with all our allies and friends in this effort.

Construction has begun on a commercial scale coal liquefaction plant in West Virginia co-financed by the United States, Japan and West Germany. An interagency task force has just reported to me on a series of measures we need to take to increase coal production and exports. This report builds on the work of the International Energy Agency's Coal Industry Advisory Board. With the assurances of a reliable United States steam coal supply at reasonable prices, many of the electric power plants to be built in the 1980's and 1990's can be coal-fired rather than oil-burning.

We are working cooperatively with other nations to increase energy security in other areas as well. Joint research and development with our allies is underway in solar energy, nuclear power, industrial conservation and other areas. In addition, we are assisting rapidly industrializing nations to carefully assess their basic energy policy choices, and our development assistance program helps the developing countries to increase indigenous energy production to meet the energy needs of their poorest citizens. We support the proposal for a new World Bank energy affiliate to these same ends, whose fulfillment will contribute to a better global balance between energy supply and demand.

INTERNATIONAL MONETARY POLICY

Despite the rapid increase in oil costs, the policy measures we have taken to improve domestic economic performance have had a continued powerful effect on our external accounts and on the strength of the dollar. A strong dollar helps in the fight against inflation.

There has also been considerable forward movement in efforts to improve the functioning of the international monetary system. The stability of the international system of payments and trade is important to the stability and good health of our own economy. We have given strong support to the innovative steps being taken by the International Monetary Fund and World Bank to help promote early adjustment to the difficult international economic problems. Recent agreement to increase quotas by fifty percent will ensure the IMF has sufficient resources to perform its central role in promoting adjustment and financing payments imbalances. The World Bank's new structural adjustment lending program will also make an important contribution to international efforts to help countries achieve a sustainable level of growth and development.

SUGAR

In 1980, Congress passed U.S. implementing legislation for the International Sugar Agreement, thus fulfilling a major commitment of this Administration. The agreement is an important element in our international commodity policy with far-reaching implications for our relations with developing countries, particularly sugar producers in Latin America. Producers and consumers alike will benefit from a more stable market for this essential commodity.

COFFEE

At year's end, Congress approved implementing legislation permitting the U.S. to carry out fully its commitments under International Coffee Agreement Specifically, the legislation enables us to meet our part of an understanding negotiated last fall among members of the Agreement, which defends, by use of export quotas, a price range well below coffee prices of previous years and which commits major coffee producers to eliminate cartel arrangements that manipulated future markets to raise prices. The way is now open to a fully-functioning International Coffee Agreement which can help to stabilize this major world commodity market. The results will be positive for both consumers— who will be less likely to suffer from sharp increases in coffee prices— and producers— who can undertake future investment with assurance of greater protection against disruptive price fluctuations in their exports.

NATURAL RUBBER

In 1980, the International Natural Rubber Agreement entered into force provisionally. U.S. membership in this new body was approved overwhelmingly by the Senate last year. The natural rubber agreement is a model of its kind and should make a substantial contribution to a stable world market in this key industrial commodity. It is thus an excellent example of constructive steps to improve the operation of the world economy in ways which can benefit the developing and industrialized countries alike. In particular, the agreement has improved important U.S. relationships with the major natural rubber-producing countries of Southeast Asia.

COMMON FUND

The United States joined members of the United Nations Conference on Trade and Development, both developed and developing nations, in concluding Articles of Agreement in 1980 for a Common Fund to help international commodity agreements stabilize the prices of raw materials.

ECONOMIC COOPERATION WITH DEVELOPING NATIONS

Our relations with the developing nations are of major importance to the United States. The fabric of our relations with these countries has strong economic and political dimensions. They constitute the most rapidly growing markets for our exports, and are important sources of fuel and raw materials. Their political views are increasingly important, as demonstrated in their overwhelming condemnation of the Soviet invasion of Afghanistan. Our ability to work together with developing nations toward goals we have in common (their political independence, the resolution of regional tensions, and our growing ties of trade for example) require us to maintain the policy of active involvement with the developing world that we have pursued over the past four years.

The actions we have taken in such areas as energy, trade, commodities, and international financial institutions are all important to the welfare of the developing countries. Another important way the United States can directly assist these countries and demonstrate our concern for their future is through our multilateral and bilateral foreign assistance program. The legislation which I will be submitting to you for FY 82 provides the authority and the funds to carry on this activity. Prompt Congressional action on this legislation is essential in order to attack such high priority global problems as food and energy, meet our treaty and base rights agreements, continue our peace efforts in the Middle East, provide economic and development support to countries in need, promote progress on North-South issues, protect Western interests, and counter Soviet influence.

Our proposed FY 1982 bilateral development aid program is directly responsive to the agreement reached at the 1980 Venice Economic Summit that the major industrial nations should increase their aid for food and energy production and for family planning. We understand that other Summit countries plan similar responses. It is also important to honor our international agreements for multilateral assistance by authorizing and appropriating funds for the International Financial Institutions. These multilateral programs enhance the efficiency of U.S. contributions by combining them with those of many other donor countries to promote development; the proposed new World Bank affiliate to increase energy output in developing countries offers particular promise. All these types of aid benefit our long-run economic and political interests.

Progress was made on a number of economic issues in negotiations throughout the U.N. system. However, in spite of lengthy efforts in the United Nations, agreement has not been reached on how to launch a process of Global Negotiations in which nations might collectively work to solve such important issues as energy, food, protectionism, and population pressures. The United States continues to believe that progress can best be made when nations focus on such specific problems, rather than on procedural and institutional questions. It will continue to work to move the North-South dialogue into a more constructive phase.

FOOD— THE WAR ON HUNGER

The War on Hunger must be a continuous urgent priority. Major portions of the world's population continue to be threatened by the specter of hunger and malnutrition. During the past year, some 150 million people in 36 African countries were faced with near disaster as the result of serious drought, induced food shortages. Our government, working in concert with the U.N.'s Food and Agricultural Organization (FAO), helped to respond to that need. But the problems of hunger cannot be solved by short-term measures. We must continue to support those activities, bilateral and multilateral, which aim at improving food production especially in developing countries and assuring global food security. These measures are necessary to the maintenance of a stable and healthy world economy.

I am pleased that negotiation of a new Food Aid Convention, which guarantees a minimum annual level of food assistance, was successfully concluded in March. The establishment of the International Emergency Wheat Reserve will enable the U.S. to meet its commitment under the new Convention to feed hungry people, even in times of short supply.

Of immediate concern is the prospect of millions of Africans threatened by famine because of drought and civil disturbances. The U.S. plea for increased food aid resulted in the organization of an international pledging conference and we are hopeful that widespread starvation will be avoided.

Good progress has been made since the Venice Economic Summit called for increased effort on this front. We and other donor countries have begun to assist poor countries develop long-term strategies to improve their food production. The World Bank will invest up to $4 billion in the next few years in improving the grain storage and food-handling capacity of countries prone to food shortages.

Good progress has been made since the Tokyo Economic Summit called for increased effort on this front. The World Bank is giving this problem top priority, as are some other donor countries. The resources of the consultative Group on International Agricultural Research will be doubled over a five-year period. The work of our own Institute of Scientific and Technological Cooperation will further strengthen the search for relevant new agricultural technologies.

The goal of freeing the world from hunger by the year 2000 should command the full support of all countries. The Human Dimension of Foreign Policy

HUMAN RIGHTS

The human rights policy of the United States has been an integral part of our overall foreign policy for the past several years. This policy serves the national interest of the United States in several important ways: by encouraging respect by governments for the basic rights of human beings, it promotes peaceful, constructive change, reduces the likelihood of internal pressures for violent change and for the exploitation of these by our adversaries, and thus directly serves our long-term interest in peace and stability; by matching espousal of fundamental American principles of freedom with specific foreign policy actions, we stand out in vivid contrast to our ideological adversaries; by our efforts to expand freedom elsewhere, we render our own freedom, and our own nation, more secure. Countries that respect human rights make stronger allies and better friends.

Rather than attempt to dictate what system of government or institutions other countries should have, the U.S. supports, throughout the world, the internationally recognized human rights which all members of the United Nations have pledged themselves to respect. There is more than one model that can satisfy the continuing human reach for freedom and justice:

1980 has been a year of some disappointments, but has also seen some positive developments in the ongoing struggle for fulfillment of human rights throughout the world. In the year we have seen:

— Free elections were held and democratic governments installed in Peru, Dominica, and Jamaica. Honduras held a free election for installation of a constituent assembly. An interim government was subsequently named pointing toward national presidential elections in 1981. Brazil continues on its course of political liberalization.

— The "Charter of Conduct" signed in Riobamba, Ecuador, by Ecuador, Colombia, Venezuela, Peru, Costa Rica, Panama and Spain, affirms the importance of democracy and human rights for the Andean countries.

— The Organization of American States, in its annual General Assembly, approved a resolution in support of the Inter-American Human Rights Commission's work. The resolution took note of the Commission's annual report, which described the status of human rights in Chile, El Salvador, Paraguay and Uruguay; and the special reports on Argentina and Haiti, which described human rights conditions as investigated during on-site inspections to these countries.

— The awarding of the Nobel Prize for Peace to Adolfo Perez Esquivel of Argentina for his non-violent advocacy of human rights.

— The United States was able to rejoin the International Labor Organization after an absence of two years, as that U.N. body reformed its procedures to return to its original purpose of strengthening employer-employee-government relations to insure human rights for the working people of the world.

The United States, of course, cannot take credit for all these various developments. But we can take satisfaction in knowing that our policies encourage and perhaps influence them.

Those who see a contradiction between our security and our humanitarian interests forget that the basis for a secure and stable society is the bond of trust between a government and its people. I profoundly believe that the future of our world is not to be found in authoritarianism: that wears the mask of order, or totalitarianism that wears the mask of justice. Instead, let us find our future in the human face of democracy, the human voice of individual liberty, the human hand of economic development.

HUMANITARIAN AID

The United States has continued to play its traditional role of safehaven for those who flee or are forced to flee their homes because of persecution or war. During 1980, the United States provided resettlement opportunities for 216,000 refugees from countries around the globe. In addition, the United States joined with other nations to provide relief to refugees in country of first asylum in Africa, the Middle East, and Asia.

The great majority of refugee admissions continued to be from Indo-china. During 1980, 168,000 Indo-chinese were resettled in the United States. Although refugee populations persist in camps in Southeast Asia, and refugees continue to flee Vietnam, Laos and Kampuchea, the flow is not as great as in the past. One factor in reducing the flow from Vietnam has been the successful negotiation and commencement of an Orderly Departure Program which permits us to process Vietnamese for resettlement in the United States with direct departure from Ho Chi Minh Ville in an orderly fashion. The first group of 250 departed Vietnam for the United States in December, 1980.

In addition to the refugees admitted last year, the United States accepted for entry into the United States 125,000 Cubans who were expelled by Fidel Castro. Federal and state authorities, as well as private voluntary agencies, responded with unprecedented vigor to coping with the unexpected influx of Cubans.

Major relief efforts to aid refugees in countries of first asylum continued in several areas of the world. In December, 1980, thirty-two nations, meeting in New York City, agreed to contribute $65 million to the continuing famine relief program in Kampuchea. Due in great part to the generosity of the American people and the leadership exercised in the international arena by the United States, we have played the pivotal role in ameliorating massive suffering in Kampuchea.

The United States has taken the lead among a group of donor countries who are providing relief to some two million refugees in the Horn of Africa who have been displaced by fighting in Ethiopia. U.S. assistance, primarily to Somalia, consists of $35 million worth of food and $18 million in cash and kind. Here again, United States efforts can in large part be credited with keeping hundreds of thousands of people alive.

Another major international relief effort has been mounted in Pakistan. The United States is one of 25 countries plus the European Economic Community who have been helping the Government of Pakistan to cope with the problem of feeding and sheltering the more than one million refugees that have been generated by the Soviet invasion of Afghanistan.

In April, 1980, the Congress passed the Refugee Act of 1980 which brought together, for the first time, in one piece of legislation the various threads of U.S. policy towards refugees. The law laid down a new, broader definition of the term refugee, established mechanisms for arriving at a level of refugee admissions through consultation with Congress, and established the Office of the United States Coordinator for Refugees.

It cannot be ignored that the destructive and aggressive policies of the Soviet Union have added immeasurably to the suffering in these three tragic situations.

The Control of Nuclear Weapons

Together with our friends and allies, we are striving to build a world in which peoples with diverse interests can live freely and prosper. But all that humankind has achieved to date, all that we are seeking to accomplish, and human existence itself can be undone in an instant— in the catastrophe of a nuclear war.

Thus one of the central objectives of my Administration has been to control the proliferation of nuclear weapons to those nations which do not have them, and their further development by the existing nuclear powers— notably the Soviet Union and the United States.

NON-PROLIFERATION

My Administration has been committed to stemming the spread of nuclear weapons. Nuclear proliferation would raise the spectre of the use of nuclear explosives in crucial, unstable regions of the world endangering not only our security and that of our Allies, but that of the whole world. Non-proliferation is not and can not be a unilateral U.S. policy, nor should it be an issue of contention between the industrialized and developing states. The international non-proliferation effort requires the support of suppliers as well as importers of nuclear technology and materials.

We have been proceeding on a number of fronts:

— First, we have been seeking to encourage nations to accede to the Non-Proliferation Treaty. The U.S. is also actively encouraging other nations to accept full-scope safeguards on all of their nuclear activities and is asking other nuclear suppliers to adopt a full-scope safeguards requirement as a condition for future supply.

— Second, the International Nuclear Fuel Cycle Evaluation (INFCE), which was completed in 1980, demonstrated that suppliers and recipients can work together on these technically complex and sensitive issues. While differences remain, the INFCE effort provides a broader international basis for national decisions which must balance energy needs with non-proliferation concerns.

— Finally, we are working to encourage regional cooperation and restraint. Protocol I of the Treaty of Tlatelolco which will contribute to the lessening of nuclear dangers for our Latin American neighbors ought now to be ratified by the United States Senate.

LIMITATIONS ON STRATEGIC ARMS

I remain convinced that the SALT II Treaty is in our Nation's security interest and that it would add significantly to the control of nuclear weapons. I strongly support continuation of the SALT process and the negotiation of more far-reaching mutual restraints on nuclear weaponry.

CONCLUSION

We have new support in the world for our purposes of national independence and individual human dignity. We have a new will at home to do what is required to keep us the strongest nation on earth.

We must move together into this decade with the strength which comes from realization of the dangers before us and from the confidence that together we can overcome them.

JIMMY CARTER The White House,
January 16, 1981.

This work is in the **public domain** in the United States because it is a work of the United States *federal* government (see 17 U.S.C. 105).

Chapter 3

Presidential Debates

3.1 1976 U.S. Presidential Debate - September 23

EDWIN NEWMAN, MODERATOR: Good evening. I'm Edwin Newman, moderator of this first debate of the 1976 campaign between Gerald R. Ford of Michigan, Republican candidate for president, and Jimmy Carter of Georgia, Democratic candidate for president. We thank you, President Ford and we thank you, Governor Carter, for being with us tonight. There are to be three debates between the presidential candidates and one between the vice-presidential candidates. All are being arranged by the League of Women Voters Education Fund. Tonight's debate, the first between presidential candidates in sixteen years and the first ever in which an incumbent president has participated, is taking place before an audience in the Walnut Street Theater in Philadelphia, just three blocks from Independence Hall. The television audience may reach a hundred million in the United States and many millions overseas. Tonight's debate focuses on domestic issues and economic policy. Questions will be put by Frank Reynolds of ABC News, James Gannon of the Wall Street Journal, and Elizabeth Drew of the New Yorker magazine. Under the agreed rules the first question will go to Governor Carter. That was decided by the toss of a coin. He will have up to three minutes to answer. One follow-up question will be permitted with up to two minutes to reply. President Ford will then have two minutes to respond. The next question will go to President Ford with the same time arrangements, and questions will continue to be alternated between the candidates. Each man will make a three-minute statement at the end, Governor Carter to go first. President Ford and Governor Carter do not have any notes or prepared remarks with them this evening. Mr. Reynolds, your question for Governor Carter.

MR. REYNOLDS: Mr. President, Governor Carter. Governor, in an interview with the Associated Press last week, you said you believed these debates would alleviate a lot of concern that some voters have about you. Well, one of those concerns, not an uncommon one about uh - candidates in any year, is that many voters say they don't really know where you stand. Now, you have made jobs your number one priority and you have said you are committed to a drastic reduction in unemployment. Can you say now, Governor, in specific terms, what your first step would be next January, if you are elected, to achieve that.

MR. CARTER: Yes. First of all is to recognize a tremendous economic strength in this country and to set the putting to - back to work of our people as a top priority. This is uh - an effort that ought to be done primarily by strong leadership in the White House, the inspiration of our people, the tapping of uh - business, agriculture, industry, labor and government at all levels to work on this uh project. We'll never have uh - an end to the inflationary spiral, and we'll never have a balanced budget until we get our people back to work. There are several things that can be done specifically that are not now being done. First of all, to channel research and development funds into areas that will provide uh large numbers of jobs. Secondly, we need to have a commitment in the uh private sector uh - to cooperate with government in matters like housing. Here a very small investment of taxpayer's money - in the housing field can bring large numbers of extra jobs, and the guarantee of mortgage loans, and the uh - putting forward of uh - two-0-two programs for housing for older people and so forth to cut down the roughly 20 percent unemployment that now exists in the - in the construction industry. Another thing is to deal with our - uh needs in the central cities, where the unemployment rate is extremely high: sometimes among minority groups, or those who don't speak English, or who're black, or young people, or - 40

65

percent of the employment. Here a CCC type program would be appropriate to channel money into the ah - cha- in - in into the sharing with the private sector and also local and state governments to employ young people who are now out of work. Another very important - uh aspect of our - uh economy would be to increase production in every way possible, uh to hold down - uh taxes on individuals, and to uh shift the tax burdens onto those who have avoided paying taxes in the past. These uh - kinds of specific things, uh none of which are being done now, would be a great help in - in reducing uh unemployment. There is uh - uh an additional factor that needs to be done and covered very - very succinctly, and that is, to make sure that we have a good relationship between management - business on the one hand, and labor, on the other. In a > Transfer interrupted! ery high, we might channel specific uh targeted job - job - uh opportunities by paying part of the salary of unemployed people - uh and also sharing with uh - local governments the uh - payment of salaries which would uh - let us cut down the unemployment rate much lower, before we hit the inflationary level. But I believe that by the end of the first four years of uh - of the next term we could have the unemployment down to 3 percent adult unemployment, which is about uh - 4 to 4 and a half percent overall uh controlled inflation rate and have a uh balance of growth of about - uh 4 to 6 percent, around 5 percent which would give us a balanced budget.

MR. REYNOLDS: Governor, uh - in the event you are successful and you do achieve a drastic drop

MR. CARTER: Yes, in unemployment that is likely to create additional pressure on prices, how willing are you to consider an incomes policy, in other words, wage and price controls?

MR. CARTER: Well - we now have such uh - a low utilization of uh - our productive capacity - uh about 73 percent; I think it's about the lowest since the Great Depression years - and such a high unemployment rate now - uh 7.9 percent - that - uh we have a long way to go in getting people to work before we have the inflationary pressures. And I think this would uh - this would be uh easy to accomplish, to get jobs down, without having strong in- inflationary pressures that - that would be necessary. I would not favor the uh - payment of uh - of a given fixed income to people unless they are not able to work. But with tax incentives for the low-income groups we could build up their uh - income levels uh - above the poverty level and not uh make welfare more uh - profitable than - than work.

MR. NEWMAN: Mr. President, your response.

MR. FORD: I don't believe that uh that Mr. Carter's been any more specific in this case than he has been on many other instances. I notice particularly that he didn't endorse the Humphrey-Hawkins bill which he has on occasions and which is included as a part of the Democratic platform. That legislation uh allegedly would help our unemployment, but uh - we all know that it would've controlled our economy, it would've added uh - ten to thirty billion dollars each year in additional expenditures by the Federal Government. It would've called for export controls on agricultural products In my judgment the best way to get jobs is to uh - expand the private sector, where five out of six jobs today exist in our economy. We can do that by reducing Federal taxes as I proposed uh - about a year ago when I called for a tax reduction of $28 billion - three-quarters of it to go to private uh taxpayers and uh one-quarter to the business sector. We could add to jobs in the major metropolitan areas by a proposal that I recommended that would give tax incentives to business to move into the inner city and to expand or to build new plants so that they would take a plant, or expand a plant where people are, and people are currently unemployed. We could uh - also uh - help our youths with some of the proposals that uh - would give to young people an opportunity to work and learn at the same time just like we give money to young people who are going to college. Those are the kind of specifics that I think we have to discuss on these uh - debates, and these are the kind of programs that I'll talk about on my time.

MR. NEWMAN: Mr. Gannon, your question to President Ford.

MR. GANNON: Mr. President, I would like to continue for a moment on this uh question of taxes which you have just raised. You have said that you favor more tax cuts for middle-income Americans - even those earning up to $30 thousand a year. That presumably would cost the Treasury quite a bit of money in lost revenue. In view of the very large budget deficits that you have accumulated and that are still in prospect, how is it possible to promise further tax cuts and to reach your goal of balancing the budget?

MR. FORD: At the time, Mr. Gannon, that I made the recommendation for a $28 billion tax cut - three-quarters of it to go to individual taxpayers and 25 percent to American business. I said at the time that we had to hold the lid an federal spending, that for every dollar of a tax reduction we had to have an equal reduction in federal expenditures - a one-for-one proposition. And I recommended that to the Congress with a budget ceiling of three hundred and ninety-five billion dollars, and that would have permitted us to have a $25 billion tax reduction. In my tax reduction program for middle-income taxpayers, I recommended that the Congress increase personal exemptions from seven hundred and fifty dollars per person to one thousand dollars per person. That would mean, of course, that for a family of four that that family would have a thousand dollars more personal exemption - money that they could spend for their own purposes, money that the government wouldn't have to spend. But if we keep the lid on federal spending, which I think we can - with the help of the Congress, we can justify fully a $28 billion tax reduction. In the budget that I submitted to the Congress in January this year, I re- recommended a 50 percent cutback in the rate of growth of federal spending. For the last ten years the budget of the United States has grown from uh - about 11 percent per year. We can't afford that kind of growth in federal spending. And in the budget that I recommended we cut it in half - a growth rate of 5 to 5 and one-half percent. With that kind of limitation, on federal spending, we can fully justify the tax reductions that I have proposed. And it seems to me with the stimulant of more money in the hands of the taxpayers, and with more money in the hands of business to expand, to modernize, to provide more jobs, our economy stimulated so that we'll get more revenue and we'll have a more prosperous economy.

MR. GANNON: Mr. President, to follow up a moment, uh - the Congress has passed a tax bill which is before you now, which did not meet exactly the uh - sort of outline that you requested. What is your intention on that bill, uh - since it doesn't meet your - your requirements? Do you plan to sign that bill?

MR. FORD: That tax bill does not entirely meet the criteria that I established. I think the Congress should have uh - added another $10 billion reduction in personal income taxes, including the increase of personal exemptions from seven hundred and fifty to a thousand dollars. And Congress could have done that if the budget committees of the Congress, and the Congress as a whole, had not increased the spending that I recommended in the budget. I'm sure that you know that in the resolutions passed by the Congress, that have added about $17 billion in more spending, by the Congress over the budget that I recommended. So I would prefer in that tax bill to have an additional tax cut and a further limitation on federal spending. Now this tax bill - that hasn't reached the White House yet, but is expected in a day or two - it's about fifteen hundred pages. It has some good provisions in it. It has - uh left out some that I have recommended, unfortunately. On the other hand, uh when you have a bill of that magnitude, with - tho- those many provisions, a president has to sit and decide if there's more good than bad. And from the a- analysis that I've made so far, it seems to me that that tax bill does uh - justify my signature and my approval.

MR. NEWMAN: Governor Carter, your response.

MR. CARTER: Well, Mr. Ford is - is uh changing uh considerably his previous philosophy. The present tax structure is a disgrace to this country; it's just a welfare program for the rich. As a matter of fact, uh - 25 percent of the total tax deductions, go for only 1 percent of the richest people in this country, and over 50 percent of the tax uh credits go for the 14 percent of the richest people in this country. When Mr. Ford first became president in - in August of 1974, the first thing he did in - in October was to ask for a $4.7 billion increase in taxes on our people in the midst of the heaviest recession, since uh - since the great depression of nineteen uh - of the 1940s. In uh - January of 1975 he asked for a tax change: a $5.6 billion increase on low-and-middle-income private individuals, a six and a half billion dollar decrease on the corporations and the special interests. In uh - December of uh - 1975 he vetoed the roughly 18 to 20 billion dollar uh tax-reduction bill that had been passed by the Congress, and then he came back later on in January of this year and he did advocate a $10 billion tax reduction, but it would be offset by a $6 billion increase this coming January in deductions for Social Security payments and for unemployment compensation. The whole philosophy of the Republican party, including uh - my opponent, has been to pile on taxes on low-income people to take 'em off on the corporations. As a matter fact, in - sin- since the late sixties when Mr. Nixon took office, we've had a reduction in uh - in the percentage of taxes paid by corporations from 30 percent down to about 20 percent. We've had an increase in taxes paid by individuals, payroll taxes, from14 Percent up to 20 percent. And this is what the Republicans have done to us. And this is why a tax reform is so important.

MR. NEWMAN: Mrs. Drew, your question to Governor Carter.

MS. DREW: Uh Governor Carter, you proposed a number of new or enlarged programs, including jobs, health, welfare reform, child care, aid to education, aid to cities, changes in social security and housing subsidies. You've also said that you wanna balance the budget by the end of your first term. Now you haven't put a price tag on those programs, but even if we price them conservatively and we count for full employment by the end of your first term, and we count for the economic growth that would occur during that period, there still isn't enough money to pay for those programs and balance the budget by any - any estimates that I've been able to see. So, in that case what would give?

MR. CARTER: Well, as a matter of fact there is. If we assume the ah - uh - a rate of growth of our economy, equivalent to what it was during President Johnson, President Kennedy, even before the - the - the - uh wa uh - Vietnese- namese War, and if we assume that at the end of the four-year period we can cut our unemployment rate down to 4 to 4 and a half percent - under those circumstances, even assuming no elimination of unnecessary programs and assuming an increase in the ad- in the allotment of money to finance programs, increasing as the inflation rate does - my economic projections, I think confirmed by the House uh - and the Senate committees, have been with the $60 billion extra amount of money that can be spent in fiscal year '81 which will be the last year of this next term. Within that sixty-billion dollars increase there would be fit the programs that I promised the American people. I might say too, that - that if we see that these goals cannot be reached - and I believe they're reasonable goals - then I would cut back on the rate of implement- implementation of new programs in order to accommodate a balanced budget by fiscal year '81 which is the last year of the next term. I believe that we ought to have a balanced budget during normal economic circumstances. And uh - these projections have been very carefully made. I stand behind them. And if they should be in error slightly on the down side, then I'll phase in the programs that we've uh - advocated, more slowly.

MS. DREW: Governor, uh - according to the budget committees of the Congress tha- tha- tha- that you referred to, if we get to full employment - what they project at a 4 percent unemployment - and, as you say, even allowing for the inflation in the programs, there would not be anything more than a surplus of $5 billion by the end of ninet- by 1981. And conservative estimates of your programs would be that they'd be about 85 to a hundred billion dollars. So how - how do you say that you're going to be able to do these things and balance the budget?

MR. CARTER: Well, the uh - the assumption that - that you uh - have described as different is in the rate of growth of our economy.

MS. DREW: No, they took that into account in those figures.

MR. CARTER: I believe that it's accurate to say that - that the - that the committees to whom you refer with the - the employment that you uh - state, and with the 5 to 5 and a half percent growth rate in our economy, that the uh - projections would be a uh - a $60 billion increase in the amount of money that we'd have to spend in 1981 compared to now. And uh - with that uh - in that framework would befit the - any improvements in the programs. Now this does not include uh - any uh - uh extra control over uh unnecessary spending, the weeding out of obsolete or obsolescent programs. Uh - we'll have uh - a safety version built in with complete reorganization of the executive branch of government which I am pledged to do. The present bureaucratic structure of the - of the Federal Government is a mess. And if I'm elected president that's gonna be a top priority of mine to completely revise the structure of the federal government, to make it economical, efficient, purposeful and manageable for a change. And also, I'm going to institute zero-based budgeting which I used four years in Georgia, which uh - assesses every program every year, and eliminates those programs that are obsolete or obsolescent. But with these projections, we will have a balanced budget by fiscal year 1981, if I'm elected president. Keep my promises to the American people. And it's just predicated on very modest, but I think accurate, projections of employment increases and uh - a growth in our national economy equal to what was experienced under Kennedy, Johnson, before the Vietnam War.

MR. NEWMAN: President Ford.

MR. FORD: If it is uh true that there will be a $60 billion surplus by fiscal year 1981, rather than spend that money for all the new programs that Governor Carter recommends and endorses, and which are included in the Democratic platform, I think the American taxpayer ought to get an additional tax break - a tax reduction of that magnitude. I feel that the taxpayers are the ones that need the relief: I don't think we should add additional programs of the magnitude that Governor Carter talks about. It seems to me that our tax structure today has rates that are too high. But I am uh - very glad to point out that since 1969, during a Republican administrations, we have had ten million people taken off of the tax rolls at the lower end of the taxpayer area. And at the same time, assuming that I sign the tax bill that was mentioned by Mr. Gannon, we will in the last two tax bills have increased the minimum tax on all wealthy taxpayers. And I believe that by eliminating ten million taxpayers in the last uh eight years, and by putting a heavier tax burden on those in the higher tax brackets, plus the other actions that've been taken uh - we can give taxpayers adequate tax relief. Now it seems to me that uh - as we look at the recommendations of the budget committees and our own projections, there isn't going to be any $60 billion dividend. I've heard of those dividends in the past; it always happens. We expected one at the time of the Vietnam War, but it was used up before we ever ended the war and taxpayers never got the adequate relief they deserved.

MR. NEWMAN: Mr. Reynolds.

MR. REYNOLDS: Mr. President, when you came into office you spoke very eloquently of the need for a time for healing, and very early in your administration you went out to Chicago and you announced, you proposed a program of uh case-by-case pardons for draft resisters to restore them to full citizenship. Some fourteen thousand young men took advantage of your offer, but another ninety thousand did not. In granting the pardon to former President Nixon, sir, part of your rationale was to put Watergate behind us to - if I may quote you again - truly end our long national nightmare. Why does not the same rationale apply now, today, in our Bicentennial year, to the young men who resisted in Vietnam, and many of them still in exile abroad?

MR. FORD: The amnesty program that I recommended in Chicago in September of 1974 would give to all draft evaders and - uh military deserters the opportunity to earn their uh - good record back. About fourteen to fifteen thousand did take advantage of that program. We gave them ample time. I am against- an across-the-board pardon of draft evaders or military deserters. Now in the case of Mr. Nixon, the reason the - the pardon was given, was that, when I took office this country was in a very, very divided condition. There was hatred, there was divisiveness - uh people had lost faith in their government in many, many respects. Mr. Nixon resigned, and I became president. It seemed to me that if I was to uh adequately and effectively handle the problems of high inflation, a growing recession, the uh - involvement of the United States still in Vietnam that I had to give a hundred percent of my time to those two major problems. Mr. Nixon resigned. That is disgrace. The first President out of thirty-eight that ever resigned from public office under pressure. So when you look at the penalty that he paid, and when you analyze the requirements that I had - to spend all of my time working on the economy, which was in trouble, that I inherited; working on our problems in Southeast Asia - which were still plaguing us - it seemed to me that Mr. Nixon had been penalized enough by his resignation in disgrace and the need, and necessity for me to concentrate on the problems of the country fully justified the action that I took.

MR. REYNOLDS: I take it then, sir, that you do not believe that uh - it is - that you are going to reconsider and uh - think about those ninety thousand who are still abroad. Uh - have they not been penalized enough - many of 'em been there for years?

MR. FORD: Well, Mr. Carter has uh indicated that uh - he would give a blanket pardon to all uh - draft evaders. I do not agree with that point of view. I gave, in September of 1974, an opportunity for all draft evaders, all deserters, to come in voluntarily, clear their records by earning an opportunity to restore their good citizenship. I think we gave them a good opportunity - we're - I don't think we should go any further.

MR. NEWMAN: Governor Carter.

MR. CARTER: Well I think it's uh... very difficult for President Ford to uh - explain the difference between the pardon of President Nixon and - and uh - his attitude toward those who violated the draft laws. As a matter of fact - now- I don't advocate amnesty; I advocate pardon. There's a difference in my opinion - uh and in accordance with the ruling of the Supreme Court and accordance with the definition in the dictionary. Amnesty means that - that you uh - that what you did was right. Pardon means that what you did, whether it's right or wrong, you're forgiven for it. And I do advocate a pardon for - for draft evaders. I think it's accurate to say that in uh - two years ago when Mr. Nixon - Mr. Ford put in this uh amnesty that three times as many deserters were uh - excused as were - as were the uh - the ones who evaded the draft. But I think that now is the time to heal our country after the Vietnam War and I think that what the people are concerned about is not the - uh pardon or the amnesty of uh - those who evaded the draft, but - but whether or not our crime system is - is fair. We've got a - a sharp distinction drawn between white collar crime - the - the - the big shots who are rich, who are influential uh very seldom go to jail; those who are poor and - and who have uh no influence - uh quite often are the ones who are punished. And - and the whole uh subject of crime is one that concerns our people very much, and I believe that the fairness of it is - is what - uh - is a - is a major problem that addresses our - our leader and this is something that hasn't been addressed adequately by - by this administration. But I - I hope to have a complete uh responsibility on my shoulders to help bring about a - a fair uh - criminal justice system and also to - to bring about uh - an end to the - to the divise- divisiveness that has occurred in our country uh as a result of the Vietnam War.

MR. NEWMAN: Mr. Gannon.

MR. GANNON: Governor Carter, you have promised a sweeping overhaul of the federal government, including a reduction in the number of government agencies - you say it would go down about two hundred from some nineteen hundred. That sounds, indeed, like a very deep cut in the federal government. But isn't it a fact that you're not really talking about fewer federal employees or less government spending, but rather that you are talking about reshaping the federal government, not making it smaller?

MR. CARTER: Well, I've been through this before, Mr. Gannon, as the governor of Georgia. When I took aver we had uh a bureaucratic mess, like we have in Washington now, and we had three hundred agencies, departments, bureaus, commissions - uh some uh - fully budgeted, some not, but all having responsibility to carry out that was in conflict. And we cut those three hundred - uh agencies and so forth down substantially. We eliminated two hundred and seventy-eight of them. We set up a simple structure of government that could be administrated fairly and it was a - a tremendous success.

It hasn't been undone since I was there. It resulted also in an ability to reshape our court system, our prison system, our education system, our mental health programs and - and a clear assignment of responsibility and - and authority and also to have uh our people once again understanding control our government. I intend to do the same thing if I'm elected president. When I get to Washington, coming in as an outsider, one of the major responsibilities that - that I will have on my shoulder is a complete reorganization of the - of the executive branch of government. We now have uh - a greatly expanded White House staff. When Mr. Nixon went in office, for instance, we had three and a half million dollars spent on - on the White House and its staff. That has escalated now to sixteen and a half million dollars, in the last uh Republican administration. This needs to be changed. We need to put the responsibilities back on the cabinet members. We also need to have a great reduction in agencies and programs. For instance, we now have uh - in the health area three hundred and two different programs administered by eleven major departments and agencies, sixty other advisory commissions responsible for this. Medicaid's in one agency; Medicare is in a different one. The - the check on the quality of health care is in a different one. None of them uh are responsible for health care itself. This makes it almost impossible for us to have a good health program. We have uh - just advocated uh - this past week a consolidation of the responsibilities for energy. Our country now has no comprehensive energy program or policy. We have twenty different agencies in the federal government responsible for the production, the regulation, the uh - information about energy, the conservation of energy, spread all over government. This is a - a gross waste of money, so tough, competent management of government, giving us a simple efficient purposeful and manageable government would be a great step forward and if I'm elected - and I intend to be - then it's gonna be done.

MR. GANNON: Well, I'd like to - to press my question on the number of federal employees - whether you would really plan to reduce the overall - uh number, or - or merely put them in different departments and relabel them. Uh - in your energy plan, you consolidate a number of a - agencies into one, or you would, but uh does that really change the overall?

MR. CARTER: I can't say for sure that we would have fewer federal employees when I go out of office than when I come in. It took me about three years to completely reorganize the Georgia government. The last year I was in office uh - our budget was - was actually less than it was a year before, uh which showed a great uh improvement. Also, we had a - a 2 percent increase in the number of employees the last year. But it was a tremendous shift from administrative jobs into the delivery of services. For instance, we uh - completely revised our prison system. We established eighty-four new mental health treatment centers. And we shifted people out of administrative jobs into the field to deliver better services. The same thing will be done uh - at the federal government level. I - I accomplished this with s - substantial reductions in employees in some departments. For instance, in the Transportation Department uh we had uh - we cut back about 25 percent of the total number of employees. In giving our people better mental health care, we increased the number of employees. But the efficiency of it, the simplicity of it, the uh ability of people to understand their own government and control it was a - was a uh - substantial benefit derived from complete reorganization. We uh - have got to do that at the federal government level. If we don't, the bureaucratic mess is going to continue. There's no way for our people now to understand what their government is. There's no way to get the answer to a question. When you come to Washington to try to - as a governor - to try to begin a new program for your people, like uh the treatment of drug addicts, I found there were thirteen different federal agencies that I had to go to, to manage the uh drug treatment program. In the Georgia government we only had one agency responsible for drug treatment. This is the kind of change that would be made. And uh - it would be of - of tremendous benefit in long-range planning, in tight budgeting, uh saving the taxpayers' money, making the government more efficient, cutting down on bureaucratic waste, having a clear delineation of authority and responsibility of employees, and giving our people a better chance to understand and control their government.

MR. NEWMAN: President Ford.

MR. FORD: I think the record should show, Mr. Newman, that uh - the Bureau of Census - we checked it just yesterday - indicates that uh - in the four years that uh - Governor Carter was governor of the state of Georgia, uh - expenditures by the government went up over 50 percent Uh - employees of the government in Georgia during his term of office went up over 25 percent; and the figures also show that the uh, uh - bonded indebtedness of the state of Georgia during his governorship went up over 20 percent. And there was some very interesting testimony given by Governor Carter's successor, Governor Busby, before a Senate committee a few uh - months ago on how he found the Medicaid program when he came into office following Governor Carter. He testified, and these are his words - the present governor of Georgia - he says he found the Medicaid program in Georgia in shambles. Now let me talk about what we've done in the White House as far as federal employees are concerned The first order that I issued after I became president was to cut or eliminate the prospective forty-thousand increase in federal employees that had been scheduled by my predecessor. And in the term that I've been president - some two years - we have reduced federal employment by eleven thousand. In the White House staff itself, when I became president, we had roughly five hundred and forty employees. We now have about four hundred and eighty-five employees, so we've made a rather significant reduction in the number of employees on the White House staff working for the president. So I think our record of cutting back employees, plus the failure on the part of the Governor's programs to actually save employment in Georgia, shows which is the better plan.

MR. NEWMAN: Mrs. Drew.

MS. DREW: Mr. President, at Vail, after the Republican convention, you announced that you would now emphasize five new areas; among those were jobs and housing and health and improved recreational facilities for Americans. And you also added crime. You also mentioned education. For two years you've been telling us that we couldn't do very much in these areas because we couldn't afford it; and in fact we do have a $50 billion deficit now. In rebuttal to Governor Carter a little bit earlier, you said that if there were to be any surplus in the next few years you thought it should be turned back to the people in the form of tax relief. So how are you going to pay for any new initiatives in these areas you announced at Vail you were going to now stress?

MR. FORD: Well, in the uh - last two years, as I indicated before, we had a very tough time. We were faced with uh - heavy inflation, over 12 percent; we were faced with substantial unemployment. But in the last uh - twenty-four months we've turned the economy around and we've brought inflation down to under 6 percent, and we have reduced the uh - well, we have added employment of about four million in the last seventeen months to the point where we have eighty-eight million people working in America today - the most in the history of the country. The net result is we are going to have some improvement in our receipts. And I think we'll have some decrease in our disbursements. We expect to have a lower deficit in fiscal year 1978. We feel that with this improvement in the economy; we feel with more receipts and fewer disbursements we can in a moderate way increase, as I recommended, over the next ten years a new parks program that would cast a billion and a half dollars, doubling our national park system. We have recommended that in the h-housing program we can reduce down payments and moderate monthly payments. But that doesn't cost any more as far as the federal treasury is concerned. We believe that we can uh do a better job in the area of crime, but that requires a tougher sentencing, mandatory certain prison sentences for those who violate our criminal laws. We - uh believe that uh you can revise the federal criminal code, which has not been revised in a good many years. That doesn't cost any more money. We believe that you can uhh - do something more effectively with a moderate increase in money in the drug abuse program. We feel that uh - in education we can have a slight increase - not a major increase. It's my understanding that Governor Carter has indicated that uh - he approves of a $30 billion uh - expenditure by the federal government as far as education is concerned. At the present time we're spending roughly three billion five hundred million dollars. I don't know where that money would come from. But as we look at the quality-of-life programs - jobs, health, education, crime, recreation - we feel that as we move forward with a healthier economy, we can absorb the small necessary cost that will be required.

MS. DREW: Sir, in the next few years would you try to reduce the deficit, would you spend more money far these programs that you have just outlined, or would you, as you said earlier, return whatever surplus you got to the people in the form of tax relief?

MR. FORD: We feel that uh - with the programs that I have recommended, the additional $10 billion tax cut, with the moderate increases in the quality-of-life area, we can still have a balanced budget which I will submit to the Congress in January of 1978. We won't wait one year or two years longer, as Governor Carter uh - indicates. As the economy improves, and it is improving, our gross national product this year will average about 6 percent increase over last year. We will have the lower rate of inflation for the uh - calendar year this year - something slightly under 6 percent. Employment will be up, revenues will be up. We'll keep the lid on some of these programs that we can hold down as we have a little extra money to spend for those quality-of-life programs which I think are needed and necessary. Now I cannot, and would not, endorse the kind of program that uh - Governor Carter recommends. He endorses the Democratic uh - platform which, as I read it, calls for approximately sixty additional programs. We estimate that those programs would add a hundred billion dollars minimum and probably two hundred billion dollars - uhh maximum each year to the federal budget. Those programs you cannot afford and give tax relief. We feel that you can hold the line and restrain federal spending, give a tax reduction and still have a balanced budget by 1978.

MR. NEWMAN: Governor Carter.

MR. CARTER: Well, Mr. Ford takes the uh - same attitude that the Republicans always take. In the last three months before an election, they're always for the programs that they always fight the other three-and-one-half years. Uh - I remember when uh - Herbert Hoover was against uh - jobs for people. I remember when Alf Landon was against Social

Security and uh - later President Nixon, sixteen years ago, was telling the public that John Kennedy's proposals would bankrupt the country and would double the cost. The best thing to do is to look at the record uh - of Mr. Ford's Administration and Mr. Nixon's before his. Uh - we had last year a $65 billion deficit - the largest deficit in the history of our country - more of a deficit spending than we had in the entire eight-year period under President Johnson and President Kennedy. We've got five hundred thousand more Americans out of jobs today than were out of work three months ago and since Mr. Ford's been in office two years, we've had a 50 percent increase in unemployment from five million people out of work to two and a half million more people out of work and a total of seven and a half million. We've also got uh - a comparison between himself and Mr. Nixon. He's got four times the size of the deficits that Mr. Nixon even had himself. This uh - talking about more people at work - uh is distorted because with a 14 percent increase in the cost of living in the last uh - two years, it means that - that women and young people have had to go to work when they didn't want to because their fathers didn't make enough to pay the increased cost of uh - food and uh housing and clothing. We have uh - in this last uh two years alone a hundred and twenty billion dollars total deficits under President Ford and uh - at the same time we've had, in the last eight years, a doubling in the number of bankruptcies for small business: we've had a negative growth in our - in our national economy measured in real dollars. The take-home pay of a worker in this country is actually less now than it was in 1968 - measured in real dollars. This is the kind of record that's there and talk about the future and a drastic change or conversion on the part of Mr. Ford as of last minute is one that just doesn't go.

MR. NEWMAN: Mr. Reynolds.

MR. REYNOLDS: Governor Carter, I'd like to turn uh - to what we used to call the energy crisis. Yesterday a British uh - government commission on air pollution, but one headed by a nuclear physicist, recommended that any further expansion of nuclear energy be delayed in Britain as long as possible. Now this is a subject that is quite controversial among our own people and there seems to be a clear difference between you and the President on the use of nuclear power plants, which you say you would use as a last priority. Why, sir, are they unsafe?

MR. CARTER: Well among my other experiences in the past, I've - I've been a nuclear engineer, and did graduate work in this field. I think I know the - the uh capabilities and limitations of atomic power. But the energy - uh policy of our nation is one that uh has not yet been established under this administration. I think almost every other developed nation in the world has an energy policy except us. We have seen uh - the Federal Energy Agency established, for instance. Uh - in the crisis of 1973 it was supposed to be a temporary agency, uh now it's permanent, it's enormous, it's growing every day. I think the Wall Street Journal uh reported not too long ago they have a hundred and twelve public relations experts working for the Federal Energy Agency to try to justify to the American people its own existence. We've got to have a - a firm way to handle the energy question. The reorganization proposal that I have put forward is one uh first step. In addition to that, we need to have - uh a realization that we've got uh about thirty-five years worth of oil left in the whole world. We're gonna run out of oil. When Mr. Nixon made his famous uh speech on Operation Independence we were importing about 35 percent of our oil. Now we've increased that amount 25 percent. We now import about 44 percent of our oil. We need to shift from oil to coal. We need to concentrate our research and development effort on uh coal burning and extraction, with safer mines, but also it's clean burning. We need to shift very strongly toward solar energy and have strict conservation measures. And then as a last resort only, continue to use atomic power. I would certainly uh - not cut out atomic power altogether. We can't afford to give up that opportunity until later. But to the extent that we continue to use atomic power, I would be responsible as president to make sure that the safety precautions were initiated and maintained. For instance, some that have been forgotten; we need to have the reactor core - below ground level, the entire power plant that uses atomic uh - power tightly sealed and a heavy - heavy vacuum maintained. There ought to be a standardized design. There ought to be a full-time uh - atomic energy specialist, independent of the power company in the control room, full time, twenty-four hours a day, to shut down a plant if an abnormality develops. These kinds of uh - procedures, along with evacuation procedures, adequate insurance, ought to be initiated. So, shift from oil to coal, emphasize research and development on coal use and also on solar power, strict conservation measures, not yield every time that the special interest groups uh - put pressure on the president like uh this administration has done, and use atomic energy only as a last resort with the strictest possible safety precautions. That's the best overall energy policy in the brief time we have to discuss it.

MR. REYNOLDS: Well Governor, on that same subject, would you require mandatory conservation efforts to try to conserve fuel?

MR. CARTER: Yes, I would. Some of the things that can be done about this is a change in the rate structure of electric power companies. We uh - now encourage people to waste electricity, and uh - by giving uh - the lowest rates to the biggest users. We don't do anything to cut down on peak load requirements. We don't have an adequate requirement for the insulation of homes, for the efficiency of automobiles. And whenever the uh - automobile manufacturers come forward and say they can't meet the uh - amendments that the Congress has put forward, this Republican administration has delayed the implementation dates. In addition to that, we ought to have a - a shift toward the use of coal, particularly in the Appalachian regions where the coal is located. A lot of uh - very high quality, low-carbon coal, uh - low-sulfur coal is there, it's where our employment is needed. Uh - this would - would help a great deal. So mandatory conservation measures - yes. Encouragement by the president for people to uh voluntarily conserve - yes. And also the private sector ought to be encouraged to - to bring forward to the public the benefits from efficiency. One bank in uh - Washington, fo- for instance, gives lower interest loans for people who adequately insulate their homes or who buy efficient automobiles. And some major uh - uh - manufacturing companies, like Dow Chemical, have through uh - very effective efficiency mechanism cut down the use of energy by uh - as much as 40 percent with the same out-product. These kinds of things uh - ought to be done, uh they ought to be encouraged and supported, and even required uh by the government, yes.

MR. NEWMAN: President Ford.

MR. FORD: Governor Carter skims over a very serious and a very broad subject. In January of uh - 1975 I submitted to the Congress and to the American people the first comprehensive energy program recommended by any president. It called for an increase in the production of energy in the United States. It called for uh - conservation measures so that we would save the energy that we have. If you're going to increase domestic oil and gas production - and we have to - you have to give those producers an opportunity to uh - develop their land or their wells. I recommended to the Congress that we should increase production in this country from six hundred million tons a year to twel- a- a billion two hundred million tons by 1985. In order to do that we have to improve our extraction of coal from the ground; we have to improve our utilization of coal - make it more efficient, make it cleaner. In addition we uh - have to expand our research and development. In my program for energy independence we have increased, for example, solar energy research from about $84 million a year to about a hundred and twenty million dollars a year. We're going as fast as the experts say we should. In nuclear power we have increased the research and development, uh - under the Energy Research and Development Agency uh - very substantially, to insure that our ener- uh - nuclear power plants are safer, that they are more efficient, and that we have adequate safeguards. I think you have to have greater oil and gas production, more coal production, more nuclear production, and in addition you have to have energy conservation.

MR. NEWMAN: Mr. Gannon.

MR. GANNON: Mr. President, I'd like to return for a moment to this problem of unemployment. You have vetoed or threatened to veto number of job bills passed or uh - in development in the Democratic Congress - Democratic-controlled Congress. Yet at the same time the government is paying out, uh - I think it is $17 billion, perhaps $20 billion a year in unemployment compensation caused by the high unemployment. Why do you think it is better to pay out unemployment compensation to idle people than to put them to work in public service jobs?

MR. FORD: The bills that I vetoed, the one for an additional $6 billion, was not a bill that would have solved our unemployment problems. Even the proponents of it admitted that no more than four hundred thousand jobs would be uh - made available. Our analysis indicates that something in the magnitude of about one hundred fifty to two hundred thousand jobs would uh - be made available. Each one of those jobs would've cost the taxpayers $25 thousand. In addition, the jobs would not be available right now. They would not have materialized for about nine to eighteen months. The immediate problem we have is to stimulate our economy now so that we can get rid of unemployment. What we have done is to hold the lid on spending in an effort to reduce the rate of inflation. And we have proven, I think very conclusively, that you can reduce the rate of inflation and increase jobs. For example, as I have said, we have added some four million jobs in the last seventeen months. We have now employed eighty-eight million people in America, the largest number in the history of the United States. We've added five hundred thousand jobs in the last two months. Inflation is the quickest way to destroy jobs. And by holding the lid on federal spending we have been able to do an- a good job, an affirmative job in inflation and as a result have added to the jobs in this country. I think it's uh - also appropriate to point out that through our tax policies we have stimulated uhh - added employment throughout the country, the investment tax credit, the tax incentives for expansion and modernization of our industrial capacity. It's my - my opinion that the private sector, where five out of six jobs are, where you have permanent jobs, with the opportunity for advancement, is a better place than make-work jobs under the program recommended by the Congress.

MR. GANNON: Just to follow up, Mr. President: the - the Congress has just passed a three point seven billion dollar appropriation bill which would provide money for the public works jobs program that you earlier tried to kill by your veto of the authorization legislation. In light of the fact that uh - unemployment again is rising - or has in the past three months

- I wonder if you have rethought that question at all; whether you would consider uh - allowing this program to be funded, or will you veto that money bill?

MR. FORD: Well, that bill has not yet come down to the Oval Office, so I am not in a position to make any judgment on it tonight. But that is an extra $4 billion that would uh - add to the deficit which would add to the inflationary pressures, which would help to destroy jobs in the private sector - not make jobs, where the jobs really are. These make-work, temporary jobs - dead end as they are - are not the kind of jobs that we want for our people. I think it's interesting to point out that uh - in the uh - two years that I've been president I've vetoed fifty-six bills. Congress has sustained forty-two vetoes. As a result, we have saved over $9 billion in federal expenditures. And the Congress by overriding the bills that I did veto, the Congress has added some $13 billion to the federal expenditures and to the federal deficit. Now Governor Carter complains about the deficits that uh - uh - this administration has had. And yet he condemns the vetoes that I have made that has - that have saved the taxpayer $9 billion and could have saved an additional $13 billion. Now he can't have it both ways. And therefore, it seems to me that we should hold the lid, as we have, to the best of our ability so we can stimulate the private economy and get the jobs where the jobs are - five out of six in this economy.

MR. NEWMAN: Governor Carter.

MR. CARTER: Well, Mr. Ford doesn't seem to put into perspective the fact that when - when uh five hundred thousand more people are out of work than there were three months ago, while we have two and a half million more people out of work than were when he took office, that this touches human beings. I was in uh - a city in uh - Pennsylvania not too long ago, near here, and uh - there were about four or five thousand people in the audience - it was on a - on a train trip. And I said, "How many uh - adults here are out of work?" About a thousand raised their hands. Mr. Ford uh - actually has fewer people now in the private sector in non-farm jobs than when he took office. And still he talks about - uh success. Seven point nine percent unemployment is a terrible tragedy in this country. He says he's learned how to match unemployment with inflation. That's right. We've got the highest inflation we've had in twenty-five years right now, except under this administration, and that was fifty years ago. And we've got uh - the highest unemployment we've had uh - under Mr. Ford's administration, since the Great Depression. This affects human beings, and - and his insensitivity in providing those people a chance to work has made this a welfare administration, and not a work administration. He hasn't saved $9 billion with his vetoes. There's only been uh - a net savings of $4 billion. And the cost in unemployment compensation, welfare compensation, and lost revenues has increased $23 billion in the last two years. This is a - a typical attitude that really causes havoc in people's lives, and then it's covered over by saying that our country has naturally got a 6 percent unemployment rate, or 7 percent unemployment rate and a 6 percent inflation. It's a travesty. It shows a lack of leadership. And we've never had a president since the War between the States that vetoed more bills. Mr. Ford has vetoed four times as many bills as Mr. Nixon - per year. And eleven of 'em have been overridden. One of his bills that was overridden - he only got one vote in the Senate and seven votes in the House, from Republicans.

MR. NEWMAN: Governor Carter. So this shows a breakdown in leadership.

MR. NEWMAN: Under the rules, I must stop you there. And Mrs. Drew.

MS. DREW: Governor Carter, I'd like to come back to the subject of taxes. You have said that you want to cut taxes for the middle and lower income groups.

MR. CARTER: Right.

MS. DREW: But unless you're willing to do such things as reduce the itemized deductions for charitable contributions or home mortgage payments, or interest, or taxes, or capital gains, you can't really raise sufficient revenue to provide an overall tax cut of any size. So how are you gonna provide that tax relief that you're talking about?

MR. CARTER: Now we have uh such a grossly unbalanced tax system - as I said earlier, that it is a disgrace - ah of all the tax - benefits now, 25 percent of 'em go to the 1 percent of the richest people in this country. Over 50 percent - 53 to be exact - percent of the tax benefits go to the 14 percent richest people in this country, and we've had a 50 percent increase in payroll deductions since Mr. Nixon went in office eight years ago. Mr. Ford has - has advocated since he's been in office over $5 billion in reductions for corporations, special interest groups, and the very, very wealthy who derive their income - not from labor - but from investments. That's got to be changed. A few things that can be done: we have now a deferral system so that the multinational corporations who invest overseas - if they make a million dollars in profits overseas - they don't have to pay any of their taxes unless they bring their money back into this country. When they don't pay their taxes, the average American pays the taxes for them. Not only that, but it robs this country of jobs, because instead of coming back with that million dollars and creating a shoe factory, say in New Hampshire or Vermont, if the company takes the money down to Italy and - and builds a shoe factory, they don't have to pay any taxes on the money. Another thing is a system called DISC which was originally designed, proposed by Mr. Nixon, to encourage exports. This permits a company to create uh - a dummy corporation, to export their products, and then not to pay the full amount of taxes on them. This costs our uh - government about uh - $1.4 billion a year. And when those rich corporations don't pay that tax, the average American taxpayer pays it for 'em. Another one that's uh - that's very important is the uh - is the business deductions, uh - jet airplanes, uh - first class travel, the fifty-dollar martini lunch. The average working person can't - uh - can't take advantage of that, but the - the wealthier people - uh can. Uh - another system is where uhh - a dentist can invest money in say, raising cattle and uh - can put in a hundred thousand dollars of his own money, borrow nine hundred thousand dollars - nine hundred mi- thousand dollars - that makes a million - and mark off a great amount of uh - of loss uh - through that procedure. Uh - there was one example, for instance, where uh - somebody uh - produced pornographic movies. They put in $30 thousand of their own money and got a hundred and twenty thousand dollars in tax savings. Well, these special kinds of programs have - have robbed the average taxpayer and have benefited those who are powerful, and who can employ lobbyists, and who can have their CPAs and their lawyers to help them benefit from the roughly uh - eight thousand pages of the tax code. The average uh American person can't do it. You can't hire a lobbyist uh out of unemployment compensation checks.

MS. DREW: Ah - Governor, to follow up on your answer. Uh - in order for any kind of tax relief to really be felt by the middle and lower-income people

MR. CARTER: Yes. You need about, according to Congressional committees on this, you need about $10 billion. Now you listed some things - the uh - deferral on foreign income as estimated: that would save about $500 million. DISC, you said, was about 1.4 billion. uh - The estimate of the outside, if you eliminated all tax shelters, is 5 billion. So where else would you raise the revenue to provide this tax relief - would you, in fact, do away with all business deductions, and what other kinds of preferences would you do away with?

MR. CARTER: No, I wouldn't do away with all - uh business deductions. I think that would be a - a very serious mistake. But uh - if - if you could just do away with the ones that are unfair, you could lower taxes for everyone. I would never do anything that would increase the taxes for those who work for a living, or who are presently required to list all their income. What I wanna do is not to raise taxes, but to eliminate loopholes. And this is uh - the point of my first statistics that I gave you - that - that the present tax benefits that have been carved out over a long period of years - fifty years - by sharp tax lawyers and by lobbyists have benefited just the rich. These programs that I described to you earlier - the tax deferrals for overseas, the DISC, and the tax shelters, uh - they only apply to people in the $50 thousand-a-year bracket or up, and I think this is the very best way to approach it. It's to make sure that everybody pays taxes on the income that they earn and make sure that you take whatever savings there is from the higher income levels and give it to the lower- and middle-income families.

MR. NEWMAN: President Ford.

MR. FORD: Governor Carter's answer tonight does not coincide with the answer that he gave in an interview to the Associated Press a week or so ago. In that interview uh - Governor Carter indicated that uh - he would raise the taxes on those in the medium or middle-income brackets or higher. Now if you uh - take the medium or middle-income taxpayer - that's about $14 thousand per person - uh - Governor Carter has indicated, publicly, in an interview that he would increase the taxes on about 50 percent of the working people of this country. I think uh - the way to get tax equity in this country is to give tax relief to the middle-income people who have an income from roughly $8 thousand up to twenty-five or thirty thousand dollars. They have been short-changed as we have taken ten million taxpayers off the tax rolls in the last eight years, and as we have uh - added to the minimum tax uh - provision to make all people pay more taxes. I believe in tax equity for the middle-income taxpayer, increasing the personal exemption. Mr. Carter wants to increase taxes for roughly half of the taxpayers of this country. Now, the Governor has also played a little fast and loose with the facts about vetoes. The records show that President Roosevelt vetoed an average of fifty-five bills a year. President Truman vetoed on the average, while he was president, about thirty-eight bills a year. I understand that Governor Carter, when he was Governor of Georgia, vetoed between thirty-five and forty bills a year. My average in two years is twenty-six. But in the process of that we have saved uhh - $9 billion. And one final comment, uh - Governor Carter talks about the tax bills and all of the inequities that exist in the present law. I must remind him the Democrats have controlled the Congress for the last twenty-two years and they wrote all the tax bills.

MR. NEWMAN: Mr. Reynolds.

MR. REYNOLDS: I suspect that uhh - we could continue on this tax argument for some time. But I'd like to move on to another area. Mr. President, uh everybody seems to be running against Washington this year. And I'd like to raise two coincidental events and ask you whether you think perhaps this may have a bearing on the attitude throughout the country. The House Ethics Committee has just now ended its investigation of Daniel Schorr, after several months and many thousands of dollars, trying to find out how he obtained and caused to be published a report of the Congress that probably is the property of the American people. At the same time. the Senate Select Committee on Standards and Conduct has voted not really to begin an investigation of a United States senator because of allegations against him that he may have been receiving corporate funds illegally over a period of years. Do you suppose, sir, that events like this contribute to the feeling in the country that maybe there's something wrong in Washington, and I don't mean just in the executive branch but throughout the whole government?

MR. FORD: There is a considerable anti-Washington feeling throughout the country. But I think the feeling is misplaced. In the last two years, we have restored integrity in the White House, and we've set high standards in the executive branch of the government. The anti-Washington feeling, in my opinion, ought to be focused on the Congress of the United States. For example, this Congress, very shortly, will spend a billion dollars a year for its housekeeping, its salaries, its expenses and the like. It - the next Congress will probably be the first billion-dollar Congress in the history of the United States. I don't think the American people are getting their money's worth from the majority party that run this Congress. We, in addition, see that uh - in the last uh - four years the number of employees hired by the Congress has gone up substantial- uh much more than uh - the gross national product, much more than any other increase throughout our society. Congress is hiring people by the droves, and the cast as a result has gone up. And I don't see any improvement in the performance of the Congress under the present leadership. So it seems to me instead of the anti-Washington feeling being aimed at everybody in Washington, it seems to me that the focus should be where the problem is, which is the Congress of the United States, and particularly the majority in the Congress. They spend too much money on themselves. They have too many employees. There's some question about their morality. It seems to me that in this election, the focus should not be on the executive branch but the corrections should come as the voters vote for their members of the House of Representatives or for their United States senator. That's where the problem is and I hope there'll be some corrective action taken so we can get some new leadership in the Congress of the United States.

MR. REYNOLDS: Mr. President, if I may follow up. Uh - I think you've made it plain that you take a dim view of the uh - majority in the Congress. Isn't it quite likely, sir, that you will have a Democratic Congress in the next session, if you are elected president? And hasn't the country uh - a right to ask whether you can get along with that Congress, or whether we'll have continued confrontation?

MR. FORD: Well, It seems to me that uh - we have a chance - the Republicans - to get a majority in the House of Representatives. We will make some gains in the United States Senate. So there will be different ratios in the House, as well as in the Senate, and as president I will be able to uh - work with that Congress. But let me take the other side of the coin, if I might. Supposing we had - had a Democratic Congress for the last two years and we'd had uh - Governor Carter as President. He has, in effect, said that he would agree with all of - he would disapprove of the vetoes that I have made, and would have added significantly to expenditures and the deficit in the federal government. I think it would be contrary to one of the basic concepts in our system of government - a system of checks and balances. We have a Democratic Congress today, and fortunately we've had a Republican president to check their excesses with my vetoes. If we have a Democratic Congress next year, and a president who wants to spend an additional one hundred billion dollars a year, or maybe two hundred billion dollars a year, with more programs, we will have in my judgment, greater deficits with more spending, more dangers of inflation. I think the American people want a Republican president to check on any excesses that come out of the next Congress, if it is a Democratic Congress.

MR. NEWMAN: Governor Carter.

MR. CARTER: Well, it's not a matter of uh - Republican and Democrat. It's a matter of leadership or no leadership. President Eisenhower worked with a Democratic Congress very well. Even President Nixon, because he was a strong leader at least, worked with a Democratic Congress very well. Uh - Mr. Ford has vetoed, as I said earlier, four times as many bills per year as Mr. Nixon. Mr. Ford quite often puts forward a program just as a public relations stunt, and never tries to put it through the Congress by working with the Congress. I think under presidents For- uh - Nixon and Eisenhower they passed about 60 to 75 percent of their legislation. This year Mr. Ford will not pass more than 26 percent of all the legislative proposals he puts forward. This is government by stalemate, and we've seen almost a complete breakdown in the proper relationship between the president, who represents this country, and the Congress, who collectively also represent this country. We've had uh - Republican presidents before who've tried to run against a Democratic - uh Congress. And I don't think it's uh - the Congress is Mr. Ford's opponent; but if uh - if - if he insists that uh - that I be responsible for the Democratic Congress, of which I'm - have not been a part, then I think it's only fair that he be responsible for the Nixon administration in its entirety, of which he was a part. That, I think, is a good balance. But the point is, that - that a president ought to lead this country. Mr. Ford, so far as I know, except for avoiding another Watergate, has not accomplished one single major program for this country. And there's been a constant squabbling between the president and the Congress, and that's not the way this country ought to be run. I might go back to one other thing. Mr. Ford has uh - misquoted an AP uh - news story that was in error to begin with. That story reported several times that I would lower taxes for low and middle-income families and uh - that correction was delivered to the White House and I am sure that the president knows about this uh - correction, but he still insists uh - on repeating an erroneous statement.

MR. NEWMAN: President Ford, Governor Carter, we no longer have enough time for two complete sequences of questions. We have only about six minutes left for questions and answers. For that reason we will drop the follow-up questions at this point but each candidate will still be able to respond to the other's answers. Uh - to the extent that you can, gentlemen, please keep your remarks brief. Mr. Gannon.

MR. GANNON: Governor Carter, one uh - important uh - part of the Government's economic policy uh - apparatus we haven't talked about is the Federal Reserve Board. I'd like to ask you something about what you've said and that is that uh - you believe that a president ought to have a chairman of the Federal Reserve Board whose views are compatible with his own. Based on the record of the last few years, would you say that your views are compatible with those of Chairman Arthur Burns? And if not, would you seek his resignation if you are elected?

MR. CARTER: What I have said is that the president ought to have a chance to appoint a chairman of the Federal Reserve Board to have a coterminous uh term; in other words, both of 'em serve the same four - four years. The Congress can modify the supply of money by modifying the income uh tax laws. The president can modify the uh - economic structure of a country by public statements and general attitudes in the budget that he proposes. The Federal Reserve has uh - an independent status that ought to be preserved; I think that Mr. uh - Burns did take a typical, erroneous Republican attitude in the 1973 year when inflation was so high. They assumed that the uh - inflation rate was because of excessive demand and uh - therefore put into effect tight constraint on the economy, very high interest rates, which is typical also of the Republican administration, uh - tried to increase the uh - the tax uh - payments by individuals, and cut the tax payments by corporations. I would have uh - done it opposite. I think the uh - problem should've been addressed by increasing productivity, by having uh - put - put people back to work so they could purchase more goods, lower income taxes on individuals, perhaps raise them, if necessary, on corporations in comparison. But uh - Mr. Burns uh - in that respect made a very serious mistake. I would not wanna destroy the - the independence of the uh Federal Reserve - uh Board. But I do think we ought to have a cohesive economic policy with at - at least the chairman of the Federal Reserve Board and the president's terms being uh - the same and letting the Congress, of course, be the third uh - entity with uh - with independence subject only to the president's veto.

MR. NEWMAN: President Ford, your response.

MR. FORD: The chairman of the Federal Reserve Board should be independent. Fortunately, he has been during Democratic as well as Republican administrations. As the result in the last uh - two years uh - we have had a responsible monetary policy. Uh the Federal Reserve Board indicated that the supply of money would be held between four to four and a half and seven and seven and a half. They have done a good job in integrating the money supply with the uh - fiscal policy of the uh - executive and legislative branches of the government. It would be catastrophic if the chairman of the Federal Reserve Board became the tool of the political uh - party that was in power. It's important for our future uhh - economic security that that job be nonpolitical and uh - separate from the executive and the Legislative branches.

MR. NEWMAN: Mrs. Drew.

MS. DREW: Uh Mr. President, the real problem with the FBI and, in fact, all of the intelligence agencies is there are no real laws governing them. Such laws as there are tend to be vague and open-ended. Now, you have issued some executive orders, but we've learned that leaving these agencies to executive discretion and direction can get them and, in fact, the country in a great deal of trouble. One president may be a decent man, the next one might not be. So, what do you think about trying to write in some more protection by getting some laws governing these agencies?

MR. FORD: You are familiar, of course, with the fact that I am the first president in thirty years who has reorganized the intelligence agencies in the federal government: the CIA, the Defense Intelligence Agency, the National Security Agency and the others. We've done that by executive order. Uhh - and I think uh - we've tightened it up; we've uh - straightened out their problems that developed over the last few years. It doesn't seem to me that it's needed or necessary to have legislation in this particular regard. Uhh - I have recommended to the Congress, however - I'm sure you're familiar with this - legislation that would uhh - make it uhh - very uhh - proper in - in the right way, that the attorney general could go in and get the right for wiretapping under security cases. This was an effort that was made by the attorney general and myself, working with the Congress. But even in this area, where I think new legislation would be justified, uh the Congress has not responded. So, I feel in that case, as well as in the reorganization of the intelligence agencies, as I've done, we have to do it by executive order. And I'm glad that we have a good director in George Bush. We have good executive orders, and the CIA and the DIA and NASA uh - uh - NSA are now doing a good job under proper supervision.

MR. NEWMAN: Governor Carter.

MR. CARTER: Well, one of the very serious things that's happened in our government in recent years, and has continued up until now, is a breakdown in the trust among our people in the [twenty-seven-minute delay]

MR. NEWMAN: failure in the broadcasting of the debate, it occurred twenty-seven minutes ago. Uh the fault has been dealt with and uh - we want to thank President Ford and Governor Carter for being so patient and understanding while this uh delay went on. Uh we very much regret the technical failure that lost the sound as it - as it was leaving this theater. It occurred during uh Governor Carter's response to what would have been and what was the last question put to the candidates. That question went to President Ford. It dealt with the control of government intelligence agencies. Uh Governor Carter was making that response and had very nearly finished it. Uh - he will conclude his response now after which uh - President Ford and Governor Carter will make their closing statements. Governor.

MR. CARTER: There has been too much government secrecy and not uh - not enough respect for the personal privacy of American citizens.

MR. NEWMAN: It is now time for the closing statements, which are to be up to four minutes long. Governor Carter, by the same toss of the coin that directed the first question to you, you are to go first now.

MR. CARTER: Well, tonight we've had a chance to talk a lot about the past. But I think it's time to talk about the future. Our nation in the last eight years has been divided as never before. It's a time for unity. It's a time to draw ourselves together: to have a president and a Congress that can work together with mutual respect for a change, cooperating for a change, in the open for a change, so the people can understand their own government. It's time for government, industry, labor, manufacturing, agriculture, education, other entities in our society to cooperate. And it's a time for government to understand and to cooperate with our people. For a long time our American citizens have been excluded, sometimes misled, sometimes have been lied to. This is uh - not compatible with the purpose of our nation. I believe in our country. It needs to be competent. The government needs to be well-managed, efficient, economical, We need to have a government that's sensitive to our people's needs - to those who are poor, who don't have adequate health care, who have been cheated too long with our tax programs, who've been out of jobs, whose families have been torn apart. We need to restore the faith and the trust of the American people in their own government. In addition to that, we've suffered because we haven't had leadership in this administration. We've got a government of stalemate. We've lost the vision of what our country can and ought to be. This is not the America that we've known in the past. It's not the America that we have to have in the future. I don't claim to know all the answers. But I've got confidence in my country. Our economic strength is still there. Our system of government - in spite of Vietnam, Cambodia, CIA, Watergate - is still the best system of government on earth. And the greatest resource of all are the two hundred and fifteen million Americans who have within us the strength, the character, the intelligence, the experience, the patriotism, the idealism, the compassion, the sense of brotherhood on which we can rely in the future to restore the greatness to our country We ought not to be excluded from our government anymore. We need a president who can go in - who derives his strength from the people. I owe the special interests nothing. I owe everything to you, the people of this country. And I believe that we can bind our wounds. I believe that we can work together. And I believe that if we can tap the tremendous untapped reservoir of innate strength in this country, that we can once again have a government as good as our people, and let the world know what we still know and hope for - that we still live in the greatest and the strongest and the best country on earth.

MR. NEWMAN: President Ford.

MR. FORD: On November second all of you will make a very, very important decision. One of the major issues in this campaign is trust. A president should never promise more than he can deliver and a president should always deliver everything that he's promised. A president can't be all things to all people. A president should be the same thing to all people. Another issue in this campaign, Governor Carter has endorsed the Democratic platform, which calls for more spending, bigger deficits, more inflation or mare taxes. Governor Carter has embraced the record of the present Congress, dominated by his political party. It calls for more of the same. Governor Carter in his acceptance speech called for more and more programs, which means more and more government. I think the real issue in this campaign, and that which you must decide on November second, is whether you should vote for his promise or my performance in two years in the White House. On the fourth of July we had a wonderful two hundredth birthday - for our great country. It was a superb occasion. It was a glorious day. In the first century of our nation's history our forefathers gave us the finest form of government in the history of mankind. In the second century of our nation's history, our forefathers developed the most productive industrial nation in the history of the globe. Our third century should be the century of individual freedom for all our two hundred and fifteen million Americans today and all that join us. In the last few years government has gotten bigger and bigger; industry has gotten larger and larger; labor unions have gotten bigger and bigger; and our children have been the victims of mass education. We must make this next century the century of the individual. We should never forget that a government big enough to give us everything we want is a government big enough to take from us everything we have. The individual worker in the plants throughout the United States should not be a small cog in a big machine. The member of a labor union must have his rights strengthened and broadened and our children in their education should have an opportunity to improve themselves based on their talents and their abilities. My mother and father, during the Depression, worked very hard to give me an opportunity to do better in our great country. Your mothers and fathers did the same thing for you and others. Betty and I have worked very hard to give our children a brighter future in the United States, our beloved country. You and others in this great country have worked hard and done a great deal to give your children and your grandchildren the blessings of a better America. I believe we can all work together to make the individuals in the future have more and all of us working together can build a better America.

MR. NEWMAN: Thank you President Ford. Thank you Governor Carter. Our thanks also to the questioners and to the audience in this theater. Ahh - we much regret the technical failure that caused a twenty-eight-minute delay in the broadcast of the debate. We believe, however, that everyone will agree that it did not detract from the effectiveness of the debate or from its fairness. The next presidential debate is to take place on Wednesday, October sixth, in San Francisco at nine-thirty P. M., Eastern Daylight Time. The topics are to be foreign and defense issues. As with all three debates between the presidential candidates and the one between the vice-presidential candidates, it is being arranged by the League of Women Voters Education Fund in the hope of promoting a wider and better informed participation by the American people in the election in November. Now, from the Walnut Street Theater in Philadelphia, good night.

3.2   1976 U.S. Presidential Debate - October 6

MS. FREDERICK: Good evening. I'm Pauline Frederick of NPR, moderator of this second of the historic debates of the 1976 campaign between Gerald R, Ford of Michigan, Republican candidate for president, and Jimmy Carter of Georgia, Democratic candidate for president. Thank you, President Ford and thank you, Governor Carter, for being with us tonight. This debate takes place before an audience in the Palace of Fine Arts Theater in San Francisco. An estimated one hundred million Americans are watching on television as well. San Francisco was the site of the signing of the United Nations Charter, thirty one years ago. Thus, it is an appropriate place to hold this debate, the subject of which is foreign and defense issues. The questioners tonight are Max Frankel, associate editor of the New York Times, Henry L. Trewhitt, diplomatic correspondent of the Baltimore Sun, and Richard Valeriani, diplomatic correspondent of NBC News. The ground rules are basically the same as they were for the first debate two weeks ago. The questions will be alternated between candidates. By the toss of a coin, Governor Carter will take the first question. Each question sequence will be as follows: The question will be asked and the candidate will have up to three minutes to answer. His opponent will have up to two minutes to respond. And prior to the response, the questioner may ask a follow-up question to clarify the candidate's answer when necessary with up to two minutes to reply. Each candidate will have three minutes for a closing statement at the end. President Ford and Governor Carter do not have notes or prepared remarks with them this evening, but they may take notes during the debate and refer to them. Mr. Frankel, you have the first question for Governor Carter.

MR. FRANKEL: Governor, since the Democrats last ran our foreign policy, including many of the men who are advising you, country has been relieved of the Vietnam agony and the military draft, we've started arms control negotiations with the Russians, we've opened relations with China, we've arranged the disengagement in the Middle East, we've regained influence with the Arabs without deserting Israel, now, maybe we've even begun a process of peaceful change in Africa. Now you've objected in this campaign to the style with which much of this was done, and you've mentioned some other things that - that you think ought to have been done. But do you really have a quarrel with this Republican record? Would you not have done any of those things?

MR. CARTER: Well I think this Republican administration has been almost all style, and spectacular, and not substance. We've uh - got a chance tonight to talk about, first of all, leadership, the character of our country, and a vision of the future. In every one of these instances, the Ford administration has failed, and I hope tonight that I and Mr. Ford will have a chance to discuss the reasons for those failures. Our country is not strong anymore; we're not respected anymore. We can only be strong overseas if we're strong at home; and when I became president we'll not only be strong in those areas but also in defense - a defense capability second to none. We've lost in our foreign policy, the character of the American people. We've uh - ignored or excluded the American people and the Congress from participation in the shaping of our foreign policy. It's been one of secrecy and exclusion. In addition to that we've had a chance to became now, contrary to our long-standing beliefs and principles, the arms merchant of the whole world. We've tried to buy success from our enemies, and at the same time we've excluded from the process the normal friendship of our allies. In addition to that we've become fearful to compete with the Soviet Union on an equal basis. We talk about detente. The Soviet Union knows what they want in detente, and they've been getting it. We have not known what we've wanted and we've been out-traded in almost every instance. The other point I wanna make is about our defense. We've got to be a nation blessed with a defense capability that's efficient, tough, capable, well organized, narrowly focused - fighting capability. The ability to fight, if necessary, is the best way to avoid the chance for, or the requirement to fight. And the last point I wanna make is this: Mr. Ford, Mr. Kissinger have uh - continued on with the policies and failures of Richard Nixon. Even the Republican platform has criticized the lack of leadership in Mr. Ford and they've criticized the foreign policy of this administration. This is one instance where I agree with - with the Republican platform. I might say this in closing, and that is that as far as foreign policy goes, Mr. Kissinger has been the president of this country. Mr. Ford has shown an absence of leadership, and an absence of a grasp of what this country is and what it ought to be. That's got to be changed. And that's one of the major issues in this uh - campaign of 1976.

MS. FREDERICK: President Ford, would you like to respond?

MR. FORD: Governor Carter again is talking in broad generalities. Let me take just one question that he raises - the military strength and capability of the United States. Governor Carter in November of 1975 indicated that he wanted to cut the defense budget by $15 billion. A few months later, he said he wanted to cut the defense budget by eight or nine billion dollars. And more recently, he talks about cutting the defense budget by five to seven billion dollars. There is no way you can be strong militarily and have those kind of reductions in our military uh - appropriation. Now let me just tell you a little story. About uh - late October of 1975, I asked the then Secretary of Defense, Mr. Schlesinger, to tell me what had to be done if we were going to reduce the defense budget by uh - three to five billion dollars. A few days later, Mr. Schlesinger came back and said if we cut the defense budget by three to five billion dollars, we will have to cut military personnel by two hundred and fifty thousand, civilian personnel by a hundred thousand, jobs in America by a hundred thousand. We would have to stretch out our aircraft procurement, we would have to reduce our naval construction program, we would have to reduce the uh - research and development for the Army, the Navy, the Air Force and Marines by 8 percent. We would have to close twenty military bases in the United States immediately. That's the kind of defense program that uh - Mr. Carter wants. Let me tell you this straight from the shoulder. You don't negotiate with Mr. Brezhnev from weakness. And the kind of defense program that Mr. Carter wants will mean a weaker defense and a poor negotiating position.

MS. FREDERICK: Mr. Trewhitt, a question for President Ford.

MR. TREWHITT: Mr. President, my question really is the other side of the coin from Mr. Frankel's. For a generation the United States has had a foreign policy based on containment of Communism. Yet we have lost the first war in Vietnam; we lost a shoving match in Angola. Uh - the Communists threatened to come to power by peaceful means in Italy and relations generally have cooled with the Soviet Union in the last few months. So le- let me ask you first, what do you do about such cases as Italy? And secondly, does this general drift mean that we're moving back toward something like an old cold - cold-war relationship with the Soviet Union?

MR. FORD: I don't believe we should move to a cold-war relationship. I think it's in the best interest of the United States, and the world as a whole that the United States negotiate rather than go back to the cold-war relationship with the Soviet Union. I don't uh - look at the picture as bleakly as you have indicated in your question, Mr. Trewhitt. I believe that the United States ha- had many successes in recent years, in recent months, as far as the Communist movement is concerned. We have been successful in Portugal, where a year ago it looked like there was a very great possibility that the uh - Communists would take over in Portugal. It didn't happen. We have a democracy in Portugal today. A few uh - months ago, or I should say, maybe two years ago, the Soviet Union looked like they had continued strength in the Middle East. Today, according to Prime Minister Rabin, the Soviet Union is weaker in the Middle East than they have been in many, many years. The facts are, there - the Soviet Union relationship with Egypt is uh - at a low level. The Soviet Union relationship with Syria is at a very low point. The United States today, according to Prime Minister Rabin of Israel, is a- at a peak in its uh - influence and power in the Middle East. But let's turn for a minute to the uhh - southern African operations that are now going on. The United States of America took the initiative in southern Africa. We wanted to end the bloodshed in southern Africa. We wanted to have the right of self-determination in southern Africa. We wanted to have majority rule with the full protection of the rights of the minority. We wanted to preserve human dignity in southern Africa. We have taken the initiative, and in southern Africa today the United States is trusted by the black front-line nations and black Africa. The United States is trusted by other elements in southern Africa. The United States foreign policy under this administration has been one of progress and success. And I believe that instead of talking about Soviet progress, we can talk about American successes. And may I make an observation - part of the question you asked, Mr. Trewhitt? I don't believe that it's in the best interest of the United States and the NATO nations to have a Communist government in NATO. Mr. Carter has indicated he would look with sympathy to a Communist government in NATO. I think that would destroy the integrity and the strength of NATO, and I am totally opposed to it.

MR. CARTER: Well, Mr. Ford, unfortunately, has just made a statement that's not true. I have never advocated a Communist government for Italy. That would obviously be a ridiculous thing for anyone to do who wanted to be president of this country. I think that this is uh - an instance of uh - deliberate distortion, and this has occurred also in the question about defense. As a matter of fact, uh - I've never advocated any cut of $15 billion in our defense budget. As a matter of fact, Mr. Ford has made a political football out of the defense budget. About a year ago he cut the Pentagon budget six point eight billion dollars. After he fired James Schlesinger, the political heat got so great that he added back about $3 billion. When Ronald Reagan won the Texas primary election, Mr. Ford added back another one and a half billion dollars. Immediately before the Kansas City convention, he added back another one point eight billion dollars in the defense budget. And his own uh - Office of Management and Budget testified that he had a $3 billion cut insurance added to the defense budget - defense budget under the pressure from the Pentagon. Obviously, this is another indication of trying to use the defense budget for political purposes, which he's trying to do tonight. Now, we went into south Africa late, after Great Britain, Rhodesia, the black nations had been trying to solve this problem for many, many years. We didn't go in until right before the election, similar to what was taking place in 1972, when Mr. Kissinger announced peace is at hand just before the election at that time. And we have weakened our position in NATO because the other countries in Europe supported the democ- democratic forces in Portugal long before we did; we stuck to the Portugal dictatorships much longer than other democracies did in this world.

MS. FREDERICK: Mr. Valeriani, a question for Governor Carter.

MR. VALERIANI: Governor Carter, much of what the United States does abroad is done in the name of the national interest. What is your concept of the national interest? What should the role of the United States in the world be? And in that connection, considering your limited experience in foreign affairs, and the fact that you take same pride in being a Washington outsider, don't you think it would be appropriate for you to tell the American voters before the election the people that you would like to have in key positions, such as Secretary of State, Secretary of Defense, national security affairs advisor at the White House?

MR. CARTER: Well, I'm not gonna name my cabinet before I get elected. I've got a little ways to go before I start doing that. But I have uh - an adequate background, I believe. I am a graduate of the U.S. Naval Academy, the first military graduate since uh - Eisenhower. I've served as the Governor of Georgia and have traveled extensively in foreign countries and South America, Central America, Europe, the Middle East and in Japan. I've traveled the last twenty-one months among the people of this country. I've talked to them and I've listened. And I've seen at first hand, in a very vivid way, the deep hurt that's come to this country in the aftermath of Vietnam and Cambodia, Chile, and Pakistan, and Angola, and Watergate, CIA revelations. What we were formerly so proud of - the strength of our country, its uh - moral integrity, the representation in foreign affairs of what our people are, what our Constitution stands for, has been gone. And in the secrecy that has surrounded our foreign policy in the last few years, uh - the American people, the Congress have been excluded. I believe I know what this country ought to be. I've uh - been one who's loved my nation as many Americans do, and I believe that there's no limit placed on what we can be in the future, if we can harness the tremendous resources - militarily, economically, and the stature of our people, the meaning of the Constitution, in the future. Every time we've made a serious mistake in foreign affairs, it's been because the American people have been excluded from the process. If we can just tap the intelligence and ability, the sound common sense and the good judgment of the American people, we can once again have a foreign policy to make us proud instead of ashamed. And I'm not gonna exclude the American people from that process in the future, as Mr. Ford and Kissinger have done. This is what it takes to have a sound foreign policy strong at home, strong defense, permanent commitments, not betray the principles of our country, and involve the American people and the Congress in the shaping of our foreign policy. Every time Mr. Ford speaks from a position of secrecy in negotiations, in secret - in secret treaties that've been uh - pursued and achieved, in supporting dictatorships, in ignoring human rights, we are weak and the rest of the world knows it. So these are the ways that we can restore the strength of our country, and they don't require long experience in foreign policy. Nobody has that except a president who has served a long time or a secretary of state. But my background, my experience, my knowledge of the people of this country, my commitment to our principles that don't change - those are the best bases to correct the horrible mistakes of this administration and restore our own country to a position of leadership in the world.

MR. VALERIANI: How specifically, uh - Governor, are you going to bring the American people into the decision-making process in foreign policy? What does that mean?

MR. CARTER: First of all, I would quit conducting the decision-making process in secret, as has been a characteristic of Mr. Kissinger and Mr. Ford. In many instances we've made agreements, like in Vietnam, uh - that have uh - been revealed later on to our uh - embarrassment. Recently Ian Smith, the uh - president of uh - Rhodesia, announced that he had unequivocal commitments from Mr. Kissinger that he could not reveal. The American people don't know what those commitments are. We've seen uh - in the past the destruction of elected governments, like in Chile, and the strong support of military dictatorship there. These kinds of things have hurt us very much. I would restore the concept of the fireside chat, which was an integral part of the administration of Franklin Roosevelt. And I would also restore the involvement of the Congress. When Harry Truman was president he was not afraid to have a strong secretary of defense. Dean Acheson, George Marshall were strong secretaries of uh - state - excuse me - state. But he also made sure that there was a bipartisan support. The members of Congress, Arthur Vandenberg, Walter George, were part of the process, and before our nation made a secret agreement, or before we made a bluffing statement, we were sure that we had the backing not only of the president and the secretary of state, but also of the Congress and the people. This is a responsibility of the president. And I think it's very damaging to our country for Mr. Ford to have turned over this responsibility to the secretary of state.

MS. FREDERICK: President Ford, do you have a response?

MR. FORD: Governor Carter again contradicts himself. He complains about secrecy and yet he is quoted as saying that in the attempt to find a solution in the Middle East that he would hold unpublicized meetings with the Soviet Union - I presume for the purpose of an - imposing a settlement on Israel and the Arab nations. But let me talk just a minute about what we've done to avoid secrecy in the Ford administration. After the United States took the initiative in working with Israel and with Egypt and achieving the Sinai II agreement - and I'm proud to say that not a single Egyptian or Israeli soldier has lost his life since the signing of the Sinai agreement. But at the time that uh - I submitted the Sinai agreement to the Congress of the United States, I submitted every single document that was applicable to the Sinai II agreement. It was the most complete documentation by any president of any agreement signed by a president on behalf of the United States. Now as far as meeting with the Congress is concerned, during the twenty-four months that I've been the president of the United States I have averaged better than one meeting a month with responsible groups or committees of the Congress - both House and Senate. The secretary of state has appeared in the several years that he's been the secretary before eighty different uh - committee hearings in the House and in the Senate. The secretary of state has made better than fifty speeches all over the United States explaining American foreign policy. I have made myself at least ten uh - speeches in various parts of the country where I have discussed with the American people defense and foreign policy.

MS. FREDERICK: Mr. Frankel, a question for President Ford.

MR. FRANKEL: Mr. President, I'd like to explore a little more deeply our relationship with the Russians. They used to brag back in Khrushchev's day that because of their greater patience and because of our greed for - for business deals that they would sooner or later get the better of us. Is it possible that despite some setbacks in the Middle East, they've proved their point? Our allies in France and Italy are now flirting with Communism. We've recognized the permanent Communist regime in East Germany. We've virtually signed, in Helsinki, an agreement that the Russians have dominance in Eastern Europe. We've bailed out Soviet agriculture with our huge grain sales. We've given them large loans, access to our best technology and if the Senate hadn't interfered with the Jackson Amendment, maybe we - you would've given them even larger loans. Is that what you call a two-way street of traffic in Europe?

MR. FORD: I believe that we have uh - negotiated with the Soviet Union since I've been president from a position of strength. And let me cite several examples. Shortly after I became president in uh - December of 1974, I met with uh - General Secretary Brezhnev in Vladivostok and we agreed to a mutual cap on the ballistic missile launchers at a ceiling of twenty-four hundred - which means that the Soviet Union, if that becomes a permanent agreement, will have to make a reduction in their launchers that they now have or plan to have. I've negotiated at Vladivostok with uh - Mr. Brezhnev a limitation on the MIRVing of their ballistic missiles at a figure of thirteen-twenty, which is the first time that any president has achieved a cap either on launchers or on MIRVs. It seems to me that we can go from there to uh - the uh - grain sales. The grain sales have been a benefit to American agriculture. We have achieved a five and three quarter year uh - sale of a minimum six million metric tons, which means that they have already bought about four million metric tons this year and are bound to buy another two million metric tons to take the grain and corn and wheat that the American farmers have produced in order to uh - have full production. And these grain sales to the Soviet Union have helped us tremendously in meeting the costs of the additional oil and - the oil that we have bought from overseas. If we turn to Helsinki - I'm glad you raised it, Mr. uh - Frankel. In the case of Helsinki, thirty-five nations signed an agreement, including the secretary of state for the Vatican - I can't under any circumstances believe that the - His Holiness, the Pope would agree by signing that agreement that the thirty-five nations have turned over to the Warsaw Pact nations the domination of the - Eastern Europe. It just isn't true. And if Mr. Carter alleges that His Holiness by signing that has done it, he is totally inaccurate. Now, what has been accomplished by the Helsinki agreement? Number one, we have an agreement where they notify us and we notify them of any uh - military maneuvers that are to be be undertaken. They have done it. In both cases where they've done so, there is no Soviet domination of Eastern Europe and there never will be under a Ford administration.

MS. FREDERICK: Governor Carter?

MR. FRANKEL: I'm sorry, I - could I just follow - did I understand you to say, sir, that the Russians are not using Eastern Europe as their own sphere of influence in occupying mo- most of the countries there and in - and making sure with their troops that it's a - that it's a Communist zone, whereas on our side of the line the Italians and the French are still flirting with the possibility of Communism?

MR. FORD: I don't believe, uh - Mr. Frankel that uh - the Yugoslavians consider themselves dominated by the Soviet Union. I don't believe that the Rumanians consider themselves dominated by the Soviet Union. I don't believe that the Poles consider themselves dominated by the Soviet Union. Each of those countries is independent, autonomous: it has its own territorial integrity and the United States does not concede that those countries are under the domination of the Soviet Union. As a matter of fact, I visited Poland, Yugoslavia and Rumania to make certain that the people of those countries understood that the president of the United States and the people of the United are dedicated to their independence, their autonomy and their freedom.

MS. FREDERICK: Governor Carter, may I have your response?

MR. CARTER: (chuckle) Well, in the first place, I'm not criticizing His Holiness the Pope. I was talking about Mr. Ford. The uh - fact is that secrecy has surrounded the decisions made by the Ford administration. In the case of the Helsinki agreement - it may have been a good agreement at the beginning, but we have failed to enforce the so-called basket three part, which insures the right of people to migrate, to join their families, to be free, to speak out. The Soviet Union is still jamming Radio Free Europe - Radio - uh- uh - Radio Free Europe is being jammed. We've also seen a very serious uh - problem with the so-called Sonnenfeldt document, which apparently Mr. Ford has just endorsed, which said that there's an organic linkage between the Eastern European countries and the Soviet Union. And I would like to see Mr. Ford convince the Polish-Americans and the Czech-Americans and the Hungarian-Americans in this country that those countries don't live under the domination and supervision of the Soviet Union behind the Iron - uh - Curtain. We also have seen Mr. Ford exclude himself from access to the public. He hasn't had a tough cross-examination-type press conference in over thirty days. One press conference he had without sound. He's also shown a weakness in yielding to pressure. The Soviet Union, for instance, put pressure on Mr. Ford and he refused to see a symbol of human freedom recognized around the world, Aleksandr Solzhenitsyn. The Arabs have put pressure on Mr. Ford, and he's yielded, and has permitted a boycott by the Arab countries of American businesses who trade with Israel, or who have American Jews owning or taking part in the management of American - companies. His own secretary of commerce had to be subpoenaed by the Congress to reveal the names of businesses who were subject to this boycott. They didn't volunteer the information. He had to be subpoenaed. And the last thing I'd like to say is this: This grain deal with the Soviet Union in '72 was terrible, and Mr. Ford made up for it with three embargoes, one against our own ally in Japan. That's not the way to run our foreign policy, including international trade.

MS. FREDERIC: Mr. Trewhitt, a question for Governor Carter.

MR. TREWHITT: Governor, I'd like to pick up on that point, actually, and on your appeal for a greater measure of American idealism in foreign affairs. Foreign affairs come home to the American public pretty much in such issues as oil embargoes and grain sales, that sort of thing. Would you be willing to - to risk an oil embargo in order to promote human rights in Iran and Saudi Arabia, withhold arms from Saudi Arabia for the same purpose? Uh - or uh - I think you - matter of fact, you've perhaps answered this final part, but would you withhold grain from the Soviet Union in order to promote civil rights in the - in the Serviette Union?

MR. CARTER: I would never single out food as a trade embargo item. If I ever decided to impose an embargo because of a crisis in international relationships, it would include all shipments of all equipment. For instance, if the Arab countries ever again declare an embargo against our nation on oil I would consider that not a military but an economic declaration of war, and I would respond instantly and in kind. I would not ship that Arab country anything - no weapons, no spare parts for weapons, no oil-drilling rigs, no oil pipe, no nothing. I wouldn't single out just food. Another thing that I'd like to say is this: In our international trade, as I said in my op- opening statement, we have become the arms merchant of the world. When this Republican administration came into office we were shipping about $1 billion worth of arms overseas, now ten to twelve billion dollars worth of arms overseas to countries that quite often use these weapons to fight each other. The shift in emphasis has been very disturbing to me, speaking about the Middle East. Under the last Democratic administration 60 percent of all weapons that went into the Middle East were for Israel. Nowadays - 75 percent were for Israel before. Now 60 percent go to the Arab countries, and this does not include Iran. If you include Iran, our present shipment of weapons to the Middle East, only 20 percent goes to Israel. This is a deviation from idealism; it's a deviation from a commitment to our major ally in the Middle East, which is Israel; it's a yielding to economic pressure on the part of the Arabs on the oil issue; and it's also a tremendous indication that under the Ford administration we have not addressed the energy policy adequately. We still have no comprehensive energy policy in this country. And it's an overall sign of weakness. When we are weak at home economically - high unemployment, high inflation, a confused government, a wasteful defense establishment, this encourages the kind of pressure that's been put on us successfully. It would've been inconceivable ten - fifteen years ago, for us to be brought to our knees with an Arab oil embargo. But it was done three years ago and they're still putting pressure on us from the Arab countries to our discredit around the world. These are the weaknesses that I see, and I believe it's not just a matter of idealism. It's a matter of being tough. It's a matter of being strong. It's a matter of being consistent. Our priorities ought to be first of all to meet our own military needs, secondly to meet the needs of our allies and friends, and only then should we ship military equipment to foreign countries. As a matter of fact, Iran is gonna get eighty F-14s before we even meet our own Air Force orders for F-l4s. And the shipment of Spruance-class destroyers to Iran are much more highly sophisticated than the Spruance-class destroyers that are present being delivered to our own Navy. This is ridiculous and it ought to be changed.

MR. TREWHITT: Governor, let me pursue that if I may. If I understand you correctly you would in fact to use my examples, withhold arms from Iran and Saudi Arabia even if the risk was an oil embargo and if they should be securing those arms from somewhere else, and then if the embargo came, then you'd respond in kind. Do I have it correctly?

MR. CARTER: If - Iran is not an Arab country, as you know, it is a Moslem country - but if Saudi Arabia should declare an oil embargo against us, then I would consider that an economic declaration of war. And I would make sure that the uh - Saudis understood this ahead of time so there would be no doubt in their mind. I think under those circumstances they would refrain from pushing us to our knees as they did in 1973 with their previous oil embargo.

MS. FREDERICK: President Ford?

MR. FORD: Governor Carter uh - apparently doesn't realize that since I've been president we have sold to the Israelis over $4 billion in military hardware. We have made available to the Israelis over 45 percent of the total economic and military aid since the establishment of Israel twenty-seven years ago. So the Ford administration has done a good job in helping our good ally, Israel, and we're dedicated to the survival and security of Israel. I believe that Governor Carter doesn't realize the need and necessity for arms sales to Iran. He indicates he would not make those. Iran is bordered very extensively by the Soviet Union. Iran has Iraq as one of its neighbors. The Soviet Union and the Communist-dominated government of Iraq are neighbors of Iran, and Iran is an ally of the United States. It's my strong feeling that we ought to sell arms to Iran for its own national security, and as an ally - a strong ally of the United States. The history of our relationship with Iran goes back to the days of President Truman when he decided that it was vitally necessary for our own security as well as that of Iran, that we should help that country, and Iran has been a good ally. In 1973 when there was an oil embargo, Iran did not participate. Iran continued to sell oil to the United States. I believe that it's in our interest and in the interest of Israel and Iran, and Saudi Arabia, for the United States to sell arms to those countries. It's for their security as well as ours.

MS. FREDERICK: Mr. Valeriani, a question for President Ford.

MR. VALERIANI: Mr. President, the policy of your administration is to normalize relations with mainland China. And that means establishing at some point full diplomatic relations and obviously doing something about the mutual defense treaty with Taiwan. If you are elected, will you move to establish full diplomatic relations with Peking, and will you abrogate the mutual defense treaty with Taiwan? And, as a corollary, would you provide mainland China with military equipment if the Chinese were to ask for it?

MR. FORD: Our relationship with the People's Republic of China is based upon the Shanghai Communique, of 1972, and that communique, calls for the normalization of relations between the United States and the People's Republic. It doesn't set a times schedule. It doesn't uh - make a determination as to how uh - that relationship should be achieved in relationship to our current uhh - diplomatic recognition and obligations to the Taiwanese Government. The Shanghai Communique, does say that the differences between the People's Republic on the one hand and Taiwan on the other shall be settled by peaceful means. The net result is this administration, and during my time as the president for the next four years, we will continue to move for normalization of relations in the traditional sense, and we will insist that the disputes between Taiwan and the People's Republic be settled peacefully, as was agreed in the Shanghai Communique, of 1972. The Ford administration will not let down, will not eliminate or forget our obligation to the people of Taiwan. We feel that there must be a continued obligation to the people, the some nineteen or twenty million people in Taiwan. And as we move during the next four years, those will be the policies of this administration.

MR. VALERIANI: And sir, the military equipment for the mainland Chinese?

MR. FORD: There is no policy of this government to give to the People's Republic, or to sell to the People's Republic of China, military equipment. I do not believe that we, the United States, should sell, give or otherwise transfer military hardware to the People's Republic of China, or any other Communist nation, such as the Soviet Union and the like.

MS. FREDERICK: Governor Carter.

MR. CARTER: Well, I'd like to go back just one moment to the previous question, where uh - Mr. Ford, I think, confused the issue by trying to say that we are shipping Israel 40 percent of our aid. As a matter of fact, during this current year uh we are shipping Iran, or have contracted to ship to Iran, about seven and a half billion dollars worth of arms and also to Saudi Arabia, about seven and a half billion dollars worth of arms. Also in 1975, we almost brought Israel to their knees after the uh - Yom Kippur War by the so-called reassessment of our relationship to Israel. We in effect tried to make Israel the scapegoat for the problems in the Middle East. And this weakened our relationships with Israel a great deal and put a cloud on the total commitment that our people feel toward the Israelis. There ought to be a clear, unequivocal commitment without change to Israel. In the Far East I think we need to continue to be uh - strong and uh - I would certainly uh - pursue the uh - normalization of uh - relationships with the People's Republic of China. We opened a great opportunity in 1972, which has pretty well been frittered - frit- frittered away under Mr. Ford, that ought to be a constant uh - inclination toward - uh - toward friendship. But I would never let that friendship with the People's Republic of China stand in the way of the preservation of the independence and freedom of the people on Taiwan.

MS. FREDERICK: Mr. Frankel, a question for Governor Carter.

MR. FRANKEL: Governor, we always seem in our elections, and maybe in between too, to argue about uh - who can be tougher in the world. Give or take a - a few billion dollars, give or take one weapons systems, our leading politicians, and I think you, too, gentlemen, seem to settle roughly on the same strategy in the world at roughly the same Pentagon budget cost. How bad do things have to get in our own economy, or how much backwardness and hunger would it take in the world to persuade you that our national security and our survival required very drastic cutbacks in arms spending and dramatic new efforts in other directions?

MR. CARTER: Well, always in the past we've had an ability to have a strong defense and also have - to have a strong uh - domestic economy, and also to be strong in our reputation and influence within the community of nations. These uh - characteristics of our country have been endangered under Mr. Ford. We're no longer respected in a showdown vote in the United Nations or in - in any other international council we're lucky to get 20 percent of the other nations to vote with us. Our allies feel that we've neglected them. The so-called Nixon shock against Japan had weakened our relationships there. Under this administration we've also had an inclination to keep separate the European countries, thinking that if they are separate, then we can dominate them and proceed with our secret, Lone Ranger-type diplomatic efforts. I would uh - also like to point out that we, in this country, have let our economy go down the drain. The worst inflation since the Great Depression. The highest unemployment of any developed nation of the world. We have a higher unemployment rate in this country than Great Britain, and West Germany. Our unemployment rate is twice as high as it is in Italy; it's three or four times as high as it is - as it is in Japan. And that terrible circumstance in this country is exported overseas. We comprise about 30 percent of the world's economic trade power influence. And when we're weak at home - weaker than all our allies - that weakness weakens the whole free world. So strong economy is very important. Another thing that we need to do is to reestablish the good relationships that we ought to have between the United States and our natural allies and friends. They have felt neglected. And using that base of strength, and using the idealism, the honesty, the predictability, the commitment, the integrity of our own country, that's where our strength lies. And that would permit us to deal with the developing nations in a position of strength. Under this administration we've had a continuation of the so-called balance of power politics, where everything is looked on as a struggle between us on the one side, the Soviet Union on the other. Our allies - the smaller countries get trampled in the rush. What we need is to try to seek individualized bilateral relationships with countries, regardless of their size, and to establish world-order politics, which means that we want to preserve peace through strength. We also wanna revert back to the stature and the respect that our country had in previous administrations. Now, I can't say when this can come. But I can guarantee it will not come if Gerald Ford is reelected and this present policy is continued; it will come if I'm elected.

MR. FRANKEL: If I hear you right, sir, you're saying guns and butter both, but President Johnson also had trouble uh - keeping up both Vietnam and his domestic programs. I was really asking when do the - the needs of the cities and our own needs and those of other backward an- and - and even more needy countries and societies around the world take precedence over some of our military spending? Ever?

MR. CARTER: Well let me say very quickly that under President Johnson, in spite of the massive investment in the Vietnam War, he turned over a balanced budget to Mr. Nixon. The unemployment rate was less than 4 percent. The inflation rate under Kennedy and Johnson was about 2 percent - one-third what it is under this administration. So we did have at that time with good management, the ability to do both. I don't think that anybody can say that Johnson and Kennedy neglected the poor and the destitute people in this country or around the world. But I can say this: The number one responsibility of any president, above all else, is to guarantee the security of our nation - an ability to be free of the threat of attack, or blackmail and to carry out our obligations to our allies and friends, and to carry out a legitimate foreign policy. They must go hand in hand, but the security of this nation has got to come first.

MS. FREDERICK: President Ford.

MR. FORD: Let me say very categorically you cannot maintain the security of the United States with the kind of defense budget cuts that Governor Carter has indicated. In 1975 he wanted to cut the budget $15 billion. He's now down to a figure of five to seven billion dollars. Reductions of that kind will not permit the United States to be strong enough to deter aggression and maintain the peace. Governor Carter apparently doesn't know the facts. As soon as I became president, I initiated a meeting with the NATO heads of state and met with them in Brussels to discuss how we could improve the re-defense relationship in Western Europe. In uh - November of 1975 I met with the leaders of the five industrial nations in France for the purpose of seeing what we could do acting together to meet the problems of uh - the coming recession. In Puerto Rico this year, I met with six of the leading industrial nations' heads of state to meet the problem of inflation so we would be able to solve it before it got out of hand. I have met with the heads of government bilaterally as well as multilaterally. Our relations with Japan have never been better. I was the first United States president to visit Japan. And we uh - had the emperor of Japan here this uh - past year and the net result is Japan and the United States are working more closely together now than at any time in the history of our relationship. You can go around the world - and let me take Israel for example. Just recently, President Rabin said that our relations were never better.

MS. FREDERICK: Mr. Trewhitt, a question for President Ford.

MR. TREWHITT: Mr. President, uh - you referred earlier to your meeting with Mr. Brezhnev at Vladivostok in 1974. At - you agreed on that occasion to try to achieve another strategic arms limitation - SALT - agreement, ah - within the year. Ah - nothing happened in 1975, or not very much publicly at least. And those talks are still dragging and things got quieter as the current season approached. Is there - is there a bit of politics involved there, perhaps on both sides? Or perhaps more important are interim weapons developments - and I'm thinking of such things as the cruise missile and the Soviet SS-20, an intermediate-range rocket - making SALT irrelevant, bypassing the SALT negotiations?

MR. FORD: First we have to understand that SALT I expires October third 1977. Uh - Mr. Brezhnev and I met in Vladivostok in December of 1974 for the purpose of trying to take the initial step so we could have a SALT II agreement that would go to 1985. As I indicated earlier, we did agree on a twenty-four-hundred limitation on uh - uh - launchers of ballistic missiles. Uh - that would mean a cutback in the Soviet program; it would not interfere with our own program. At the same time, we put a limitation of thirteen hundred and twenty on MIRVs. Our technicians have been working since that time in Geneva, trying to put into technical language a - an agreement that can be verified by both parties. In the meantime, there has developed the problem of the Soviet Backfire - their high-performance aircraft which they say is not a long-range aircraft and which some of our people say is a intercontinental aircraft. In the interim, there has been the development on our part primarily, the cruise missiles; cruise missiles that could be launched from land-based mobile installations; cruise missiles that could be launched - launched from high-performance aircraft, like the B-52s or the B-1s, which I hope we proceed with; cruise missiles which could be launched from either surface or submarine uh - naval vessels. Those gray-area weapons systems are creating some problems in a - the agreement for a SALT II negotiation. But I can say that I am dedicated to proceeding, and I met just last week with the foreign minister of the Soviet Union, and he indicated to me that uh - the Soviet Union was interested in narrowing the differences and making a realistic and a sound compromise. I hope and trust, in the best interest of both countries, and in the best interests of all people throughout this globe, that the Soviet Union and the United States can make a mutually beneficial agreement. Because if we do not and SALT I expires on October three, 1977, you will unleash again an all-out nuclear arms race with the potential of a nuclear holocaust of unbelievable dimensions. So it's the obligation of the president to do just that, and I intend to do so.

MR. TREWHITT: Mr. President, let me follow that up by - I'll submit that the cruise missile adds a - a whole new dimension to the - to the arms competition - and then cite a statement by your office to the Arms Control Association a few days ago in which you said the cruise missile might eventually be included in a comprehensive arms limitation agreement but that in the meantime it was an essential of the American strategic arsenal. Now, uh - may I assume that from that you're tending to exclude the cruise missile from the next SALT agreement, or is it still negotiable in that context?

MR. FORD: I believe that the cruise missiles which we are now developing in research and development across the spectrum from air, from the sea, or from the land, uh - can be uh - included within a SALT II agreement. They are a new weapons system that has a great potential, both conventional and nuclear armed. At the same time, we have to make certain that the Soviet Union's Backfire, which they claim is not an intercontinental aircraft and which some of our people contend is, must also be included if we are to get the kind of agreement which is in the best interest of both countries. And I really believe that it - it's far better for us and for the Soviet Union, and more importantly for the people around the world, that these two superpowers find an answer for a SALT II agreement before October three, 1977. I think good will on both parts, hard bargaining by both parties and a reasonable compromise will be in the best interests of all parties.

MS. FREDERICK: Governor Carter.

MR. CARTER: Well, Mr. Ford acts like he's uh - running for president for the first time. He's been in office two years, and there has been absolutely no progress made toward a new SALT agreement. He has learned the date of the expiration of SALT I, apparently. We've seen, in this world, a development of a tremendous threat to us. As a nuclear engineer myself, I know the limitations and capabilities of atomic power. I also - know that as far as the human beings on this earth are concerned that the nonproliferation of atomic weapons is number one. Only the last few days with the election approaching, has Mr. Ford taken any interest in a nonproliferation movement. I advocated last May in a speech at the United Nations that we move immediately as a nation to declare a complete moratorium on the testing of all nuclear devices, both weapons and peaceful devices; that we not ship any more atomic fuel to a country that refuses to comply with strict controls over the waste which can be reprocessed into explosives. I've also advocated that we stop the sale by Germany and France of - processing plants for Pakistan and Brazil. Mr. Ford hasn't moved on this. We also need to provide an adequate supply of enriched uranium. Mr. Ford, again, under pressure from the atomic energy lobby, has insisted that this reprocessing or rather re-en- enrichment be done by private industry and not by the existing uh - government uh - plants. This kind of confusion and absence of leadership has let us drift now for two years with a constantly increasing threat of atomic weapons throughout the world. We now have five nations that have atomic bombs that we know about. If we continue under Mr. Ford's policy by 1985 or '90 we'll have twenty nations that have the capability of exploding atomic weapons. This has got to be stopped. That is one of the major challenges and major undertakings that I will assume as the next president.

MS. FREDERICK: Mr. Valeriani, a question for Governor Carter.

MR. VALERIANI: Governor Carter, earlier tonight you said America is not strong any more; America is not respected any more. And I feel that I must ask you: Do you really believe that the United States is not the strongest country in the world, do you really believe that the United States is not the most respected country in the world? Or is that just campaign rhetoric?

MR. CARTER: No, it's not just campaign rhetoric. I think that militarily we are as strong as any nation on earth. I think we got to stay that way and continue to increase our capabilities to meet any potential threat. But as far as strength derived from commitment to principles, as far as strength derived from the unity within our country, as far as strength derived from the people, the Congress, the secretary of state, the president, sharing in the evolution and carrying-out of a foreign policy, as far as strength derived from the respect of our own allies and friends, their assurance that we will be staunch in our commitment, that we will not deviate and that we'll give them adequate attention, as far as - as strength derived from doing what's right - caring for the poor, providing food, becoming the breadbasket of the world instead of the arms merchant of the world - in those respects, we're not strong. Also, we'll never be strong again overseas, unless we're strong at home. And with our economy in such terrible disarray and getting worse by the month. We've got five-hundred thousand more Americans unemployed today than we had three months ago. We've got two and a half million more Americans out of work now than we had when Mr. Ford took office. This kind of deterioration in our economic strength is bound to weaken us around the world. And we not only have uh problems at home but we export those problems overseas. So as far as the respect of our own people toward our own government, as far as participating in the shaping of uh - concepts and commitments, as far as the trust of our country among the nations of the world, as far as dependence of our country in meeting the needs and obligations that we've expressed to our allies, as far as the respect of our country - even among our potential adversaries - we are weak. Potentially we're strong. Under this administration that strength has not been realized.

MS. FREDERICK: President Ford.

MR. FORD: Governor Carter uh - brags about the unemployment during Democratic administrations and condemns the unemployment at the present time. I must remind him that we're at peace and during the period that he brags about unemployment being low, the United States was at war. Now let me correct one other comment that uh - Governor Carter has made. I have recommended to the Congress that we develop the uranium enrichment plant at Portsmouth, Ohio, which is a publicly owned - U.S. government facility and have indicated that the private program which would follow on in Alabama is one that may or may not uhh - be constructed. But I am committed to the one at Portsmouth, Ohio. The governor also talks about morality in foreign policy. The foreign policy of the United States meets the highest standards of morality. What is more moral than peace, and the United States is at peace today? What is more moral in foreign policy than for the administration to take the lead in the World Food Conference in Rome in 1974 when the United States committed six million metric tons of food - over 60 percent of the food committed for the disadvantaged and underdeveloped nations of the world? The Ford administration wants to eradicate hunger and disease in our underdeveloped countries throughout the world. What is more moral than for the United States under the Ford administration to take the lead in southern Africa, in the Middle East? Those are initiatives in foreign policy which are of the highest moral standard and that is indicative of the foreign policy of this country.

MS. FREDERICK: Mr. Frankel, a question for President Ford.

MR. FRANKEL: Mr. President, can we stick with morality? Uh - for a lot of people it seems to cover uh - a bunch of sins. Uh - Mr. Nixon and Mr. Kissinger used to tell us that instead of morality we had to worry in the - in the world about living and letting live all kinds of governments that we really don't like. North and South Korean dictators, Chilean fascists, uh - Chinese Communists, Iranian emperors and so on. They said the only way to get by in a wicked world was to treat others on the basis of how they treated us and not how they treated their own people. But more recently, uhh - we seemed to've taken a different tack. Uhh - we've seemed to have decided that it - that it is part of our business to tell the Rhodesians, for instance, that the way they're treating their own black people is wrong and they've got to change their government and we've put pressure an them. We were rather liberal in our advice to the Italians as to how to vote. Umm - is this a new Ford foreign policy in the making? Can we expect that you are now going to turn to South Africa and force them to change their governments, to intervene in similar ways to end the bloodshed, as you called it, say, in Chile or Chilean prisons, and throw our weight around for the - for the values that - that we hold dear in the world?

MR. FORD: I believe that uh - our foreign policy must express the highest standards of morality. And the initiatives that we took in southern Africa are the best examples of what this administration is doing and will continue to do in the next four years. If the United States had not moved when we did in southern Africa, there's no doubt there would have been an acceleration of bloodshed in that tragic part of the world. If we had not taken our initiative, it's very, very possible that uh - the government of Rhodesia would have been overrun and that the Soviet Union and the Cubans would have dominated uh - southern Africa. So the United States, seeking to preserve the principle of self-determination, to eliminate the possibility of bloodshed, to protect the rights of the minority as we insisted upon the rights of the majority, uh - I believe followed the good conscience of the American people in foreign policy. And I believe that we used our skill. Secretary of State Kissinger has done a superb job in working with the black African nations, the so-called front-line nations. He has done a superb job in getting the prime minister of South Africa, Mr. Vorster, to agree that the time had come for a solution to the problem of Rhodesia. Secretary Kissinger, in his meeting with uh - Prime Minister Smith of Rhodesia, was able to convince him that it was in the best interests of whites as well as blacks in Rhodesia to find an answer for a transitional government and then a majority government. This is a perfect example of the kind of leadership that the United States, under this administration, has taken. And I can assure you that this administration will follow that high moral principle in our future efforts in foreign policy, including our efforts in the Middle East where it is vitally important because the Middle East is the crossroads of the world. There've been more disputes in its area where there's more volatility than any other place in the world. But because Arab nations and the Israelis trust the United States, we were able to take the lead in the Sinai II Agreement. And I can assure you that the United States will have the leadership role in moving toward a comprehensive settlement of the Middle Eastern problems, I hope and trust as soon as possible. And we will do it with the highest moral principles.

MR. FRANKEL: Mr. President, just clarify one paint: There are lots of majorities in the world that feel they're being pushed around by minority governments. And are you saying they can now expect to look to us for not just good cheer but throwing our weight on their side - in South Africa, or on Taiwan, or in Chile, uh - to help change their governments, as in Rhodesia?

MR. FORD: I would hope that as we move to one area of the world from another - and the United States must not spread itself too thinly - that was one of the problems that helped to create the circumstances in Vietnam - but as we as a nation find that we are asked by the various parties, either one nation against another or individuals within a nation, that the United States will take the leadership and try to resolve the differences. Let me take uh - South Korea as an example. I have personally told President Pack that the United States does not condone the kind of repressive measures that he has taken in that country. But I think in all fairness and equity we have to recognize the problem that South Korea has. On the north they have North Korea with five hundred thousand well-trained, well-equipped troops - they are supported by the People's Republic of China; they are supported by the Soviet Union. South Korea faces a very delicate situation. Now the United States, in this case, this administration, has recommended a year ago and we have reiterated it again this year, that the United States, South Korea, North Korea and the uh - People's Republic of China sit down at a conference table to resolve the problems of the Korean peninsula. This is a leadership role that the United States under this administration is carrying out, and if we do it, and I think the opportunities and the possibilities are getting better, we will have solved many of the internal domestic problems that exist in South Korea at the present time.

MS. FREDERICK: Governor Carter.

MR. CARTER: I notice that Mr. Ford didn't comment on the uh - prisons in Chile. This is an - a typical example, maybe of many others, where this administration overthrew an elected government and helped to establish a military dictatorship. This has not been an ancient history story. Last year under Mr. Ford, of all the Food for Peace that went to South America, 85 percent went to the military dictatorship in Chile. Another point I wanna make is this. He says we have to move from one area of the world to another. That's one of the problems with this administration's so-called shuttle diplomacy. While the secretary of state's in one country, there are almost a hundred and fifty others that are wondering what we're gonna do next, what will be the next secret agreement. We don't have a comprehensive understandable foreign policy that deals with world problems or even regional problems. Another thing that concerned me was what Mr. Ford said about unemployment, that - insinuating that under Johnson and Kennedy that unemployment could only be held down when this country is at war. Karl Marx said that the free enterprise system in a democracy can only continue to exist when they are at war or preparing far war. Karl Marx was the grandfather of Communism. I don't agree with that statement. I hope Mr. Ford doesn't either. He has put pressure on the Congress - and I don't believe Mr. Ford would even deny this - to hold up on nonproliferation legislation until the Congress agreed for an $8 billion program for private industry to start producing enriched uranium. And the last thing I wanna make is this. He talks about peace and I'm thankful for peace. We were peaceful when Mr. Ford went into office. But he and Mr. Kissinger and others tried to start a new Vietnam in Angola, and it was only the outcry of the American people and the Congress when their secret deal was discovered that prevented our involvement in that conflagration which was taking place there.

MS. FREDERICK: Gentlemen, I'm sorry we do not have time enough for two complete sequences of questions. We now have only twelve minutes left. Therefore, I would like to ask for shorter questions and shorter answers. And we also will drop the follow-up question. Each candidate may still respond, of course, to the other's answer. Mr. Trewhitt, a question for Governor Carter.

MR. TREWHITT: Governor Carter, before this event the most communications I received concerned Panama. Is - would you as president be prepared to sign a treaty which at a fixed date yielded administrative and economic control of the Canal Zone and shared defense, which, as I understand it, is the position the United States took in 1974?

MR. CARTER: Well, here again, uh - the Panamanian question is one that's been confused by Mr. Ford. Uh - he had directed his uh - diplomatic relation - uh - uh - representative to yield to the Panamanians full sovereignty over the Panama Canal Zone at the end of a certain period of time. When Mr. Reagan raised this uh - question in Florida uh - Mr. Ford not only disavowed his instructions, but he also even dropped, parenthetically, the use of the word "detente." I would never give up complete control or practical control of the Panama Canal Zone, but I would continue to negotiate with the Panamanians. When the original treaty was signed back in the early 1900s, when Theodore Roosevelt was president, Panama retained sovereignty over the Panama Canal Zone. We retained control as though we had sovereignty. Now I would be willing to go ahead with negotiations. I believe that we could share more fully responsibilities for the Panama Canal Zone with Panama. I would be willing to continue to raise the payment for shipment of goods through the Panama Canal Zone. I might even be willing to reduce to some degree our military emplacements in the Panama Canal Zane, but I would not relinquish practical control of the Panama Canal Zane any time in the foreseeable future.

MS. FREDERICK: President Ford.

MR. FORD: The United States must and will maintain complete access to the Panama Canal. The United States must maintain a defense capability of the Panama Canal. And the United States will maintain our national security interest in the Panama Canal. The negotiations far the Panama Canal started under President Johnson and have continued up to the present time. I believe those negotiations should continue. But there are certain guidelines that must be followed, and I've just defined them. Let me take just a minute to comment on something that Governor Carter said. On non - nu- oh - uh - nonproliferation, in May of 1975, I called for a conference of uh - nuclear suppliers. That conference has met six times. In May of this year, Governor Carter took the first initiative, approximately twelve months after I had taken my initiative a year ago.

MS. FREDERICK: Mr. Valeriani, a question for President Ford.

MR. VALERIANI: Mr. President, the Government Accounting Office has just put out a report suggesting that you shot from the hip in the Mayaguez rescue mission and that you ignored diplomatic messages saying that a peaceful solution was in prospect. Uh - why didn't you do more diplomatically at the time; and a related question: Did the White House try to prevent the release of that report?

MR. FORD: The White House did not uh - prevent the release of that report. On July twelfth of this year, we gave full permission for the release of that report. I was very disappointed in the fact that the uh - GAO released that report because I think it interjected political partisan politics at the present time. But let me comment on the report. Somebody who sits in Washington, D.C., eighteen months after the Mayaguez incident, can be a very good grandstand quarterback. And let me make another observation. This morning, I got a call from the skipper of the Mayaguez. He was furious because he told me that it was the action of me, President Ford, that saved the lives of the crew of the Mayaguez. And I can assure you that if we had not taken the strong and forceful action that we did, we would have been uh - criticized very, very uh - severely for sitting back and not moving. Captain Miller is thankful. The crew is thankful. We did the right thing. It seems to me that those who sit in Washington eighteen months after the incident are not the best judges of the decision-making process that had to be made by the National Security Council and by myself at the time the incident was developing in the Pacific. Let me assure you that we made every possible overture to the People's Republic of China and through them to the Cambodian Government. We made uh - diplomatic uh - protests to the Cambodian government through the United Nations. Every possible diplomatic means was utilized. But at the same time, I had a responsibility, and so did the National Security Coun- Council, to meet the problem at hand. And we handled it responsibly and I think Captain Miller's testimony to that effect is the best evidence.

MS. FREDERICK: Governor Carter.

MR. CARTER: Well, I'm reluctant to uh comment on the recent report - I haven't read it. I think the American people have only one - uh requirement - that the facts about Mayaguez be given to them accurately and completely. Mr. Ford has been there for eighteen months. He had the facts that were released today immediately after the Mayaguez incident. I understand that the report today is accurate. Mr. Ford has said, I believe, that it was accurate, and that the White House made no attempt to block the issuing of that report. I don't know if that's exactly accurate or not. I understand that both the - the uh - Department of State and the Defense Department have approved the accuracy of today's report, or yesterday's report, and also the National Security Agency. I don't know what was right, or what was wrong, or what was done. The only thing I believe is that whatever the - the knowledge was that Mr. Ford had should have been given to the American people eighteen months ago, immediately after the Mayaguez uh - incident occurred. This is uh - what the American people want. When something happens that endangers our security, or when something happens that threatens our stature in the world, or when American people are endangered by the actions of a foreign country, uh - just forty uh sailors on the Mayaguez, we obviously have to move aggressively and quickly to rescue them. But then after the immediate action is taken, I believe the president has an obligation to tell the American people the truth and not wait eighteen months later for the report to be issued.

MS. FREDERICK: Gentlemen, at this time we have time for only two very short questions. Mr. Frankel, a question for Governor Carter.

MR. FRANKEL: Governor Carter, if the price of uh - gaining influence among the Arabs is closing our eyes a little bit to their boycott against Israel, how would you handle that?

MR. CARTER: I believe that the boycott of American businesses by the Arab countries because those businesses trade with Israel or because they have American Jews who are owners or directors in the company is an absolute disgrace. This is the first time that I've - remember in the history of our country when we've let a foreign country circumvent or change our Bill of Rights. I'll do everything I can as president to stop the boycott of American businesses by the Arab countries. It's not a matter of diplomacy or trade with me. It's a matter of morality. And I don't believe that Arab countries will pursue it when we have a strong president who will protect the integrity of our country, the commitment of our Constitution and Bill of Rights and protect people in this country who happen to be Jews. It may later be Catholics; it may be - later be Baptists who are threatened by some foreign country. But we ought to stand staunch. And I think it's a disgrace that so far Mr. Ford's administration has blocked the passage of legislation that would've revealed by law every instance of the boycott and it would've prevented the boycott from continuing.

MS. FREDERICK: President Ford.

MR. FORD: Again Governor Carter is inaccurate. The Arab boycott action was first taken in 1952. And in November of 1975 I was the first president to order the executive branch to take action, affirmative action, through the Department of Commerce and other cabinet departments, to make certain that no American businessman or business organization should discriminate against Jews because of an Arab boycott. And I might add that uh - my administration - and I'm very proud of it - is the first administration that has taken an antitrust action against companies in this country that have allegedly cooperated with the Arab boycott. Just on Monday of this week I signed a tax bill that included an amendment that would prevent companies in the United States from taking a tax deduction if they have in any way whatsoever cooperated with the Arab boycott. And last week when we were trying to get the Export Administration Act through the Congress - necessary legislation - my administration went to Capitol Hill and tried to convince the House and the Senate that we should have an amendment on that legislation which would take strong and effective action against those who uh - participate or cooperate with the Arab uh boycott. One other point. Because the Congress failed to act, I am going to announce tomorrow that the Department of Commerce will disclose those companies that have uh - participated in the Arab boycott. This is something that we can do; the Congress failed to do it, and we intend to do it.

MS. FREDERICK: Mr. Trewhitt, a very brief question for President Ford.

MR. TREWHITT: Mr. President, if you get the accounting of missing in action you want from North Vietnam - or from Vietnam, I'm sorry, now would you then be prepared to reopen negotiations for restoration of relations with that country?

MR. FORD: Let me restate uh - our policy. As long as Vietnam, North Vietnam, does not give us a full and complete accounting of our missing in action, I will never uh - go along with the admission of Vietnam to the United Nations. If they do give us a bona fide, complete uh - accounting of the eight hundred MIA's, then I believe that the United States should begin negotiations for the uh - admission of Vietnam to the United Nations. But not until they have given us the full accounting of our MIAs.

MS. FREDERICK: Governor Carter.

MR. CARTER: One of the uh - most embarrassing uh - failures of the Ford administration, and one that touches specifically on human rights, is his refusal to appoint a presidential commission to go to Vietnam, to go to Laos, to go to Cambodia and try to trade for the release of information about those who are missing in action in those wars. This is what the families of MIAs want. So far, Mr. Ford has not done it. We've had several fragmentary efforts by members of the Congress and by - by private citizens. Several months ago the Vietnam government said, "We are ready to sit down and negotiate for release of information on MIAs. So far, Mr. Ford has not responded. I would never normalize relationships with Vietnam, nor permit them to join the United Nations until they've taken this action. But that's not enough. We need to have an active and aggressive action on the part of the president, the leader of his country, to seek out every possible way to get that information which has kept the MIA families in despair and doubt, and Mr. Ford has just not done it.

MS. FREDERICK: Thank you Governor Carter. That completes the questioning for this evening. Each candidate now has up to three minutes for a closing statement. It was determined by the toss of a coin that Governor Carter would take the first question, and he now goes first with his closing remarks. Governor Carter.

MR. CARTER: The purpose of this debate and the outcome of the election will determine three basic things: Leadership, upholding the principles of our country, and proper priorities and commitments for the future. This election will also determine what kind of world we leave our children. Will it be a nightmare world threatened with the proliferation of atomic bombs, not just in five major countries but dozens of smaller countries that have been permitted to develop atomic weapons because of a failure of our top leadership to stop proliferation? Will we have a world of hunger and - and hatred, and will we be living in an armed camp stripped of our friendship and allies hiding behind a tight defense that's been drawn in around us because we are fearful of the outside world? Will we have a government of secrecy that excludes the American people from participation in making basic decisions and therefore covers up mistakes and makes it possible for our government - our government - to depart from the principles of our Constitution and Bill of Rights? Or will we have a world of peace with the threat of atomic weapons eliminated, with full trade, with our people at work, inflation controlled, openness in government, our people proud once again, Congress, citizens, president, secretary of state working in harmony and unity toward a common future? Or world where people have enough to eat and a world where we care about those who don't? Can we become a breadbasket of the world instead of the arms merchant of the world? I believe we can and we ought to. Now we've been hurt in recent years in this country. In the aftermath of Vietnam, Cambodia, Chile, Pakistan, Angola, Watergate, CIA, we've been hurt. Our people feel that we've lost something precious. That's not necessary. I wanna see our nation - return to a posture and an image and a standard to make us proud once again. I remember the world with NATO, and the world of Point Four, and the world of the Marshall Plan, and the world of the Peace Corps. Why can't we have that once again? We ought to be a beacon for nations who search for peace and who search for freedom, who search for individual liberty, who search for basic human rights. We haven't been lately. We can be once again. We'll never have that world leadership until we are strong at home, and we can have that strength if we return to the basic principles. It ought not to be a strength of bombast and threats. It ought to be a quiet strength based on the integrity of our people, the vision of the Constitution, an in- innate strong will and purpose that God's given us in the greatest nation on earth - the United States.

MS. FREDERICK: President Ford.

MR. FORD: As we have seen tonight, foreign policy and defense policy are difficult and complex issues. We can debate methods, we can debate one decision or another, but there are two uh things which cannot be debated - experience and results. In the last two years, I have made policy decisions involving - long-range difficulties and policies and made day-to-day judgments not only as president of the United States but as the leader of the free world What is the result of that leadership? America is strong. America is free. America is respected. Not a single young American today is fighting or dying on any foreign battlefield. America is at peace and with freedom. Thank you, and good night.

MS. FREDERICK: Thank you, President Ford. Thank you, Governor Carter. I also want to thank our questioners and the audience here this evening. The third and final debate between President Ford and Governor Carter will take place on October the twenty-second at nine-thirty P.M. Eastern daylight time on the campus of the College of William and Mary in Williamsburg, Virginia. The subject matter will cover all issues. These debates are sponsored by the League of Women Voters Education Fund to help voters become better informed on the issues and to generate greater voter turnout in the November election. Now, from the Palace of Fine Arts Theater in San Francisco, good night.

3.3   1976 U.S. Presidential Debate - October 22

MS. WALTERS: Good evening, I'm Barbara Walters, moderator of the last of the debates of 1976 between Gerald R. Ford, Republican candidate for president, and Jimmy Carter, Democratic candidate for president. Welcome, President Ford. Welcome, Governor Carter. And thank you for joining us this evening. This debate takes place before an audience in Phi Beta Kappa Memorial Hall on the campus of the College of William and Mary in historic Williamsburg, Virginia. It is particularly appropriate that in this Bicentennial year we meet on these grounds to hear this debate. Two hundred years ago, five William and Mary students met at nearby Raleigh Tavern to form Phi Beta Kappa, a fraternity designed, they wrote, to search out and dispel the clouds of falsehood by debating without reserve the issues of the day. In that spirit of debate, without reserve, to dispel the clouds of falsehood, gentlemen, let us proceed. The subject matter of this debate is open, covering all issues and topics. Our questioners tonight are Joseph Kraft, syndicated columnist; Robert Maynard, editorial writer for the Washington Post; and Jack Nelson, Washington bureau chief of the Los Angeles Times. The ground rules tonight are as follows: Questioners will alternate questions between the candidates. The candidate has up to two and one-half minutes to answer the question. The other candidate has up to two minutes to respond. If necessary, a questioner may ask a follow-up question for further clarification, and in that case the candidate has up to two minutes to respond. As was initially agreed to by both candidates, the answers should be responsive to the particular questions. Finally, each candidate has up to three minutes for a closing statement. President Ford and Governor Carter do not have prepared notes or comments with them this evening, but they may make notes and refer to them during the debate. It has been determined that President Ford would take the first question in this last debate, and Mr. Kraft, you have that first question for President Ford.

MR. KRAFT: Mr. President, uh - I assume that the Americans all know that these are difficult times and that there's no "pie in the sky" and that they don't expect something for nothing. Uh - so, I'd like to ask you as a first question as you look ahead in the next four years, what sacrifices are you going to call on the American people to make, what price are you going to ask them to pay uh - to realize your objectives? Uh - let me add, uh - Governor Carter, that if - if you felt uh - that it was appropriate to answer that question in - in your comments uh - as to what price it would be appropriate for the American pay - people to pay uh - for a Carter administration, I think that would be proper too. Mr. President?

MR. FORD: Mr. Kraft, I believe that the American people, in the next four years under a Ford administration, will be called upon to make those necessary sacrifices to preserve the peace which we have. Which means, of course, that uh - we will have to maintain an adequate military capability - which means, of course, that we will have to add a uh - I think uh - a few billion dollars to our defense appropriations to make certain that we have adequate uh -strategic forces - adequate conventional forces. I think the American people will be called upon to uh - uh - be in the forefront in giving leadership to the solution of those problems that must be solved in the Middle East, in southern Africa, and any problems that might arise in the Pacific. The American people will be called upon to tighten their belts a bit in meeting some of the problems that we face domestically. I don't think that uh - America can go on a big spending spree with a whole lot of new programs uh - that would add significantly to the federal budget. I believe that the American people, if given the leadership that I would expect to give, would be willing to give this thrust to preserve the peace and the necessary restraint at home to hold the lid on spending so that we could, I think, have a long overdue and totally justified tax decrease for the middle-income people. And then, with the economy that would be generated from a restraint on spending, and a tax uh reduction primarily for the middle-income people, then I think the American people would be willing to make those sacrifices for peace and prosperity in the next uh - four years.

MR. KRAFT: Could I be a little bit more specific, Mr. President?

MR. FORD: Surely, surely, overlapping. Doesn't your policy really imply that we're going to have a fairly high rate of unemployment over a fairly long time, that growth is gonna be fairly slow, and that we're not gonna be able to do much - very much in the next four or five years to meet the basic agenda of our national needs in the cities, in health, uh in transit and a whole lot of things like that.

MR. FORD: Not at all. overlapping, aren't those the real costs?

MR. FORD: No, Mr. Kraft, we're spending very significant amounts of money now, some $200 billion a year, almost 50 percent of our total federal expenditure uh - by the federal government at the present time for human needs. Now we will probably need to increase that to same extent. But we don't have to have - growth in spending that will blow the lid off and add to the problems of inflation. I believe we can meet the problems within the cities of this country and still uh - give a tax reduction. I proposed, as you know, a reduction to increase the personal exemption from seven hundred and fifty to a thousand dollars. With the fiscal program that I have, and if you look at the projections, it shows that we will reduce unemployment, that we will continue to win the battle against inflation, and at the same time give the kind of quality of life that I believe is possible in America. Uh - a job, a home for all those that'll work and save for it, uh - safety in the streets, uh - health that is a - health care that is affordable. These things can be done if we have the right vision and the right restraint and the right leadership.

MS. WALTERS: Thank you. Governor Carter, your response please.

MR. CARTER: Well I might say first of all that I think in case of the Carter administration the sacrifices would be much less. Mr. Ford's own uh - environmental agency has projected a 10 percent unemployment rate by 1978 if he's uh - president. The American people are ready to make sacrifices if they are part of the process. If they know that they will be helping to make decisions and won't be excluded from being an involved party to the national purpose. The major effort we must put forward is to put our people back to work. And I think that this uh - is one example where uh - a lot of people have selfish, grasping ideas now. I remember 1973 in the depth of the uh - energy crisis when President Nixon called on the American people to make a sacrifice, to cut down on the waste of uh - gasoline, to cut down on the uh - speed of automobiles. It was a - a tremendous surge of patriotism, that "I want to make a sacrifice for my country." I think we uh - could call together, with strong leadership in the White House, business, industry and labor, and say let's have voluntary price restraints. Let's lay down some guidelines so we don't have continuing inflation. We can also have a-an end to the extremes. We now have one extreme for instance, of some welfare recipients, who by taking advantage of the welfare laws, the housing laws, the uh - Medicaid uh - laws, and the uh - food stamp laws, make over $10 thousand a year and uh - they don't have to pay any taxes on it. At the other extreme, uh - just 1 percent of the richest people in our country derive 25 percent of all the tax benefits. So both those extremes grasp for advantage and the person who has to pay that expense is the middle-income family who's still working for a living and they have to pay for the rich who have privilege, and for the poor who are not working. But I think uh - uh - a balanced approach, with everybody being part of it and a striving for unselfishness, could help as it did in 1973 to let people sacrifice for their own country. I know I'm ready for it. I think the American people are too.

MS. WALTERS: Thank you. Mr. Maynard, your question for Governor Carter.

MR. MAYNARD: Governor, by all indications, the voters are so turned off by this election campaign so far that only half intend to vote. One major reason for this apathetic electorate appears to be the low level at which this campaign has been conducted. It has digressed frequently from important issues into allegations of blunder and brainwashing and fixations on lust and Playboy. What responsibility do you accept for the low level of this campaign for the nation's highest office?

MR. CARTER: I think the major reason for a decrease in participation that we have experienced ever since 1960 has been the deep discouragement of the American people about the performance of public officials. When you've got seven and a half, eight million people out of work, and you've got three times as much inflation as you had during the last eight-year Democratic administration, when you have the highest deficits in history; when you have it uh - becoming increasingly difficult far a family to put a child through college or to own a home, there's a natural inclination to be turned off. Also, in the aftermath of Vietnam and Cambodia and uh - Watergate and uh - the CIA revelations, people have feel - have felt that they've uh been betrayed by public officials, I have to admit that in the uh - heat of the campaign - I've been in thirty primaries during the springtime, I've been campaigning for twenty-two months - I've made some mistakes. And I think this is uh - uh - part of uh - of just being a human being. I - I have to say that my campaign has been an open one. And uh - the Playboy thing has been of great - very great concern to me. I don't know how to deal with it exactly. Uh - I uh - agreed to give the interview uh - to Playboy Other people have done it who are notable - uh - Governor Jerry Brown, uh - Walter Cronkite, uh - Albert Schweitzer, Mr. Ford's own secretary of the treasury, Mr. Simon, uh - William Buckley - many other people. But they weren't running for president, and in retrospect, from hindsight, I would not have given that uh - interview had I do it - had it - I to do it over again. If I should ever decide in the future to discuss my - my deep Christian beliefs and uh - condemnation and sinfulness, I'll use another forum besides Playboy. But I can say this, uh - I'm doing the best I can to get away from that, and during the next ten days, the American people will not see the Carter campaign running uh - television advertisements and newspaper advertisements based on a personal attack on President Ford's character. I believe that the opposite is true with President Ford's campaign, and uh - I hope that we can leave those issues in this next ten days about personalities and mistakes of the past - we've both made some mistakes - and talk about unemployment, inflation, housing, education, taxation, government organization, stripping away of secrecy, and the things that are crucial to the American people. I regret the things in my own long campaign that have been mistaken, but I'm trying to do away with those the last ten days.

MS. WALTERS: Thank you, Governor Carter. President Ford, your response.

MR. FORD: I believe that the uh - American people have been turned off in this election, uh - Mr. Maynard, for a variety of reasons. We have seen on Capitol Hill, in the Congress, uh - a great many uh - allegations of wrong-doing, of uh - alleged immorality, uh - those are very disturbing to the American people. They wonder how an elected representative uh - can serve them and participate in such activities uh - serving in the Congress of the United States. Yes, and I'm certain many, many Americans were turned off by the revelations of Watergate, a very, very uh - bad period of time in American political history. Yes, and thousands, maybe millions of Americans were turned off because of the uh - problems that came out of our involvement in Vietnam. But on the other hand, I found on July fourth of this year, a new spirit born in America. We were celebrating our Bicentennial; and I find that uh - there is a - a movement as I travel around the country of greater interest in this campaign. Now, like uh - any hardworking uh - person seeking public office uh - in the campaign, inevitably sometimes you will use uh - rather graphic language and I'm guilty of that just like I think most others in the political arena. But I do make a pledge that in the next ten days when we're asking the American people to make one of the most important decisions in their lifetime, because I think this election is one of the mast vital in the history of America, that uh - we do together what we can to stimulate voter participation.

MS. WALTERS: Thank you, President Ford. Mr. Nelson, your question to President Ford.

MR. NELSON: Uh - Mr. President, you mentioned Watergate, and you became president because of Watergate, so don't you owe the American people a special obligation to explain in detail your role of limiting one of the original investigations of Watergate, that was the one by the House Banking Committee? And, I know you've answered questions on this before, but there are questions that still remain and I think people want to know what your role was. Will you name the persons you talked to in connection with that investigation, and since you say you have no recollection of talking to anyone from the White House, would you be willing to open for examination the White House tapes of conversations uh - during that period?

MR. FORD: Well, Mr. uh - Nelson, uh - I testified before two committees, House and Senate, on precisely the questions that you have asked. And the testimony under oath was to the effect that I did not talk to Mr. Nixon, to Mr. Haldeman, to Mr. Ehrlichman, or to any of the people at the White House. I said I had no recollection whatsoever of talking with any of the White House legislative liaison people. I indicated under oath that the initiative that I took was at the request of the ranking members of the House Banking and Currency Committee on the Republican side, which was a legitimate request and a proper response by me. Now that was gone into by two congressional committees, and following that investigation, both committees overwhelmingly approved me, and the House and the Senate did likewise. Now, in the meantime, the special prosecutor, within the last few days, after an investigation himself, said there was no reason for him to get involved because he found nothing that would justify it. And then just a day or two ago, the attorney general of the United States made a further investigation and came to precisely the same conclusion. Now, after all of those investigations by objective, responsible people, I think the matter is closed once and for all. But to add one other feature, I don't control any of the tapes. Those tapes are in the jurisdiction of the courts and I have no right to say "yes" or "no." But all the committees, the attorney general, the special prosecutor, all of them have given me a clean bill of health. I think the matter is settled once and for all.

MR. NELSON: Well, Mr. President, if I do say so though, the question is that I think that you still have not gone into details about what your role in it was. And I don't think there is any question about whether or not uh - there was criminal prosecution, but whether - whether you have told the American people your entire involvement in it. And whether you would be willing, even if you don't control the tapes, whether you would be willing to ask that the tapes be released for examination.

MR. FORD: That's for the uh - proper authorities who have control over those tapes to make that decision. I have given every bit of evidence, answered every question that's as- been asked me by any senator or any member of the House. Plus the fact, that the special prosecutor, on his own initiation, and the attorney general on his initiation, the highest law enforcement official in this country, all of them have given me a clean bill of health. And I've told everything I know about it. I think the matter is settled once and for all.

MS. WALTERS: Governor Carter, your response.

MR. CARTER: I don't have a response.

MS. WALTERS: Thank you. Then we'll have the next question from Mr. Kraft to Governor Carter.

MR. KRAFT: Uh - Governor Carter, the next big crisis spot in the world may be Yugoslavia. Uh - President Tito is old and sick and there are divisions in his country. Uh - it's pretty certain that the Russians are gonna do everything they possibly can after Tito dies to force Yugoslavia back into the Soviet camp. But last Saturday you said, and this is a quote, "I would not go to war in Yugoslavia, even if the Soviet Union sent in troops." Doesn't that statement practically invite the Russians to intervene in Yugoslavia? Ah - doesn't it discourage Yugoslavs who might be tempted to resist? And wouldn't it have been wiser on your part uh - to say nothing and to keep the Russians in the dark as President Ford did, and as I think every president has done since - since President Truman?

MR. CARTER: In the last uh - two weeks, I've had a chance to talk to uh - two men who have visited uh - the Soviet Union, Yugoslavia and China. One is Governor Avell- Averell Harriman, who visited the Soviet Union and Yugoslavia, and the other is James Schlesinger, whom I think you accompanied to uh - China. I got a- a complete report back from those countries from these two distinguished - uh - gentlemen. Mr. Harriman talked to the leaders in Yugoslavia, and I think it's accurate to say that there is no uh - prospect in their opinion, of the Soviet Union invading uh - Yugoslavia should uh - Mr. Tito pass away. The present leadership uh - there is uh - is fairly uniform in - in their purpose, and I think it's a close-knit group, uh - and uh - I think it would be unwise for us to say that we will go to war uh - in Yugoslavia uh - if the Soviets should invade, which I think would be an extremely unlikely thing. I have maintained from the very beginning of my campaign, and this was a standard answer that I made in response to the Yugoslavian question, that I would never uh - go to war or become militarily involved, in the internal affairs of another country unless our own security was direc- rectly threatened. And uh - I don't believe that our security would be directly threatened if the Soviet Union went uh - into Yugoslavia. I don't believe it will happen. I certainly hope it won't. I would take eh - the strongest possible measures short of uh - actual military uh - action there by our own troops, but I doubt that that would be an eventuality.

MR. KRAFT: One quick follow-up question. (GOVERNOR CARTER: Yes.) Did you clear the response you made with Secretary Schlesinger and Governor Harriman?

MR. CARTER: No, I did not.

MS. WALTERS: President Ford, your response.

MR. FORD: I firmly believe, uh - Mr. Kraft, that it's unwise for a president to signal in advance what uh - options he might exercise if any uhh - international problem arose. I think we all recall with some sadness that at uh - the period of the nin- late nineteen forties, early nineteen fifties, there were some indications that the United States would not include uh - South Korea in an area of defense. There are some who allege, I can't prove it true or untrue, that uh - such a statement uh - in effect invited the North Koreans to invade South Korea. It's a fact they did. But no president of the United States, in my opinion, should signal in advance to a prospective enemy, what his uhh - decision might be or what option he might exercise. It's far better for a person sitting in the White House uh - who has a number of options to make certain that the uh - other side, so to speak, doesn't know precisely what you're going to do. And therefore, that was the reason that I would not uh - identify any particular course of action uh - when I responded to a question a week or so ago.

MS. WALTERS: Thank you, Mr. Maynard, your question to President Ford, please.

MR. MAYNARD: Sir, this question concerns your administrative performance as president. The other day, General George Brown, the chairman of the Joint Chiefs of Staff, delivered his views on several sensitive subjects, among them Great Britain, one of this country's oldest allies. He said, and I quote him now, "Great Britain, it's a pathetic thing. It just makes you cry. They're no longer a world power. All they have are generals, admirals, and bands," end quote. Since General Brown's comments have caused this country embarrassment in the past, why is he still this nation's leading military officer?

MR. FORD: I have indicated to General Brown that uh - the words that he used in that interview, in that particular case and in several others, were very ill advised. And General Brown has indicated uh - his apology, his regrets, and I think that will, uh - in this situation, settle the matter. It is tragic that uh - the full transcript of that interview was not released and that there were excerpts, some of the excerpts, taken out of context. Not this one, however, that you bring up. General Brown has an exemply [sic] record of military performance. He served this nation with great, great skill and courage and bravery for thirty-five years. And I think it's the consensus of the people who are knowledgeable in the military field, that he is probably the outstanding military leader and strategist that we have in America today. Now he did use uh - ill-advised words, but I think in the fact that he apologized, that he was reprimanded, uh - does permit him to stay on and continue that kind of leadership that's we so badly need as we enter into uh - negotiations uh - under the SALT II agreement, or if we have operations that might be developing uh in the Middle East or southern Africa, in the Pacific, uh - we need a man with that experience, that knowledge, that know-how, and I think, in light of the fact that he has uh - apologized, uh - would not have justified my asking for his resignation.

MS. WALTERS: Thank you. Governor Carter, your response.

MR. CARTER: Well, just briefly, I - I think this is uh - the second time that General Brown has made a statement that - for which he did have to apologize. And I know that everybody uh - makes mistakes. I think the first one was related to uh - the unwarranted influence of American Jews on the media and uh - in the Congress. This one concerned uh - Great Britain. I think he said that Israel was a - a military burden on us and that Iran hoped to reestablish the Persian Empire. Ah - I'm not uh - sure that I remembered earlier that President Ford had - had expressed uh - his concern about the statement or apologized for it. This is uh - something, though, that I think uh - is indicative of the need among the American people to know how its commander-in-chief, the president, feels and - and - and I think the only criticism that I would have uh - on - of Mr. Ford is that uh - immediately when the statement was re - re - revealed, uh - perhaps a - a statement from the president would have been a clarifying and a very beneficial thing.

MS. WALTERS: Mr. Nelson, your question now to Governor Carter.

MR. NELSON: Governor, despite the fact that uh - you've been running for president a long time now, uh - many Americans uh - still seem to be uneasy about you. Uh - they don't feel that uh - they know you or the people around you. And one problem seems to be that you haven't reached out to bring people of broad background or national experience into your campaign or your presidential plans. Most of the people around you on a day-to-day basis are the people you've kno- known in Georgia. Many of them are young and relatively inexperienced in national affairs. And uh - doesn't this raise a serious question as to uh - whether you would bring into a Carter administration uh people with the necessary background to run the federal government?

MR. CARTER: I don't believe it does. Uh - I began campaigning uh - twenty-two months ago. At that time, nobody thought I had a chance to win. Uh - very few people knew who I was. I came from a tiny town, as you know, Plains, and didn't hold public office, didn't have very much money. And my first organization was just four or five people plus my wife and my children, my three sons and their wives. And we won the nomination by going out into the streets - barbershops, beauty parlors, restaurants, stores, in factory shift lines also in farmers' markets and livestock sale barns - and we talked a lot and we listened a lot and we learned from the American people. And we built up uh - an awareness among the uh - voters of this country, particularly those in whose primaries I entered - thirty of them, nobody's ever done that before - about who I was and what I stood for. Now we have a very, very wide-ranging group of advisers who help me prepare for these debates and who teach me about international economics, and foreign affairs, defense matters, health, education, welfare, government reorganization. I'd say, several hundred of them. And they're very fine and very highly qualified. The one major decision that I have made since acquiring the nomination, and I share this with President Ford, is the choice of a vice president. I think this should be indicative of the kind of leaders I would choose to help me if I am elected. I chose Senator Walter Mondale. And the only criterion I ever put forward in my own mind was who among the several million people in this country would be the best person qualified to be president, if something should happen to me and to join me in being vice president if I should serve out my term. And I'm convinced now, more than I was when I got the nomination, that Walter Mondale was the right choice, And I believe this is a good indication of the kind of people I would choose in the future. Mr. Ford has had that same choice to make. I don't want to say anything critical of Senator Dole, but I've never heard Mr. Ford say that that was his prim- primary consideration - Who is the best person I could choose in this country to be president of the United States? I feel completely at ease knowing that someday Senator Mondale might very well be president. In the last five pres- vice presidential uh - nominees, uh - incumbents, three of them have become president. But I think this is indicative of what I would do.

MS. WALTERS: President Ford, your response, please.

MR. FORD: The Governor may not have heard my uh - established criteria for the selection of a vice president, but uh - it was a well-established criteria that the person I selected would be fully qualified to be president of the United States. And Senator Bob Dole is so qualified: sixteen years in the House of Representatives and in the Senate, uhh - very high responsibilities on important committees. I don't mean to be critical of uh - Senator Mondale, but uh - I was uh - very, very surprised when I read that uh - Senator Mondale made a very derogatory, very personal comment about General Brown uh - after the news story that uh - broke about General Brown. If my recollection is correct he indicated that uh - General Brown was not qualified to be a sewer commissioner. I don't think that's a proper way to describe aayuh-chairman of the Joint Chiefs of Staff who has fought for his country for thirty-five years, and I'm sure the governor would agree with me on that. Uh - I think Senator Dole would show more good judgment and discretion than to so describe uh - a heroic and brave and very outstanding leader of the military. So I think our selection uh - of Bob Dole as vice president uh - is based on merit. And if he should ever become uh - the president of the United States, with his vast experience as member the House and a member of the Senate, as well as a vice president, I think he would do an outstanding job as president of the United States.

MS. WALTERS: Mr. Kraft, your question to President Ford.

MR. KRAFT: Uh - Mr. President, uh - uh - let me assure you then maybe some of the uh viewing audience that being on this panel hasn't been as it may seem, all torture and agony. Uh - one of the heartening things is that uh - I and my colleagues have received uh - literally hundreds and maybe even thousands of suggested questions from ordinary citizens all across the country who want answers.

MR. FORD: That's a tribute to their interest in this election.

MR. KRAFT: I'll give you that. Ahh - but, uh - let me go on, because one main subject on the minds of all of them has been the environment. Uh - they're particularly curious about your record. People - people really wanna know why you vetoed the strip-mining bill. They wanna know why you worked against strong controls on auto emissions. They wanna know why you aren't doing anything about pollution uh - of the Atlantic Ocean. Uh - they wanna know a-a bipartisan organization such as the National League of Conservation Voters says that when it comes to environmental issues, you are - and I'm quoting - "hopeless."

MR. FORD: Well, first, uh - let me set the record straight. I vetoed the strip-mining bill, Mr. Kraft, because it was the overwhelming consensus of knowledgeable people that that strip-mining bill would have meant the loss of literally uh - thousands of jobs, something around a hundred and forty thousand jabs. Number two, that strip-mining bill would've severely set back our need for more coal, and Governor Carter has said repeatedly that coal is the resource that we need to use more in the effort to become independent of the uh - Arab oil supply. So, I vetoed it because of a loss of jobs and because it would've interfered with our energy independence program. The auto emissions - uh - it was agreed by Leonard Woodcock, the head of the UAW, and by the uh - heads of all of the automobile industry, we had labor and management together saying that those auto emission standards had to be modified. But let's talk about what the Ford administration has done in the field of environment. I have increased, as president, by over 60 percent the funding for water treatment plants in the United States, the federal contribution. I have fully funded the land and water conservation program; in fact, have recommended and the Congress approved a substantially increased land and water conservation program. Uh - I have uh - added in the current year budget the funds for the National Park Service. For example, we uh - proposed about $12 million to add between four and five hundred more employees for the National Park Service. And a month or so ago I did uh - likewise say over the next ten years we should expand - double - this national parks, the wild wilderness areas, the scenic river areas. And then, of course, the - the final thing is that I have signed and approved of more scenic rivers, more wilderness areas, since I've been president than any other president in the history of the United States.

MS. WALTERS: Governor Carter.

MR. CARTER: Well, I might say that I think the League of Conservation Voters is absolutely right. This uh - administration's record on environment is very bad. Uh - I think it's accurate to say that the uh - strip-mining law which was passed twice by the Congress - uh - and was only like two votes I believe of being overridden - would have been good for the country. The claim that it would have put hundred and forty thousand miners out of work is uh - hard to believe, when at the time Mr. Ford vetoed it, the United Mine Workers was uh - supporting the bill. And I don't think they would have supported the uh - bill had they known that they would lose a hundred and forty thousand jobs. There's been a consistent policy on the part of this administration to lower or delay enforcement of air pollution standards and water pollution standards. And under both President Nixon and Ford, monies have been impounded that would've gone to uh - cities and others to control uh - water pollution. We have no energy policy. We, I think, are the only developed nation in the world that has no comprehensive energy policy, to permit us to plan in an orderly way how to shift from increasing the scarce uh - energy uh - forms: oil, and have research and development concentrated on the increased use of coal, which I strongly favor. The research and development to be used primary to make the coal burning uh - be clean. We need a heritage trust program, similar to the one we had in Georgia, to set aside additional lands that have uh - geological and archeological importance, uh natural areas for enjoyment. Uh - the lands that Mr. Ford uh - brags about having approved are in Alaska and they are enormous in uh - in size. But as far as the accessibility of them by the American people, it's very uh - far in the future. We've taken no strong position in the uh - control of pollution of our oceans, and I would say the worst uh - threat to the environment of all is nuclear proliferation. And this administration, having been in office now for two years or more, has still not taken strong and bold action to stop the proliferation of nuclear waste around the world, particularly plutonium. Those are some brief remarks about the failures of this administration. I would do the opposite in every respect.

MS. WALTERS: Mr. Maynard, to Governor Carter.

MR. MAYNARD: Governor, federal policy in this country since World War II has tended to favor the development of suburbs at the great expense of central cities. Does not the federal government now have an affirmative obligation to revitalize the American city? We have heard little in this campaign suggesting that you have an urban reconstruction program. Could you please outline your urban intentions for us tonight?

MR. CARTER: Yes, I'd be glad to. In the first place, uh - as is the case with the environmental policy and the energy policy that I just described, and the policy for nonproliferation of uh - of nuclear waste, this administration has no urban policy. It's impossible for mayors or governors to cooperate with the resident, because they can't anticipate what's gonna happen next. A mayor of a city like New York, for instance, needs to know uh - eighteen months or two years ahead of time what responsibility the city will have in administration and in financing - in things like housing, uh - pollution control, uh - crime control, education, welfare and health. This has not been done, unfortunately. I remember the headline in the Daily News that said, "Ford to New York: Drop Dead." I think it's very important that our cities know that they have a partner in the federal government. Quite often Congress has passed laws in the past designed to help people with uh - the ownership of homes and with the control of crime and with adequate health care and education programs and so forth. Uh - those uh programs were designed to help those who need it most. And quite often this has been in the very poor people and neighborhoods in the downtown urban centers. Because of the uh - great -ly- greatly uh - advantaged uh - tho- per - persons who live in the suburbs, better education, better organization, more articulate, more aware of what the laws are, quite often this money has been channeled out of the downtown centers where it's needed. Also I favor all revenue sharing money being used for local governments, and also to remove prohibitions in the use of revenue sharing money so that it can be used to improve education, and health care. We have now uh - for instance only 7 percent of the total education cost being financed by the federal government. When uh - the Nixon-Ford Administration started, this was 10 percent. That's a 30 percent reduction in the portion that the federal government contributes to education in just eight years. And as you know, the education cost has gone up uh - tremendously. The last point is that the major - uh thrust has gotta be to put people back to work. We've got an extraordinarily high unemployment rate among downtown urban ghetto areas, uh - particularly among the very poor and particularly among minority groups, sometimes 50 or 60 percent. And the concentration of employment opportunities in those areas would help greatly not only to reestablish the tax base, but also to help reduce the extraordinary welfare cost. One of the major responsibilities on the shoulders of uh - New York City is to - is to finance welfare. And I favor a shifting of the welfare cost away from the local governments altogether. And over a longer period of time, let the federal government begin to absorb part of it that's now paid by the state governments. Those things would help a great deal with the cities, but we still have a - a very serious problem there.

MS. WALTERS: President Ford.

MR. FORD: Let me uh - speak out very strongly. The Ford administration does have a very comprehensive program to help uh - our major metropolitan areas. I fought for, and the Congress finally went along with a general revenue sharing program, whereby cities and uh - states, uh - the cities two-thirds and the states one-third, get over six billion dollars a year in cash through which they can uh - provide many, many services, whatever they really want. In addition we uh - in the federal government make available to uh - cities about uh - three billion three hundred million dollars in what we call community development. In adesh- in addition, uh - uh - as a result of my pressure an the Congress, we got a major mass transit program uh - over a four-year period, eleven billion eight-hundred million dollars. We have a good housing program, uh - that uh - will result in cutting uh - the down payments by 50 percent and uh - having mortgage payments uh lower at the beginning of any mortgage period. We're expanding our homestead uh - housing program. The net result is uh - we think under Carla Hills, who's the chairman of my uh - urban development and uh - neighborhood revitalization program, we will really do a first-class job in helping uh - the communities throughout the country. As a matter of fact, that committee under Secretary Hills released about a seventy-five-page report with specific recommendations so we can do a better job uh - the weeks ahead. And in addition, the tax program of the Ford administration, which provides an incentive for industry to move into our major uh - metropolitan areas, into the inner cities, will bring jobs where people are, and help to revitalize those cities as they can be.

MS. WALTERS: Mr. Nelson, your question next to President Ford.

MR. NELSON: Uh - Mr. President, your campaign has uh - run ads in black newspapers saying that quote, "for black Americans, President Ford is quietly getting the job done." Yet, study after study has shown little progress in desegregation and in fact actual increases in segregated schools and housing in the Northeast. Now, civil rights groups have complained repeatedly that there's been lack of progress and commitment to an integrated society uh - during your administration. So how are you getting the job done for blacks and other minorities and what programs do you have in mind for the next four years.

MR. FORD: Let me say at the outset, uh - I'm very proud of the record of this administration. In the cabinet I have one of the outstanding, I think, administrators as the secretary of transportation, Bill Coleman. You're familiar, I'm sure, with the recognition given in the Air Force to uh - General James, and there was just uh - approved a three-star admiral, the first in the history of the United States Navy, so uh - we are giving full recognition to individuals of quality in the Ford administration in positions of great responsibility. In addition, uh - the Department of Justice is fully enforcing, and enforcing effectively, the Voting Rights Act, the legislation that involves jobs, housing for minorities, not only blacks but all others. Uh - the Department of uh - uh - HUD is enforcing the new legislation that uhh - outlaws, that takes care of redlining. Uh - what we're doing is saying that there are opportunities, business opportunities, educational opportunities, responsibilities uh - where people with talent, black or any other minority, can fully qualify. The Office of Minority

Business in the Department of Commerce has made available more money in trying to help uh - black businessmen or other minority businessmen than any other administration since the office was established. The Office of Small Business, under Mr. Kobelinski, has a very massive program trying to help the black community. The individual who wants to start a business or expand his business as a black businessman is able to borrow, either directly or with guaranteed loans. I believe on the record that this administration has been more responsive and we have carried out the law to the letter, and I'm proud of the record.

MS. WALTERS: Governor Carter, your response, please.

MR. CARTER: The uh - description just made of this administration's record is hard to uh - recognize. I think it's accurate to say that Mr. Ford voted against the uh - Voting Rights Acts and the uh - Civil Rights Acts in their uh - debative stage I think once it was assured they were going to pass he finally voted for it. This country uh - changed drastically in 1969 when the uh - terms of John Kennedy and Lyndon Johnson were over and Richard Nixon and - and Gerald Ford became the presidents. There was a time when there was hope for those who uh - were poor and downtrodden and who were - uh elderly or who were - uh ill or who were in minority groups, but that time has been gone. I think the greatest thing that ever happened to the South was the passage of the Civil Rights Act and the opening up of opportunities - uh to black people - the chance to vote, to hold a job, to buy a house, to go to school, and to participate in public affairs. It not only liberated - uh black people but it also liberated the whites. We've seen uh - in many instances in recent years a minority affairs uh - section of uh Small Loan Administration, uh - Small Business Administration lend uh - a black entrepreneur just enough money to get started, and then to go bankrupt. The bankruptcies have gone up - uh in an extraordinary degree. Uh - FHA, which used to be a very responsible agency, uh - that everyone looked to to help own a home, lost six million dollars last year. There've been over thirteen hundred indictments in HUD, over eight hundred convictions relating just to home loans. And now the federal government has become the world's greatest slum landlord. We've got a 30 percent or 40 percent unemployment rate among minority uh - young people. And there's been no concerted effort given to the needs of those who are both poor and black, or poor and who speak a foreign language. And that's where there's been a great uh generation of despair, and ill health, and the lack of education, lack of purposefulness, and the lack of hope for the future. But it doesn't take just a quiet uh - dormant uh minimum enforcement of the law. It requires an aggressive searching out and reaching out to help people who especially need it. And that's been lacking in the last eight years.

MS. WALTERS: Mr. Kraft, to Governor Carter.

MR. KRAFT: Ah - Governor Carter, ah - in the nearly two-hundred-year history of the Constitution, there've been only uh - I think it's twenty-five amendments, most of them on issues of the very broadest principle. Uh - now we have proposed amendments in many highly specialized causes, like gun control, school busing, balanced budgets, school prayer, abortion, things like that. Do you think it's appropriate to the dignity of the Constitution to tack on amendments in wholesale fashion? And which of the ones that I listed - that is, uh - balanced budgets, school busing, school prayer, abortion, gun con- control - which of those would you really work hard to support if you were president?

MR. CARTER: I would not work hard to support any of those. Uh - we've always had, I think, a lot of constitutional amendments proposed, but the passage of them has been uh - fairly slow, and uh - few and far between. In the two-hundred-year history there's been a very uh - cautious approach to this. We - quite often we have a transient problem. I - I'm strongly against a- abortion. I think abortion's wrong. I don't think the government oughta do anything to encourage abortion. But I don't favor a constitutional amendment on the subject. But short of the constitutional amendment, and within the confines of the Supreme Court rulings, I'll do everything I can to minimize the need for abortions with better sex education, family planning, with better adoptive procedures. I personally don't believe that the federal government oughta finance abortions, but I - I draw the line and don't support a constitutional amendment. However, I honor the right of people who seek the constitutional amendments on school busing, on uh - prayer in the schools and an abortion. But among those you named, I won't actively work for the passage of any of them.

MS. WALTERS: President Ford, your response, please.

MR.FORD: support the uh - Republican uh - platform, which calls for the constitutional amendment that would uh - outlaw abortions. I favor the particular constitutional amendment that would turn over to the states the uh - individual right to the voters in those states uh - the chance to make a decision by public referendum. Uh I call that the people amendment. I think if you really believe that the people of a state ought to make a decision on a matter of this kind that uh - we ought to have a federal constitutional amendment that would permit each one of the fifty states to make the choice. Uh - I think this is a responsible and a proper way to proceed. Uhh - I believe also that uh - there is some merit to a - an amendment that uh - uh - Senator Everett Dirksen uh - proposed very frequently, an amendment that would uh - change the court decision as far as voluntary prayer in public schools. Uh - it seems to me that there should have - be an opportunity, uh - as long as it's voluntary, as long as there is no uh - compulsion whatsoever, that uh - an individual ought to have that right. So in those two cases I think uh - such uh - a constitutional amendment would be proper, and I really don't think in either case they're trivial matters. I think they're matters of very deep conviction, as far as many, many people in this country believe. And therefore, they shouldn't be treated lightly. But they're matters that are ah - important. And in those two cases, I would favor them.

MS. WALTERS: Mr. Maynard to President Ford.

MR. MAYNARD: Mr. President, twice you have been the intended victim of would-be assassins using handguns. Yet, you remain a steadfast opponent of substantive handgun control. There are now some forty million handguns in this country, going up at the rate of two point five million a year. And tragically, those handguns are frequently purchased for self-protection and wind up being used against a relative or a friend. In light of that, why do you remain so adamant in your opposition to substantive gun control in this country?

MR. FORD: Uh - Mr. Maynard, uh - the record of gun control, whether it's one city or another or in some states, does not show that the registration of a gun, handgun, or the registration of the gun owner, has in any way whatsoever decreased the crime rate or the use of that gun in the committing of a crime. The record just doesn't prove that such legislation or action by a local city council is effective. What we have to do, and this is the crux of the matter, is to make it very, very uh - difficult for a person who uses a gun in the commission of a crime to stay out of jail. If we make the use of a gun in the commission. of a crime a serious criminal offense, and that person is prosecuted, then, in my opinion, we are going after the person who uses the gun for the wrong reason. I don't believe in the registration of handguns or the registration of the handgun owner. That has not proven to be effective, and therefore, I think the better way is to go after the criminal, the individual who commits a crime in the possession of a gun and uses that gun for a part of his criminal activity. Those are the people who ought to be in jail. And the only way to do it is to pass strong legislation so that once apprehended, indicted, convicted, they'll be in jail and off the streets and not using guns in the commission of a crime.

MR. MAYNARD: But Mr. President, don't you think that the proliferation of the availability of handguns contributes to the possibility of those crimes being committed. And, there's a second part to my follow-up, very quickly. There are, as you know and as you've said, jurisdictions around the country with strong gun-control laws. The police officials in those cities contend that if there were a national law, to prevent other jurisdictions from providing the weapons that then came into places like New York, that they might have a better handle on the problem. Have you considered that in your analysis of the gu- the handgun proliferation problem?

MR. FORD: Yes, I have. And uh - the individuals that uh - with whom I've consulted have not uh - convinced me that uh - a national registration of handguns or handgun owners will solve the problem you're talking about. The person who wants to use a gun for an illegal purpose can get it whether it's registered or outlawed. They will be obtained. And they are the people who ought to go behind bars. You should not in the process penalize the legitimate handgun owner. And when you go through the process of registration, you in effect, are penalizing that individual who uses his gun for a very legitimate purpose.

MS. WALTERS: Governor Carter.

MR. CARTER: I - I think it's accurate to say that Mr. Ford's position on gun control has changed. Uh - earlier, uh - Mr. Levi, his uh - attorney general, put forward a gun control proposal, which Mr. Ford later, I believe, espoused, that called for the prohibition against the uh sale aw- of the uh - so-called Saturday Night Specials. And it would've put uh - very strict uh - uh - control over who owned a handgun. I have been a hunter all my life and happen to own both shotguns, rifles, and a handgun. And uh - the only purpose that I would see in registering uh - handguns and not long guns of any kind would be to prohibit the uh - ownership of those guns by those who've used them in the commission of a crime, or who uh - have been proven to be mentally incompetent to own a gun. I believe that limited approach to the - to the question would be uh - advisable, and - and I think, adequate. But that's as far as I would go with it.

MS. WALTERS: Mr. Nelson to Governor Carter.

MR. NELSON: Uh Governor, you've said the uh - Supreme Court of today is, uh - as you put it, moving back in a proper direction uh - in rulings that have limited the rights of criminal defendants. And you've compared the present Supreme Court under Chief Justice Burger very favorably with the more liberal court that we had under Chief Justice Warren. So exactly what are you getting at, and can you elaborate on the kind of court you think this country should have? And can you tell us the kind of qualifications and philosophy you would look for as president in making Supreme Court appointments?

MR. CARTER: While I was governor of Georgia, although I'm not a lawyer, we had complete reform of the Georgia court system. We uh - streamlined the structure of the court, put in administrative officers, put a unified court system in, required that all uh - severe sentences be reviewed far uniformity. And, in addition to that put forward a proposal that was adopted and used throughout my own term of office of selection of - for all judges and district attorneys or prosecuting attorneys, on the basis of merit. Every time I had a vacancy on the Georgia Supreme Court - and I filled five of those vacancies out of seven total and about half the court of appeals judges, about 35 percent of the trial judges - I was given from an objective panel the five most highly qualified persons in Georgia. And from those five, I always chose the first one or second one. So merit selection of judges is the most important single criterion. And I would institute the same kind of procedure as president, not only in judicial appointments, but also in diplomatic appointments. Secondly, I think that the Burger Court has fairly well confirmed the major and - and most far-reaching and most controversial decisions of the Warren Court. Civil rights - uh has been confirmed by the Burger Court, hasn't been uh - reversed, and I don't think there's any inclination to reverse those basic decisions. The one-man, one-vote rule, which is a very important one that uh - s- struck down the unwarranted influence in the legislature of parsley - uh populated areas of - of the states. The uh - right of indigent or very poor accused persons to uh - legal counsel. Uh - I think the Burger Court has confirmed that basic and very controversial decision of the Warren Court. Also the - the protection of an arrested person against unwarranted persecution in trying to get a false uh - confession. But now I think there have been a couple of instances where the Burger Court has made technical rulings where an obviously guilty person was later found to be guilty. And I think that in that case uh - some of the more liberal uh - members of the uh - so-called Warren Court agreed with those decisions. But the only uh - thing I uh - have pointed out was, what I've just said, and that there was a need to clarify the technicalities so that you couldn't be forced to release a person who was obviously guilty just because of a - of a small technicality in the law. And - and that's a reversal of position uh by the Burger Court with which I do agree.

MR. NELSON: Governor, I don't believe you ans- you answered my question though about the kinds of uh people you would be looking for the court, the type of philosophy uh - you would be looking for if you were making appointments to the Supreme Court as president.

MR. CARTER: Okay, I thought I answered it by saying that it would be on the basis of merit. Once the uh - search and analysis procedure had been completed, and once I'm given a list of the five or seven or ten uh - best qualified persons in the country, I would make a selection from among those uh - persons. If the uh - list was, uh - in my opinion, fairly uniform, if there was no outstanding person, then I would undoubtedly choose someone who would most accurately reflect my own basic politi- political philosophy as best I could determine it. Which would be uh - to continue the progress that has been made under the last two uh - courts - the Warren Court and the Burger Court. I would also like to uh - completely revise our criminal justice system - to do some of the things at the federal level in court reform that I've just described, as has been done in Georgia and other states. And then I would like to appoint people who would be interested in helping with that. I know that uh Chief Justice Burger is. He hasn't had help from the administration, from the Congress, to carry this out. The uh - emphasis, I think, of the - of the court system uh - should be to interpret the uh - the Constitution and the laws uh - equally between property protection and personal protection. But when there's uh - a very narrow decision - which quite often there's one that reaches the Supreme Court - I think the choice should be with human rights. And uh - that would be another factor that I would follow.

MS. WALTERS: President Ford.

MR. FORD: Well, I think the answer uh - as to the kind of person that I would select uh - is obvious. I had one opportunity to nominate uh - an individual to the Supreme Court and I selected the Circuit Court of Appeals judge from Illinois, uh - John Paul Stevens. I selected him because of his outstanding record as a Circuit Court of Appeals Judge, and I was very pleased that uh - an overwhelming Democratic United States Senate, after going into his background, came to the conclusion that he was uh - fit and should serve, and the vote in his behalf was overwhelming. So, I would say somebody in the format of uh - Justice Stevens would be the kind of an individual that I would uh - select in the future, as I did him in the past. I uh - believe, however, a comment ought to be made about the direction of the uh - Burger Court, vis-a-vis the uh - court uh - that preceded it. It seems to me that the Miranda case was a case that really made it very, very difficult for the - uh police, the law enforcement people in this country to uh - do what they could to make certain that the victim of a crime was protected and that those that commit crimes uh - were properly handled and uh - sent to jail. The Miranda case, uh - the Burger Court uh - is gradually changing, and I'm pleased to see that there are some steps being made by the uh - Burger Court to modify the so-called Miranda decision. Uh - I might make a correction uh - of what uh - Governor

Carter said, uh speaking of uh - uh - gun control, uh - yes, it is true, I believe that the sale of uh - Saturday Night S-Specials should be cut out, but he wants the registration of handguns.

MS. WALTERS: Mr. Kraft.

MR. KRAFT: Uh - Mr. President, uh - the country is now uh - in uh - in something that your uh - advisors call an economic pause. I think to most Americans that sounds like a - a antiseptic term for uh - low growth, uh - unemployment standstill at a high, high level, uhh - decline in take-home pay, uh - lower factory earnings, more layoffs. Uh, isn't that a really rotten record and doesn't your administration bear most of the blame for it?

MR. FORD: Well, Mr. Kraft, uh - I violently disagree with your assessment. And I don't think the record justifies the conclusion that you come to. Uh - let me uh - talk about uh - the economic announcements that were made just this past week. Yes, it was announced that the uh - GNP real growth in the third quarter was at 4 percent. But do you realize that over the last ten years that's a higher figure than the average growth during that ten-year period? Now it's lower than the nine-point-point-two percent growth in the first quarter, and it's lower than the uh 5 percent growth in the second quarter. But every economist - liberal, conservative that I'm familiar with - recognizes that in the fourth quarter of this year and in the fifth quar- uh - the first quarter of next year that we'll have an increase in real GNP. But now let's talk about the pluses that came out this week. We had an 18 percent increase in housing starts. We had a substantial increase in new permits for housing. As a matter of fact, based on the announcement this week, there will be at an annual rate of a million, eight hundred and some thousand new houses built, which is a tremendous increase over last year and a substantial increase over the earlier part of this year. Now in addition, we had a very - some very good news in the reduction in the rate of inflation. And inflation hits everybody: those who are working and those who are on welfare. The rate of inflation, as announced just the other day, is under 5 percent; and the uh - 4.4 percent that was indicated at the time of the 4 percent GNP was less than the 5.4 percent. It means that the American buyer is getting a better bargain today because inflation is less.

MR. KRAFT: Mr. President, let me ask you this. Uh - there has been an increase in layoffs and that's something that bothers everybody because even people that have a job are afraid that they're going to be fired. Did you predict that layoff, uh - that increase in layoffs? Didn't that take you by surprise? Hasn't the gov- hasn't your administration been surprised by this pause? Uh - in fact, haven't you not - haven't you been so obsessed with saving money uh - that you didn't even push the government to spend funds that were allocated?

MR. FORD: Uh Mr. Kraft, uh - I think the record can be put in this uh - in this way, which uh - is the way that I think satisfies most Americans. Since the depths of the recession, we have added four million jobs. Im- most importantly, consumer confidence as surveyed by the reputable organization at the University of Michigan is at the highest since 1972. In other words, there is a growing public confidence in the strength of this economy. And that means that there will be more industrial activity. It means that there will be a reduction in the uhh - unemployment. It means that there will be increased hires. It means that there will be increased employment. Now we've had this pause, but most economists, regardless of their political philosophy, uh - indicate that this pause for a month or two was healthy, because we could not have honestly sustained a 9.2 percent rate of growth which we had in the first quarter of this year. Now, uh - I'd like to point out as well that the United States' economic recovery from the recession of a year ago is well ahead of the economic recovery of any major free industrial nation in the world today. We're ahead of all of the Western European country. We're ahead of Japan. The United States is leading the free world out of the recession that was serious a year, year and a half ago. We're going to see unemployment going down, more jobs available, and the rate of inflation going down. And I think this is a record that uh - the American people understand and will appreciate.

MS. WALTERS: Governor Carter.

MR. CARTER: With all due respect to President Ford, I think he ought to be ashamed of mentioning that statement, because we have the highest unemployment rate now than we had at any time between the Great Depression caused by Herbert Hoover and the time President Ford took office. We've got seven and a half million people out of jobs. Since he's been in office, two and a half million more American people have lost their jobs. In the last four months alone, five hundred thousand Americans have gone on the unemployment roll. In the last month, we've had a net loss of one hundred and sixty-three thousand jobs. Anybody who says that the inflation rate is in good shape now ought to talk to the housewives. One of the overwhelming results that I've seen in the polls is that people feel that you can't plan anymore. There's no way to make a prediction that my family might be able to own a home or to put my kid through college. Savings accounts are losing money instead of gaining money. Inflation is robbing us. Under the present administration - Nixon's and Ford's - we've had three times the inflation rate that we experienced under President Johnson and President Kennedy.

The economic growth is less than half today what it was at the beginning of this year. And housing starts - he compares the housing starts with last year. I don't blame him, because in 1975 we had fewer housing starts in this country, fewer homes built, than any year since 1940. That's thirty-five years. And we've got a 35 percent unemployment rate in many areas of this country among construction workers. And Mr. Ford hasn't done anything about it. And I think this shows a callous indifference to the families that have suffered so much. He has vetoed bills passed by Congress within the congressional budget guidelines job opportunities for two million Americans. We'll never have a balanced budget, we'll never meet the needs of our people, we'll never control the inflationary spiral, as long as we have seven and a half or eight million people out of work, who are looking for jobs. And we've probably got two and a half more million people who are not looking for jobs any more, because they've given up hope. That is a very serious indictment of this administration. It's probably the worst one of all.

MS. WALTERS: Mr. Maynard.

MR. MAYNARD: Governor Carter, you entered this race against President Ford with a twenty-point lead or better in the polls. And now it appears that this campaign is headed for a photo finish. You've said how difficult it is to run against a sitting president. But Mr. Ford was just as much an incumbent in July when you were twenty points ahead as he is now. Can you tell us what caused the evaporation of that lead in your opinion?

MR. CARTER: Well, that's not exactly an accurate description of what happened. When I was that far ahead, it was immediately following the Democratic Convention, and before the Republican Convention. At that time, uh - 25 or 30 percent of the Reagan supporters said that they would not support President Ford. But as occurred at the end of the con- Democratic Convention, the Republican Party unified itself. And I think immediately following the Republican Convention, there was about a ten-point spread. I believe that to be accurate, I had 49 percent; President Ford, 39 percent. Uh - the polls uh - are good indications of fluctuations, but they vary widely one from another. And the only poll I've ever followed is the one that uh - you know, is taken on election day. I was in uh - thirty primaries in the spring, and uh - at first it was obvious that I didn't have any standing in the poll. As a matter of fact, I think when Gallup ran their first poll in December of 1975 they didn't put my name on the list. They had thirty-five people on the list. My name wasn't even there. And at the beginning of the year I had about 2 percent. So the polls to me are interesting, but they don't determine, you know, my hopes or - or my despair. I campaign among people. I've never depended on powerful political figures to put me in office. I have a direct relationship with hundreds of people around - hundreds of thousands around the country who actively campaign for me. In Georgia alone, for instance, I got 84 percent of the vote, and I think there were fourteen people uh - in addition to myself on the ballot, and Governor Wallace had been very strong in Georgia. That's an overwhelming support from my own people who know me best. And today, we have about five hundred Georgians at their own expense - just working people who believe in me - spread around the country uh - involved in the political campaign. So, the polls are interesting, but uh - I don't know how to explain the fluctuation. I think a lot of it uh - depends on current events - uh - sometimes foreign affairs, sometimes domestic affairs. But I think our hold uh - of support among those who uh - are crucial to the election has been fairly steady. And my success in the primary season was, I think, notable for a newcomer, from someone who's from outside Washington, who - who never has been a part of the Washington establishment. And I think that we'll have good results uh - on November the second for myself and I hope for the country.

MS. WALTERS: President Ford, your response.

MR. FORD: I think uh - the uh - increase and the uh - prospects as far as I'm concerned and the I - less favorable prospects for Governor Carter, reflect that Governor Carter uh - is inconsistent in many of the positions that he takes. He tends to distort on a number of occasions. Uh - just a moment ago, for example, uh - he uh - was indicating that uh - uh - in the 1950s, for example, uh - unemployment was very low. He fails to point out that uh - in the 1950s we were engaged in the war in Vietnam. We - I mean in Korea - we had uh - three million five hundred thousand young men uh - in the Army, Navy, Air Force and Marines. That's not the way to end unemployment or to reduce unemployment. At the present time we're at peace. We have reduced the number of people in the Army, Navy, Air Force and Marines from three million, one hundred - three million, five hundred thousand to two mil- lion one hundred thousand. We are not at war. We have reduced the military manpower by a million four hundred thousand. If we had that many more people in the Army, the Navy, the Air Force, and Marines, our unemployment figure would be considerably less. But this administration doesn't believe the way to reduce unemployment is to go to war, or to increase the number of people in the military. So you cannot compare unemployment, as you sought to, uh - with the present time with the 1950s, because the then administration had people in the military - they were at war, they were fighting overseas, and this administration has reduced the size of the military by a million four hundred thousand. They're in the civilian labor market and they're not fighting anywhere around the world today.

MS. WALTERS: Thank you, gentlemen. This will complete our questioning for this debate. We don't have uh - time for more questions and uh - full answers. So now each candidate will be allowed up to four minutes for a closing statement. And at the original coin toss in Philadelphia a month ago it was determined that President Ford would make the first closing statement tonight. President Ford.

MR. FORD: For twenty-five years I served in the Congress under five presidents. I saw them work, I saw them make very hard decisions. I didn't always agree with their decisions, whether they were Democratic or Republican presidents. For the last two years, I've been the president, and I have found from experience that it's much more difficult to make those decisions than it is to second-guess them. I became president at the time that the United States was in a very troubled time. We had inflation of over 12 percent, we were on the brink of the worst recession in the last forty years, we were still deeply involved in the problems of Vietnam. The American people had lost faith and trust and confidence in the presidency itself. That uh - situation called for me to first put the United States on a steady course and to keep our keel well balanced, because we had to face the difficult problems that had all of a sudden hit America. I think most people know that I did not seek the presidency. But I am asking for your help and assistance to be president for the next four years. During this campaign we've seen a lot of television shows, a lot of bumper stickers, and a great many uh - slogans of one kind or another. But those are not the things that count. What counts is, that the United States celebrated its 200th birthday on July fourth. As a result of that wonderful experience all over the United States, there is a new spirit in America. The American people are healed, are working together. The American people are moving again, and moving in the right direction. We have cut inflation by better than half. We have came out of the recession and we're well on the road to real prosperity in this country again. There has been a restoration of faith and confidence and trust in the presidency because I've been open, candid and forthright. I have never promised more than I could produce and I have produced everything that I promised. We are at peace. Not a single young American is fighting or dying on any foreign soil tonight. We have peace with freedom. I've been proud to be president of the United States during these very troubled times. I love America just as all of you love America. It would be the highest honor for me to have your support on November second and for you to say, "Jerry Ford, you've done a good job, keep on doing it." Thank you, and good night.

MS. WALTERS: Thank you President Ford. Governor Carter.

MR. CARTER: Thank you Barbara (barely audible). The major purpose of an election for president is to choose a leader. Someone who can analyze the depths of feeling in our country to set a standard for our people to follow, to inspire our people to reach for greatness, to correct our defects, to answer difficult questions, to bind ourselves together in a spirit of unity. I don't believe the present administration has done that. We have been discouraged and we've been alienated. Sometimes we've been embarrassed and sometimes we've been ashamed. Our people are out of work, and there's a sense of withdrawal. But our country is innately very strong. Mr. Ford is a good and decent man, but he's in - been in office now more than eight hundred days approaching almost as long as John Kennedy was in office. I'd like to ask the American people what, what's been accomplished. A lot remains to be done. My own background is different from his. I was a school board member, and a library board member. I served an a hospital authority. And I was in the state senate and I was governor and I'm an engineer, a Naval officer, a farmer, a businessman. And I believe we require someone who can work harmoniously with the Congress, who can work closely with the people of this country, and who can bring a new image and a new spirit to Washington. Our tax structure is a disgrace, it needs to be reformed. I was Governor of Georgia for four years. We never increased sales taxes or income tax or property tax. As a matter of fact, the year before I went out of office we gave a $50 million refund to the property taxpayers of Georgia. We spend six hundred dollars per person in this country - every man, woman and child - for health care. We still rank fifteenth among all the nations of the world in infant mortality. And our cancer rate is uh - higher than any country in the world. We don't have good health care. We could have it. Employment ought to be restored to our people. We've become almost a welfare state. We spend now 700 percent more on unemployment compensation than we did eight years ago when the Republicans took over the White House. Our people wanna go back to work. Our education system can be improved. Secrecy ought to be stripped away from government and a maximum of personal privacy ought to be maintained. Our housing programs have uh - gone bad. It used to be that the average - uh family could own a house. But now less than a third of our people can afford to buy their own homes. The budget was more grossly out of balance last year than ever before in the history of our country - $65 billion - primarily because our people are not at work. Inflation is robbing us, as we've already discussed, and the government bureaucracy is uh - just a horrible mess. This doesn't have to be. Now I don't know all the answers. Nobody could. But I do know that if the president of the United States and the Congress of the United States and the people of the United States said, "I believe our nation is greater than what we are now." I believe that if we are inspired, if we can achieve a degree of unity, if we can set our goals high enough and work toward recognized goals with industry and labor and agriculture along with government at all levels, then we can achieve great things. We might have to do it slowly. There are no magic answers to do it. But I believe together we can make great progress. We can correct our difficult mistakes and answer those very tough questions. I believe in the greatness of our country, and I believe the American people are ready for a change in Washington. We've been drifting too long. We've been dormant too long. We've been discouraged too long. And we have not set an example for our own people. But I believe that we can now establish in the White House a good relationship with Congress, a good relationship with our people, set very high goals for our country. And with inspiration and hard work we can achieve great things. And let the world know - that's very important. But more importantly, let the people in our own country realize that we still live in the greatest nation on earth. Thank you very much.

MS. WALTERS: Thank you, Governor Carter, and thank you, President Ford. I also would like to thank the audience and my three colleagues - Mr. Kraft, Mr. Maynard and Mr. Nelson - who have been our questioners. This debate has, of course, been seen by millions of Americans and, in addition, tonight is being broadcast to one hundred and thirteen nations throughout the world. This concludes the 1976 presidential debates, a truly remarkable exercise in democracy, for this is the first time in sixteen years that the presidential candidates have debated. It is the first time ever that an incumbent president has debated his challenger. And the debate included the first between the two vice presidential candidates. President Ford and Governor Carter, we not only want to thank you, but we commend you for agreeing to come together to discuss the issues before the American people. And our special thanks to the League of Women Voters for making these events possible. In sponsoring these events, the League of Women Voters Education Fund has tried to provide you with the information that you will need to choose wisely. The election is now only eleven days off. The candidates have participated in presenting their views in three ninety-minute debates, and now it's up to the voters, now it is up to you, to participate. The League urges all registered voters to vote on November second for the candidate of your choice. And now, from Phi Beta Kappa Memorial Hall an the campus of the College of William and Mary, this is Barbara Walters wishing you all a good evening.

3.4   1980 U.S. Presidential Debate - October 28

RUTH HINERFELD, LEAGUE OF WOMEN VOTERS, EDUCATION FUND: Good evening. I'm Ruth Hinerfeld of the League of Women Voters Education Fund. Next Tuesday is Election Day. Before going to the polls, voters want to understand the issues and know the candidates' positions. Tonight, voters will have an opportunity to see and hear the major party candidates for the Presidency state their views on issues that affect us all. The League of Women Voters is proud to present this Presidential Debate. Our moderator is Howard K. Smith.

MR. SMITH, ABC NEWS: Thank you, Mrs. Hinerfeld. The League of Women Voters is pleased to welcome to the Cleveland, Ohio, Convention Center Music Hall President Jimmy Carter. the Democratic Party's candidate for reelection to the Presidency. and Governor Ronald Reagan of California, the Republican Party's candidate for the Presidency. The candidates will debate questions on domestic, economic, foreign policy, and national security issues. The questions are going to be posed by a panel of distinguished journalists who are here with me. They are: Marvin Stone, the editor of U.S. News & World Report; Harry Ellis, national correspondent of the Christian Science Monitor; William Hilliard, assistant managing editor of the Portland Oregonian; Barbara Walters, correspondent, ABC News. The ground rules for this, as agreed by you gentlemen, are these: Each panelist down here will ask a question, the same question, to each of the two candidates. After the two candidates have answered, a panelist will ask follow-up questions to try to sharpen the answers. The candidates will then have an opportunity each to make a rebuttal. That will constitute the first half of the debate, and I will state the rules for the second half later on. Some other rules: The candidates are not permitted to bring prepared notes to the podium, but are permitted to make notes during the debate. If the candidates exceed the allotted time agreed on, I will reluctantly but certainly interrupt. We ask the Convention Center audience here to abide by one ground rule. Please do not applaud or express approval or disapproval during the debate. Now, based on the toss of the coin, Governor Reagan will respond to the first question from Marvin Stone.

MARVIN STONE, U.S. NEWS AND WORLD REPORT: Governor, as you're well aware, the question of war and peace has emerged as a central issue in this campaign in the give and take of recent weeks. President Carter has been criticized for responding late to aggressive Soviet impulses, for insufficient build-up of our armed forces. and a paralysis in dealing with Afghanistan and Iran. You have been criticized for being all too quick to advocate the use of lots of muscle

- military action - to deal with foreign crises. Specifically, what are the differences between the two of you on the uses of American military power?

MR. REAGAN: I don't know what the differences might be, because I don't know what Mr. Carter's policies are. I do know what he has said about mine. And I'm only here to tell you that I believe with all my heart that our first priority must be world peace, and that use of force is always and only a last resort, when everything else has failed, and then only with regard to our national security. Now, I believe, also, that this meeting this mission, this responsibility for preserving the peace, which I believe is a responsibility peculiar to our country, and that we cannot shirk our responsibility as a leader of the free world because we're the only ones that can do it. Therefore, the burden of maintaining the peace falls on us. And to maintain that peace requires strength. America has never gotten in a war because we were too strong. We can get into a war by letting events get out of hand, as they have in the last three and a half years under the foreign policies of this Administration of Mr. Carter's, until we're faced each time with a crisis. And good management in preserving the peace requires that we control the events and try to intercept before they become a crisis. I have seen four wars in my lifetime. I'm a father of sons; I have a grandson. I don't ever want to see another generation of young Americans bleed their lives into sandy beachheads in the Pacific, or rice paddies and jungles in the in Asia or the muddy battlefields of Europe.

MR. SMITH: Mr. Stone, do you have a follow-up question for the Governor?

MR. STONE: Yes. Governor, we've been hearing that the defense build-up that you would associate yourself with would cost tens of billions of dollars more than is now contemplated. Assuming that the American people are ready to bear this cost, they nevertheless keep asking the following question: How do you reconcile huge increases in military outlays with your promise of substantial tax cuts and of balancing the budget, which in this fiscal year, the one that just ended, ran more than $60 billion in the red?

MR. REAGAN: Mr. Stone, I have submitted an economic plan that I have worked out in concert with a number of fine economists in this country, all of whom approve it, and believe that over a five year projection, this plan can permit the extra spending for needed refurbishing of our defensive posture, that it can provide for a balanced budget by 1983 if not earlier, and that we can afford - along with the cuts that I have proposed in Government. spending - we can afford the tax cuts I have proposed and probably mainly because Mr. Carter's economic policy has built into the next five years, and on beyond that, a tax increase that will be taking $86 billion more out of the people's pockets than was taken this year. And my tax cut does not come close to eliminating that $86 billion increase. I'm only reducing the amount of the increase. In other words, what I'm talking about is not putting government back to getting less money than government's been getting, but simply cutting the increase in in spending.

MR. SMITH: The same question now goes to President Carter. President Carter, would you like to have the question repeated?

MR. STONE: Yes, President Carter, the question of war and peace, a central issue in this campaign. You've been criticized for, in the give and take, for responding late to aggressive Soviet impulses, for an insufficient build-up of our armed forces, and a paralysis in dealing with Afghanistan and Iran. Governor Reagan, on the other hand, has been criticized for being all too quick to advocate the use of lots of muscle - military action - to deal with foreign crises such as I have mentioned. Specifically, what are the differences between the two of you on the uses of American military power?

MR. CARTER: Mr. Stone, I've had to make thousands of decisions since I've been President, serving in the Oval Office. And with each one of those decisions that affect the future of my country, I have learned in the process. I think I'm a much wiser and more experienced man than I was when I debated four years ago against President Ford. I've also learned that there are no simple answers to complicated questions. H. L. Mencken said that for every problem there's a simple answer. It would be neat and plausible and wrong. The fact is that this nation, in the eight years before I became President, had its own military strength decreased. Seven out of eight years, the budget commitments for defense went down, 37% in all. Since I've been in office, we've had a steady, carefully planned, methodical but, very effective increase in our commitment for defense. But what we've done is use that enormous power and prestige and military strength of the United States to preserve the peace. We've not only kept peace for our own country, but we've been able to extend the benefits of peace to others. In the Middle East, we've worked for a peace treaty between Israel and Egypt, successfully, and have tied ourselves together with Israel and Egypt in a common defense capability. This is a very good step forward for our nation's security, and we'll continue to do as we have done in the past. I might also add that there are decisions that are made in the Oval Office by every President which are profound in nature. There are always trouble spots in the world, and how those troubled areas are addressed by a President alone in that Oval Office affects our nation directly, the involvement of the United States and also our American interests. That is a basic decision that has to be made so frequently, by every

President who serves. That is what I have tried to do successfully by keeping our country at peace.

MR. SMITH: Mr. Stone, do you have a follow-up for?

MR. STONE: Yes. I would like to be a little more specific on the use of military power and let's talk about one area for a moment. Under what circumstances would you use military forces to deal with, for example, a shut-off of the Persian Oil Gulf [sic] if that should occur, or to counter Russian expansion beyond Afghanistan into either Iran or Pakistan? I ask this question in view of charges that we are woefully unprepared to project sustained - and I emphasize the word sustained - power in that part of the world.

MR. CARTER: Mr. Stone, in my State of the Union address earlier this year, I pointed out that any threat to the stability or security of the Persian Gulf would be a threat to the security of our own country. In the past, we have not had an adequate military presence in that region. Now we have two major carrier task forces. We have access to facilities in five different areas of that region. And we've made it clear that working with our allies and others, that we are prepared to address any foreseeable eventuality which might interrupt commerce with that crucial area of the world. But in doing this, we have made sure that we address this question peacefully, not injecting American military forces into combat, but letting the strength of our nation be felt in a beneficial way. This, I believe, has assured that our interests will be protected in the Persian Gulf region, as we have done in the Middle East and throughout the world.

MR. SMITH: Governor Reagan, you have a minute to comment or rebut.

MR. REAGAN: Well yes, I question the figure about the decline in defense spending under the two previous Administrations in the preceding eight years to this Administration. I would call to your attention that we were in a war that wound down during those eight years, which of course made a change in military spending because of turning from war to peace. I also would like to point out that Republican presidents in those years, faced with a Democratic majority in both houses of the Congress, found that their requests for defense budgets were very often cut. Now, Gerald Ford left a five-year projected plan for a military build-up to restore our defenses, and President Carter's administration reduced that by 38%, cut 60 ships out of the Navy building program that had been proposed, and stopped the the B-1, delayed the cruise missile, stopped the production line for the Minuteman missile, stopped the Trident or delayed the Trident submarine, and now is planning a mobile military force that can be delivered to various spots in the world which does make me question his assaults on whether I am the one who is quick to look for use of force.

MR. SMITH: President Carter, you have the last word on this question.

MR. CARTER: Well, there are various elements of defense. One is to control nuclear weapons, which I hope we'll get to later on because that is the most important single issue in this campaign. Another one is how to address troubled areas of the world. I think, habitually, Governor Reagan has advocated the injection of military forces into troubled areas, when I and my predecessors - both Democrats and Republicans - have advocated resolving those troubles in those difficult areas of the world peacefully, diplomatically, and through negotiation. In addition to that, the build-up of military forces is good for our country because we've got to have military strength to preserve the peace. But I'll always remember that the best weapons are the ones that are never fired in combat, and the best soldier is one who never has to lay his life down on the field of battle. Strength is imperative for peace, but the two must go hand in hand.

MR. SMITH: Thank you gentlemen. The next question is from Harry Ellis to President Carter.

MR. ELLIS, CHRISTIAN SCIENCE MONITOR: Mr. President, when you were elected in 1976, the Consumer Price Index stood at 4.8%. It now stands at more than 12%. Perhaps more significantly, the nation's broader, underlying inflation rate has gone up from 7% to 9%. Now, a part of that was due to external factors beyond U.S. control, notably the more than doubling. of oil prices by OPEC last year. Because the United States remains vulnerable to such external shocks, can inflation in fact be controlled? If so, what measures would you pursue in a second term?

MR. CARTER: Again it's important to put the situation in perspective. In 1974, we had a so-called oil shock, wherein the price of OPEC oil was raised to an extraordinary degree. We had an even worse oil shock in 1979. In 1974, we had the worst recession, the deepest and most penetrating recession since the Second World War. The recession that resulted this time was the briefest since the Second World War. In addition, we've brought down inflation. Earlier this year, in the first quarter, we did have a very severe inflation pressure brought about by the OPEC price increase. It averaged about 18% in the first quarter of this year. In the second quarter, we had dropped it down to about 13%. The most recent figures, the last three months, on the third quarter of this year, the inflation rate is 7% - still too high, but it illustrates very vividly that in addition to providing an enormous number of jobs - nine million new jobs in the last three and a half years - that the inflationary threat is still urgent on us. I notice that Governor Reagan recently mentioned the Reagan-

Kemp-Roth proposal. which his own running mate, George Bush, described as voodoo economics, and said that it would result in a 30% inflation rate. And Business Week, which is not a Democratic publication, said that this Reagan-Kemp-Roth proposal - and I quote them, I think - was completely irresponsible and would result in inflationary pressures which would destroy this nation. So our proposals are very sound and very carefully considered to stimulate jobs, to improve the industrial complex of this country, to create tools for American workers, and at the same time would be anti-inflationary in nature. So to add nine million new jobs, to control inflation, and to plan for the future with an energy policy now intact as a foundation is our plan for the years ahead.

MR. SMITH: Mr. Ellis, do you have a follow-up question for Mr. Carter?

MR. ELLIS: Yes. Mr. President, you have mentioned the creation of nine million new jobs. At the same time, the unemployment rate still hangs high, as does the inflation rate. Now, I wonder, can you tell us what additional policies you would pursue in a second administration in order to try to bring down that inflation rate? And would it be an act of leadership to tell the American people they are going to have to sacrifice to adopt a leaner lifestyle for some time to come?

MR. CARTER: Yes. We have demanded that the American people sacrifice, and they have done very well. As a matter of fact, we're importing today about one-third less oil from overseas than we did just a year ago. We've had a 25% reduction since the first year I was in office. At the same time, as I have said earlier, we have added about nine million net new jobs in that period of time - a record never before achieved. Also, the new energy policy has been predicated on two factors: One is conservation, which requires sacrifice, and the other one, increase in production of American energy, which is going along very well - more coal this year than ever before in American history, more oil and gas wells drilled this year than ever before in history. The new economic revitalization program that we have in mind, which will be implemented next year, would result in tax credits which would let business invest in new tools and new factories to create even more new jobs - about one million in the next two years. And we also have planned a youth employment program which would encompass 600,000 jobs for young people. This has already passed the House, and it has an excellent prospect to pass the Senate.

MR. SMITH: Now, the same question goes to Governor Reagan. Governor Reagan, would you like to have the question repeated?

MR. ELLIS: Governor Reagan, during the past four years, the Consumer Price Index has risen from 4.8% to currently over 12%. And perhaps more significantly, the nation's broader, underlying rate of inflation has gone up from 7% to 9%. Now, a part of that has been due to external factors beyond U.S. control, notably the more than doubling of OPEC oil prices last year, which leads me to ask you whether, since the United States remains vulnerable to such external shocks, can inflation in fact be controlled? If so, specifically what measures would you pursue`?

MR. REAGAN: Mr. Ellis, I think this idea that has been spawned here in our country that inflation somehow came upon us like a plague and therefore it's uncontrollable and no one can do anything about it, is entirely spurious and it's dangerous to say this to the people. When Mr. Carter became President, inflation was 4.8%, as you said. It had been cut in two by President Gerald Ford. It is now running at 12.7%. President Carter also has spoken of the new jobs created. Well, we always, with the normal growth in our country and increase in population, increase the number of jobs. But that can't hide the fact that there are eight million men and women out of work in America today, and two million of those lost their jobs in just the last few months. Mr. Carter had also promised that he would not use unemployment as a tool to fight against inflation. And yet, his 1980 economic message stated that we would reduce productivity and gross national product and increase unemployment in order to get a handle on inflation, because in January, at the beginning of the year, it was more than 18%. Since then, he has blamed the people for inflation, OPEC, he has blamed the Federal Reserve system, he has blamed the lack of productivity of the American people, he has then accused the people of living too well and that we must share in scarcity, we must sacrifice and get used to doing with less. We don't have inflation because the people are living too well. We have inflation because the Government is living too well. And the last statement, just a few days ago, was a speech to the effect that we have inflation because Government revenues have not kept pace with Government spending. I see my time is running out here. I'll have to get this out very fast. Yes, you can lick inflation by increasing productivity and by decreasing the cost of government to the place that we have balanced budgets, and are no longer grinding out printing press money, flooding the market with it because the Government is spending more than it takes in. And my economic plan calls for that. The President's economic plan calls for increasing the taxes to the point that we finally take so much money away from the people that we can balance the budget in that way. But we will have a very poor nation and a very unsound economy if we follow that path.

MR. SMITH: A follow-up, Mr. Ellis?

MR. ELLIS: Yes. You have centered on cutting Government spending in what you have just said about your own policies. You have also said that you would increase defense spending. Specifically, where would you cut Government spending if you were to increase defense spending and also cut taxes, so that, presumably. Federal revenues would shrink?

MR. REAGAN: Well. most people, when they think about cutting Government spending, they think in terms of eliminating necessary programs or wiping out something, some service that Government is supposed to perform. I believe that there is enough extravagance and fat in government. As a matter of fact, one of the secretaries of HEW under Mr. Carter testified that he thought there was $7 billion worth of fraud and waste in welfare and in the medical programs associated with it. We've had the Central Accounting. Office estimate that there is probably tens of billions of dollars that is lost in fraud alone, and they have added that waste adds even more to that. We have a program for a gradual reduction of Government spending based on these theories, and I have a task force now that has been working on where those cuts could be made. I'm confident that it can be done and that it will reduce inflation because I did it in California. And inflation went down below the national average in California when we returned the money to the people and reduced Government spending.

MR. SMITH: President Carter.

MR. CARTER: Governor Reagan's proposal, the Reagan-Kemp-Roth proposal, is one of the most highly inflationary ideas that ever has been presented to the American public. He would actually have to cut Government spending by at least $130 billion in order to balance the budget under this ridiculous proposal. I notice that his task force that is working for his future plans had some of their ideas revealed in The Wall Street Journal this week. One of those ideas was to repeal the minimum wage, and several times this year, Governor Reagan has said that the major cause of unemployment is the minimum wage. This is a heartless kind of approach to the working families of our country, which is typical of many Republican leaders of the past, but, I think, has been accentuated under Governor Reagan. In California - I'm surprised Governor Reagan brought this up - he had the three largest tax increases in the history of that state under his administration. He more than doubled state spending while he was Governor - 122% increase - and had between a 20% and 30% increase in the number of employees

MR. SMITH: Sorry to interrupt, Mr. Carter.

MR. CARTER: in California. Thank you, sir.

MR. SMITH: Governor Reagan has the last word on this question.

MR. REAGAN: Yes. The figures that the President has just used about California is a distortion of the situation there, because while I was Governor of California, our spending in California increased less per capita than the spending in Georgia while Mr. Carter was Governor of Georgia in the same four years. The size of government increased only one-sixth in California of what it increased in proportion to the population in Georgia. And the idea that my tax-cut proposal is inflationary: I would like to ask the President why is it inflationary to let the people keep more of their money and spend it the way that they like, and it isn't inflationary to let him take that money and spend it the way he wants?

MR. SMITH: I wish that question need not be rhetorical, but it must be because we've run out of time on that. Now, the third question to Governor Reagan from William Hilliard.

WILLIAM HILLIARD, PORTLAND OREGONIAN: Yes. Governor Reagan, the decline of our cities has been hastened by the continual rise in crime, strained race relations, the fall in the quality of public education, persistence of abnormal poverty in a rich nation, and a decline in the services to the public. The signs seem to point toward a deterioration that could lead to the establishment of a permanent underclass in the cities. What, specifically, would you do in the next four years to reverse this trend?

MR. REAGAN: I have been talking to a number of Congressmen who have much the same idea that I have, and that is that in the inner city areas, that in cooperation with the local government and the national Government, and using tax incentives and with cooperating with the private sector, that we have development zones. Let the local entity, the city, declare this particular area, based on the standards of the percentage of people on welfare, unemployed, and so forth, in that area. And then, through tax incentives, induce the creation of businesses providing jobs and so forth in those areas. The elements of government through these tax incentives For example, a business that would not have, for a period of time, an increase in the property tax reflecting its development of the unused property that it was making wouldn't be any loss to the city because the city isn't getting any tax from that now. And there would simply be a delay, and on the other hand, many of the people who would then be given jobs are presently wards of the Government and it wouldn't hurt to give them a tax incentive, because they... that wouldn't be costing Government anything either. I think there are things to do in this regard. I stood in the South Bronx on the exact spot that President Carter stood on in 1977. You have to see it to believe it. It looks like a bombed-out city - great, gaunt skeletons of buildings. Windows smashed out, painted on one of them "Unkept promises;" on another, "Despair." And this was the spot at which President Carter had promised that he was going to bring in a vast program to rebuild this department. There are whole or this area there are whole blocks of land that are left bare, just bulldozed down flat. And nothing has been done, and they are now charging to take tourists there to see this terrible desolation. I talked to a man just briefly there who asked me one simple question: "Do I have reason to hope that I can someday take care of my family again? Nothing has been done."

MR. SMITH: Follow-up. Mr. Hilliard:

MR. HILLIARD: Yes. Governor Reagan. Blacks and other non-whites are increasing. in numbers in our cities. Many of them feel that they are facing a hostility from whites that prevents them from joining the economic mainstream of our society. There is racial confrontation in the schools, on jobs, and in housing, as non-whites seek to reap the benefits of a free society. What do you think is the nation's future as a multi-racial society?

MR. REAGAN: I believe in it. I am eternally optimistic, and I happen to believe that we've made great progress from the days when I was young and when this country didn't even know it had a racial problem. I know those things can grow out of despair in an inner city, when there's hopelessness at home, lack of work, and so forth. But I believe that all of us together, and I believe the Presidency is what Teddy Roosevelt said it was. It's a bully pulpit. And I think that something can be done from there, because a goal for all of us should be that one day, things will be done neither because of nor in spite of any of the differences between us - ethnic differences or racial differences, whatever they may be - that we will have total equal opportunity for all people. And I would do everything I could in my power to bring that about.

MR. SMITH: Mr. Hilliard, would you repeat your question for President Carter?

MR. HILLIARD: President Carter. the decline of our cities has been hastened by the continual rise in crime, strained race relations, the fall in the quality of public education, persistence of abnormal poverty in a rich nation, and a decline in services to the public. The signs seem to point toward deterioration that could lead to the establishment of a permanent underclass in the cities. What, specifically, would you do in the next four years to reverse this trend.

MR. CARTER: Thank you, Mr. Hilliard. When I was campaigning in 1976, everywhere I went, the mayors and local officials were in despair about the rapidly deteriorating central cities of our nation. We initiated a very fine urban renewal program, working with the mayors, the governors, and other interested officials. This has been a very successful effort. That's one of the main reasons that we've had such an increase in the number of people employed. Of the nine million people put to work in new jobs since I've been in office, 1.3 million of those has been among black Americans, and another million among those who speak Spanish. We now are planning to continue the revitalization program with increased commitments of rapid transit, mass transit. Under the windfall profits tax, we expect to spend about $43 billion in the next 10 years to rebuild the transportation systems of our country. We also are pursuing housing programs. We've had a 73% increase in the allotment of Federal funds for improved education. These are the kinds of efforts worked on a joint basis with community leaders, particularly in the minority areas of the central cities that have been deteriorating so rapidly in the past. It's very important to us that this be done with the full involvement of minority citizens. I have brought into the top level, top levels of government, into the White House, into administrative offices of the Executive branch, into the judicial system, highly qualified black and Spanish citizens and women who in the past had been excluded. I noticed that Governor Reagan said that when he was a young man that there was no knowledge of a racial problem in this country. Those who suffered from discrimination because of race or sex certainly knew we had a racial problem. We have gone a long way toward correcting these problems, but we still have a long way to go.

MR. SMITH: Follow-up question?

MR. HILLIARD: Yes. President Carter, I would like to repeat the same follow-up to you. Blacks and other non-whites are increasing in numbers in our cities. Many of them feel that they are facing a hostility from whites that prevents them from joining the economic mainstream of our society. There is racial confrontation in the schools, on jobs, and in housing, as non-whites seek to reap the benefits of a free society. What is your assessment of the nation's future as a multi-racial society?

MR. CARTER: Ours is a nation of refugees, a nation of immigrants. Almost all of our citizens came here from other lands and now have hopes, which are being realized, for a better life, preserving their ethnic commitments, their family structures, their religious beliefs, preserving their relationships with their relatives in foreign countries, but still holding themselves together in a very coherent society, which gives our nation its strength. In the past, those minority groups have often been excluded from participation in the affairs of government. Since I've been President, I've appointed, for instance, more than twice as many black Federal judges as all previous presidents in the history of this country. I've done the same thing in the appointment of women, and also Spanish-speaking Americans. To involve them in the administration of government and the feeling that they belong to the societal structure that makes decisions in the judiciary and in the executive branch is a very important commitment which I am trying to realize and will continue to do so in the future.

MR. SMITH: Governor Reagan, you have a minute for rebuttal.

MR. REAGAN: Yes. The President talks of Government programs, and they have their place. But as governor, when I was at that end of the line and receiving some of these grants for Government programs, I saw that so many of them were dead-end. They were public employment that these people who really want to get out into the private job market where there are jobs with a future. Now, the President spoke a moment ago about that I was against the minimum wage. I wish he could have been with me when I sat with a group of teenagers who were black, and who were telling me about their unemployment problems, and that it was the minimum wage that had done away with the jobs that they once could get. And indeed, every time it has increased you will find there is an increase in minority unemployment among young people. And therefore, I have been in favor of a separate minimum for them. With regard to the great progress that has been made with this Government spending, the rate of black unemployment in Detroit, Michigan, is 56%.

MR. SMITH: President Carter, you have the last word on this question.

MR. CARTER: It's obvious that we still have a long way to go in fully incorporating the minority groups into the mainstream of American life. We have made good progress, and there is no doubt in my mind that the commitment to unemployment compensation, the minimum wage, welfare, national health insurance, those kinds of commitments that have typified the Democratic party since ancient history in this country's political life are a very important element of the future. In all those elements, Governor Reagan has repeatedly spoken out against them, which, to me, shows a very great insensitivity to giving deprived families a better chance in life. This, to me, is a very important difference between him and me in this election, and I believe the American people will judge accordingly. There is no doubt in my mind that in the downtown central cities, with the, with the new commitment on an energy policy, with a chance to revitalize homes and to make them more fuel efficient, with a chance for our synthetic fuels program, solar power, this will give us an additional opportunity for jobs which will pay rich dividends.

MR. SMITH: Now, a question from Barbara Walters.

BARBARA WALTERS: Mr. President, the eyes of the country tonight are on the hostages in Iran. I realize this is a sensitive area, but the question of how we respond to acts of terrorism goes beyond this current crisis. Other countries have policies that determine how they will respond. Israel, for example, considers hostages like soldiers and will not negotiate with terrorists. For the future, Mr. President, the country has a right to know, do you have a policy for dealing with terrorism wherever it might happen, and, what have we learned from this experience in Iran that might cause us to do things differently if this, or something similar, happens again?

MR. CARTER: Barbara, one of the blights on this world is the threat and the activities of terrorists. At one of the recent economic summit conferences between myself and the other leaders of the western world, we committed ourselves to take strong action against terrorism. Airplane hijacking was one of the elements of that commitment. There is no doubt that we have seen in recent years - in recent months - additional acts of violence against Jews in France and, of course, against those who live in Israel, by the PLO and other terrorist organizations. Ultimately, the most serious terrorist threat is if one of those radical nations, who believe in terrorism as a policy, should have atomic weapons. Both I and all my predecessors have had a deep commitment to controlling the proliferation of nuclear weapons. In countries like Libya or Iraq, we have even alienated some of our closest trade partners because we have insisted upon the control of the spread of nuclear weapons to those potentially terrorist countries. When Governor Reagan has been asked about that, he makes the very disturbing comment that non-proliferation, or the control of the spread of nuclear weapons, is none of our business. And recently when he was asked specifically about Iraq, he said there is nothing we can do about it. This ultimate terrorist threat is the most fearsome of all, and it's part of a pattern where our country must stand firm to control terrorism of all kinds.

MR. SMITH: Ms. Walters, a follow up?

MS. WALTERS: While we are discussing policy, had Iran not taken American hostages. I assume that, in order to preserve our neutrality, we would have stopped the flow of spare parts and vital war materials once war broke out between Iraq and Iran. Now we're offering to lift the ban on such goods if they let our people come home. Doesn't this reward terrorism, compromise our neutrality, and possibly antagonize nations now friendly to us in the Middle East?

MR. CARTER: We will maintain our position of neutrality in the Iran and Iraq war. We have no plans to sell additional materiel or goods to Iran, that might be of a warlike nature. When I made my decision to stop all trade with Iran as a result of the taking of our hostages, I announced then, and have consistently maintained since then, that if the hostages are released safely, we would make delivery on those items which Iran owns - which they have bought and paid for - also, that the frozen Iranian assets would be released. That's been a consistent policy, one I intend to carry out.

MR. SMITH: Would you repeat the question now for Governor Reagan, please, Ms. Walters?

MS. WALTERS: Yes. Governor, the eyes of the country tonight remain on the hostages in Iran, but the question of how we respond to acts of terrorism goes beyond this current crisis. There are other countries that have policies that determine how they will respond. Israel, for example, considers hostages like soldiers and will not negotiate with terrorists. For the future, the country has the right to know, do you have a policy for dealing with terrorism wherever it might happen, and what have we learned from this experience in Iran that might cause us to do things differently if this, or something similar, should happen again?

MR. REAGAN: Barbara, you've asked that question twice. I think you ought to have at least one answer to it. I have been accused lately of having a secret plan with regard to the hostages. Now, this comes from an answer that I've made at least 50 times during this campaign to the press, when I am asked have you any ideas of what you would do if you were there? And I said, well, yes. And I think that anyone that's seeking this position, as well as other people, probably, have thought to themselves, what about this, what about that? These are just ideas of what I would think of if I were in that position and had access to the information, and which I would know all the options that were open to me. I have never answered the question, however; second, the one that says, well, tell me, what are some of those ideas? First of all, I would be fearful that I might say something that was presently under way or in negotiations, and thus expose it and endanger the hostages, and sometimes, I think some of my ideas might require quiet diplomacy where you don't say in advance, or say to anyone, what it is you're thinking of doing. Your question is difficult to answer, because, in the situation right now, no one wants to say anything that would inadvertently delay, in any way, the return of those hostages if there if there is a chance that they're coming home soon, or that might cause them harm. What I do think should be done, once they are safely here with their families, and that tragedy is over - we've endured this humiliation for just lacking one week of a year now - then, I think, it is time for us to have a complete investigation as to the diplomatic efforts that were made in the beginning, why they have been there so long, and when they came home, what did we have to do in order to bring that about - what arrangements were made? And I would suggest that Congress should hold such an investigation. In the meantime, I'm going to continue praying that they'll come home.

MR. SMITH: Follow up question.

MS. WALTERS: I would like to say that neither candidate answered specifically the question of a specific policy for dealing with terrorism, but I will ask Governor Reagan a different follow-up question. You have suggested that there would be no Iranian crisis had you been President, because we would have given firmer support to the Shah. But Iran is a country of 37 million people who are resisting a government that they regarded as dictatorial. My question is not whether the Shah's regime was preferable to the Ayatollah's, but whether the United States has the power or the right to try to determine what form of government any country will have, and do we back unpopular regimes whose major merit is that they are friendly to the United States?

MR. REAGAN: The degree of unpopularity of a regime when the choice is total authoritarianism totalitarianism, I should say, in the alternative government, makes one wonder whether you are being helpful to the people. And we've been guilty of that. Because someone didn't meet exactly our standards of human rights, even though they were an ally of ours, instead of trying patiently to persuade them to change their ways, we have, in a number of instances, aided a revolutionary overthrow which results in complete totalitarianism, instead, for those people. I think that this is a kind of a hypocritical policy when, at the same time, we're maintaining a detente with the one nation in the world where there are no human rights at all - the Soviet Union. Now, there was a second phase in the Iranian affair in which we had something to do with that. And that was, we had adequate warning that there was a threat to our embassy, and we could have done what other embassies did - either strengthen our security there, or remove our personnel before the kidnap and the takeover took place.

MR. SMITH: Governor, I'm sorry, I must interrupt. President Carter, you have a minute for rebuttal.

MR. CARTER: I didn't hear any comment from Governor Reagan about what he would do to stop or reduce terrorism in the future. What the Western allies did decide to do is to stop all air flights - commercial air flights - to any nation involved in terrorism or the hijacking of air planes, or the harboring of hijackers. Secondly, we all committed ourselves, as have all my predecessors in the Oval Office not to permit the spread of nuclear weapons to a terrorist nation, or to any other nation that does not presently have those weapons or capabilities for explosives. Third, not to make any sales of materiel or weapons to a nation which is involved in terrorist activities. And, lastly, not to deal with the PLO until and unless the PLO recognizes Israel's right to exist and recognizes UN Resolution 242 as a basis for Middle East peace. These are a few of the things to which our nation is committed, and we will continue with these commitments.

MR. SMITH: Governor Reagan, you have the last word on that question.

MR. REAGAN: Yes. I have no quarrel whatsoever with the things that have been done, because I believe it is high time that the civilized countries of the world made it plain that there is no room worldwide for terrorism; there will be no negotiation with terrorists of any kind. And while I have a last word here, I would like to correct a misstatement of fact by the President. I have never made the statement that he suggested about nuclear proliferation and nuclear proliferation, or the trying to halt it, would be a major part of a foreign policy of mine.

MR. SMITH: Thank you gentlemen. That is the first half of the debate. Now, the rules for the second half are quite simple. They're only complicated when I explain them. In the second half, the panelists with me will have no follow-up questions. Instead, after the panelists have asked a question, and the candidates have answered, each of the candidates will have two opportunities to follow up,. to question, to rebut, or just to comment on his opponent's statement. Governor Reagan will respond, in this section, to the first question from Marvin Stone.

MR. STONE: Governor Reagan - arms control: The President said it was the single most important issue. Both of you have expressed the desire to end the nuclear arms race with Russia, but by methods that are vastly different. You suggest that we scrap the SALT II treaty already negotiated, and intensify the build-up of American power to induce the Soviets to sign a new treaty - one more favorable to us. President Carter, on the other hand, says he will again try to convince a reluctant Congress to ratify the present treaty on the grounds it's the best we can hope to get. Now, both of you cannot be right. Will you tell us why you think you are?

MR. REAGAN: Yes. I think I'm right because I believe that we must have a consistent foreign policy, a strong America, and a strong economy. And then, as we build up our national security, to restore our margin of safety, we at the same time try to restrain the Soviet build-up, which has been going forward at a rapid pace, and for quite some time. The SALT II treaty was the result of negotiations that Mr. Carter's team entered into after he had asked the Soviet Union for a discussion of actual reduction of nuclear strategic weapons. And his emissary, I think, came home in 12 hours having heard a very definite nyet. But taking that one no from the Soviet Union, we then went back into negotiations on their terms, because Mr. Carter had canceled the B-I bomber, delayed the MX, delayed the Trident submarine, delayed the cruise missile, shut down the Missile Man - the three - the Minuteman missile production line, and whatever other things that might have been done. The Soviet Union sat at the table knowing that we had gone forward with unilateral concessions without any reciprocation from them whatsoever. Now, I have not blocked the SALT II treaty, as Mr. Carter and Mr. Mondale suggest I have. It has been blocked by a Senate in which there is a Democratic majority. Indeed, the Senate Armed Services Committee voted 10 to 0, with seven abstentions, against the SALT II treaty, and declared that it was not in the national security interests of the United States. Besides which, it is illegal, because the law of the land, passed by Congress, says that we cannot accept a treaty in which we are not equal. And we are not equal in this treaty for one reason alone - our B-2 bombers are considered to be strategic weapons; their Backfire bombers are not.

MR. SMITH: Governor, I have to interrupt you at that point. The time is up for that. But the same question now to President Carter.

MR. STONE: Yes. President Carter, both of you have expressed the desire to end the nuclear arms race with Russia, but through vastly different methods. The Governor suggests we scrap the SALT II treaty which you negotiated in Vienna or signed in Vienna, intensify the build-up of American power to induce the Soviets to sign a new treaty, one more favorable to us. You, on the other hand, say you will again try to convince a reluctant Congress to ratify the present treaty on the grounds it is the best we can hope to get from the Russians. You cannot both be right. Will you tell us why you think you are?

MR. CARTER: Yes, I'd be glad to. Inflation. unemployment, the cities are all very important issues, but they pale into insignificance in the life and duties of a President when compared with the control of nuclear weapons. Every President who has served in the Oval Office since Harry Truman has been dedicated to the proposition of controlling nuclear weapons. To negotiate with the Soviet Union a balanced, controlled, observable, and then reducing levels of atomic weaponry, there is a disturbing pattern in the attitude of Governor Reagan. He has never supported any of those arms control agreements - the limited test ban, SALT I, nor the Antiballistic Missile Treaty, nor the Vladivostok Treaty negotiated with the Soviet Union by President Ford - and now he wants to throw into the wastebasket a treaty to control nuclear weapons on a balanced and equal basis between ourselves and the Soviet Union, negotiated over a seven-year period, by myself and my two Republican predecessors. The Senate has not voted yet on the Strategic Arms Limitation Treaty. There have been preliminary skirmishing in the committees of the Senate, but the Treaty has never come to the floor of the Senate for either a debate or a vote. It's understandable that a Senator in the preliminary debates can make an irresponsible statement, or, maybe, an ill-advised statement. You've got 99 other senators to correct that mistake, if it is a mistake. But when a man who hopes to be President says, take this treaty, discard it, do not vote, do not debate, do not explore the issues, do not finally capitalize on this long negotiation - that is a very dangerous and disturbing thing.

MR. SMITH: Governor Reagan, you have an opportunity to rebut that. REAGAN: Yes, I'd like to respond very much. First of all, the Soviet Union if I have been critical of some of the previous agreements, it's because we've been out-negotiated for quite a long time. And they have managed, in spite of all of our attempts at arms limitation, to go forward with the biggest military build-up in the history of man. Now, to suggest that because two Republican presidents tried to pass the SALT treaty - that puts them on its side - I would like to say that President Ford, who was within 90% of a treaty that we could be in agreement with when he left office, is emphatically against this SALT treaty. I would like to point out also that senators like Henry Jackson and Hollings of South Carolina - they are taking the lead in the fight against this particular treaty. I am not talking of scrapping. I am talking of taking the treaty back, and going back into negotiations. And I would say to the Soviet Union, we will sit and negotiate with you as long as it takes, to have not only legitimate arms limitation, but to have a reduction of these nuclear weapons to the point that neither one of us represents a threat to the other. That is hardly throwing away a treaty and being opposed to arms limitation.

MR. SMITH: President Carter?

MR. CARTER: Yes. Governor Reagan is making some very misleading and disturbing statements. He not only advocates the scrapping of this treaty - and I don't know that these men that he quotes are against the treaty in its final form - but he also advocates the possibility, he said it's been a missing element, of playing a trump card against the Soviet Union of a nuclear arms race, and is insisting upon nuclear superiority by our own nation, as a predication for negotiation in the future with the Soviet Union. If President Brezhnev said, we will scrap this treaty, negotiated under three American Presidents over a seven-year period of time, we insist upon nuclear superiority as a basis for future negotiations, and we believe that the launching of a nuclear arms race is a good basis for future negotiations, it's obvious that I, as President, and all Americans, would reject such a proposition. This would mean the resumption of a very dangerous nuclear arms race. It would be very disturbing to American people. It would change the basic tone and commitment that our nation has experienced ever since the Second World War, with al Presidents, Democratic and Republican. And it would also be very disturbing to our allies, all of whom support this nuclear arms treaty. In addition to that, the adversarial relationship between ourselves and the Soviet Union would undoubtedly deteriorate very rapidly. This attitude is extremely dangerous and belligerent in its tone, although it's said with a quiet voice.

MR. SMITH: Governor Reagan?

MR. REAGAN: I know the President's supposed to be replying to me, but sometimes, I have a hard time in connecting what he's saying, with what I have said or what my positions are. I sometimes think he's like the witch doctor that gets mad when a good doctor comes along with a cure that'll work. My point I have made already, Mr. President, with regard to negotiating: it does not call for nuclear superiority on the part of the United States. It calls for a mutual reduction of these weapons, as I say, that neither of us can represent a threat to the other. And to suggest that the SALT II treaty that your negotiators negotiated was just a continuation, and based on all of the preceding efforts by two previous Presidents, is just not true. It was a new negotiation because, as I say, President Ford was within about 10% of having a solution that could be acceptable. And I think our allies would be very happy to go along with a fair and verifiable SALT agreement.

MR. SMITH: President Carter, you have the last word on this question.

MR. CARTER: I think, to close out this discussion, it would be better to put into perspective what we're talking about. I had a discussion with my daughter, Amy, the other day, before I came here, to ask her what the most important issue was. She said she thought nuclear weaponry - and the control of nuclear arms. This is a formidable force. Some of these weapons have 10 megatons of explosion. If you put 50 tons of TNT in each one of railroad cars, you would have a carload of TNT - a trainload of TNT stretching across this nation. That's one major war explosion in a warhead. We have thousands, equivalent of megaton, or million tons, of TNT warheads. The control of these weapons is the single major responsibility of a President, and to cast out this commitment of all Presidents, because of some slight technicalities that can be corrected, is a very dangerous approach.

MR. SMITH: We have to go to another question now, from Harry Ellis to President Carter.

HARRY ELLIS: Mr. President, as you have said, Americans, through conservation, are importing much less oil today than we were even a year ago. Yet U.S. dependence on Arab oil as a percentage of total imports is today much higher than it was at the time of the 1973 Arab oil embargo, and for some time to came, the loss of substantial amounts of Arab oil could plunge the U.S. into depression. This means that a bridge must be built out of this dependence. Can the United States develop synthetic fuels and other alternative energy sources without damage to the environment, and will this process mean steadily higher fuel bills for American families?

MR. CARTER: I don't think there's any doubt that, in the future, the cost of oil is going to go up. What I've had as a basic commitment since I've been President is to reduce our dependence on foreign oil. It can only be done in two ways: one, to conserve energy - to stop the waste of energy - and, secondly, to produce more American energy. We've been very successful in both cases. We've now reduced the importing of foreign oil in the last year alone by one-third. We imported today 2 million barrels of oil less than we did the same date just a year ago. This commitment has been opening up a very bright vista for our nation in the future, because with the windfall profits tax as a base, we now have an opportunity to use American technology and American ability and American natural resources to expand rapidly the production of synthetic fuels, yes; to expand rapidly the production of solar energy, yes; and also to produce the traditional kinds of American energy. We will drill more oil and gas wells this year than any year in history. We'll produce more coal this year than any year in history. We are exporting more coal this year than any year in history. And we have an opportunity now with improved transportation systems and improved loading facilities in our ports, to see a very good opportunity on a world international market, to replace OPEC oil with American coal as a basic energy source. This exciting future will not only give us more energy security, but will also open up vast opportunities for Americans to live a better life and to have millions of new jobs associated with this new and very dynamic industry now in prospect because of the new energy policy that we've put into effect.

MR. SMITH: Would you repeat the question now for Governor Reagan?

MR. ELLIS: Governor Reagan, Americans, through conservation, are importing much less oil today than we were even a year ago. And yet, U.S. reliance on Arab oil as a percentage of total imports is much higher today than it was during the 1973 Arab oil embargo. And the substantial loss of Arab oil could plunge the United States into depression. The question is whether the development of alternative energy sources, in order to reduce this dependence, can be done without damaging the environment, and will it mean for American families steadily higher fuel bills?

MR. REAGAN: I'm not so sure that it means steadily higher fuel costs, but I do believe that this nation has been portrayed for too long a time to the people as being energy-poor when it is energy-rich. The coal that the President mentioned - yes, we have it - and yet one-eighth of our total coal resources is not being utilized at all right now. The mines are closed down; there are 22000 miners out of work. Most of this is due to regulations which either interfere with the mining of it or prevent the burning of it:. With our modern technology, yes, we can burn our coal within the limits of the Clean Air Act. I think, as technology improves, we'll be able to do even better with that. The other thing is that we have only leased out - begun to explore - 2% of our outer continental shelf for oil, where it is believed, by everyone familiar with that fuel and that source of energy, that there are vast supplies yet to be found. Our Government has, in the last year or so, taken out of multiple use millions of acres of public lands that once were - well, they were public lands subject to multiple use - exploration for minerals and so forth. It is believed that probably 70% of the potential oil in the United States is probably hidden in those lands, and no one is allowed to even go and explore to find out if it is there. This is particularly true of the recent efforts to shut down part of Alaska. Nuclear power: There were 36 power plants planned in this country. And let me add the word safety; it must be done with the utmost of safety. But 32 of those have given up and canceled their plans to build, and again, because Government regulations and permits, and so forth, take - make it take - more than twice as long to build a nuclear plant in the United States as it does to build one in Japan or in Western Europe. We have the sources here. We are energy rich, and coal is one of the great potentials we have.

MR. SMITH: President Carter, your comment?

MR. CARTER: To repeat myself, we have this year the opportunity, which we'll realize, to produce 800 million tons of coal - an unequaled record in the history of our country. Governor Reagan says that this is not a good achievement, and he blames restraints on coal production on regulations - regulations that affect the life and the health and safety of miners, and also regulations that protect the purity of our air and the quality our water and our land. We cannot cast aside these regulations. We have a chance in the next 15 years, insisting upon the health and safety of workers in the mines, and also preserving the same high air and water pollution standards, to triple the amount of coal we produce. Governor Reagan's approach to our energy policy, which has already proven its effectiveness, is to repeal, or to change substantially, the windfall profits tax - to return a major portion of $227 billion back to the oil companies; to do away with the Department of Energy; to short-circuit our synthetic fuels program; to put a minimal emphasis on solar power; to emphasize strongly nuclear power plants as a major source of energy in the future. He wants to put all our eggs in one basket and give that basket to the major oil companies.

MR. SMITH: Governor Reagan.

MR. REAGAN: That is a misstatement, of course, of my position. I just happen to believe that free enterprise can do a better job of producing the things that people need than government can. The Department of Energy has a multi-billion-dollar budget in excess of $10 billion. It hasn't produced a quart of oil or a lump of coal, or anything else in the line of energy. And for Mr. Carter to suggest that I want to do away with the safety laws and with the laws that pertain to clean water and clean air, and so forth. As Governor of California, I took charge of passing the strictest air pollution laws in the United States - the strictest air quality law that has even been adopted in the United States. And we created an OSHA - an Occupational Safety and Health Agency - for the protection of employees before the Federal Government had one in place. And to this day, not one of its decisions or rulings has ever been challenged. So, I think some of those charges are missing the point. I am suggesting that there are literally thousands of unnecessary regulations that invade every facet of business, and indeed, very much of our personal lives, that are unnecessary; that Government can do without; that have added $130 billion to the cost of production in this country; and that are contributing their part to inflation. And I would like to see us a little more free, as we once were.

MR. SMITH: President Carter, another crack at that?

MR. CARTER: Sure. As a matter of fact,. the air pollution standard laws that were passed in California were passed over the objections of Governor Reagan, and this is a very well-known fact. Also, recently, when someone suggested that the Occupational Safety and Health Act should be abolished, Governor Reagan responded, amen. The offshore drilling rights is a question that Governor Reagan raises often. As a matter of fact, in the proposal for the Alaska lands legislation, 100% of all the offshore lands would be open for exploration, and 95% of all the Alaska lands, where it is suspected or believed that minerals might exist. We have, with our five-year plan for the leasing of offshore lands, proposed more land to be drilled than has been opened up for drilling since this program first started in 1954. So we're not putting restraints on American exploration, we're encouraging it in every way we can.

MR. SMITH: Governor Reagan, you have the last word on this question.

MR. REAGAN: Yes. If it is a well-known fact that I opposed air pollution laws in California, the only thing I can possibly think of is that the President must be suggesting the law that the Federal Government tried to impose on the State of California - not a law, but regulations - that would have made it impossible to drive an automobile within the city limits of any California city, or to have a place to put it if you did drive it against their regulations. It would have destroyed the economy of California, and, I must say, we had the support of Congress when we pointed out how ridiculous this attempt was by the Environmental Protection Agency. We still have the strictest air control, or air pollution laws in the country. As for offshore oiling, only 2% now is so leased and is producing oil. The rest, as to whether the lands are going to be opened in the next five years or so - we're already five years behind in what we should be doing. There is more oil now, in the wells that have been drilled, than has been taken out in 121 years that they've been drilled.

MR. SMITH: Thank you Governor. Thank you, Mr. President. The next question goes to Governor Reagan from William Hilliard.

MR. HILLIARD: Governor Reagan, wage earners in this country - especially the young - are supporting a Social Security system that continues to affect their income drastically. The system is fostering a struggle between the young and the old, and is drifting the country toward a polarization of these two groups. How much longer can the young wage earner expect to bear the ever-increasing burden of the Social Security system?

MR. REAGAN: The Social Security system was based on a false premise, with regard to how fast the number of workers would increase and how fast the number of retirees would increase. It is actuarially out of balance, and this first became evident about 16 years ago, and some of us were voicing warnings then. Now, it is trillions of dollars out of balance, and the only answer that has come so far is the biggest single tax increase in our nation's history - the payroll tax increase for Social Security - which will only put a band-aid on this and postpone the day of reckoning by a few years at most. What is needed is a study that I have proposed by a task force of experts to look into this entire problem as to how it can be reformed and made actuarially sound, but with the premise that no one presently dependent on Social Security is going to have the rug pulled out from under them and not get their check. We cannot frighten, as we have with the threats and the campaign rhetoric that has gone on in this campaign, our senior citizens - leave them thinking that in some way, they're endangered and they would have no place to turn. They must continue to get those checks, and I believe that the system can be put on a sound actuarial basis. But it's going to take some study and some work, and not just passing a tax increase to let the load - or the roof - fall in on the next administration.

MR. SMITH: Would you repeat that question for President Carter?

MR. HILLIARD: Yes. President Carter, wage earners in this country, especially the young, are supporting a Social Security System that continues to affect their income drastically. The system is fostering a struggle between young and old and is drifting the country toward a polarization of these two groups. How much longer can the young wage earner expect to bear the ever-increasing burden of the Social Security System?

MR. CARTER: As long as there is a Democratic President in the White House, we will have a strong and viable Social Security System, free of the threat of bankruptcy. Although Governor Reagan has changed his position lately, on four different occasions, he has advocated making Social Security a voluntary system, which would, in effect, very quickly bankrupt it. I noticed also in The Wall Street Journal early this week, that a preliminary report of his task force advocates making Social Security more sound by reducing the adjustment in Social Security for the retired people to compensate for the impact of inflation. These kinds of approaches are very dangerous to the security, the well being and the peace of mind of the retired people of this country and those approaching retirement age. But no matter what it takes in the future to keep Social Security sound, it must be kept that way. And although there was a serious threat to the Social Security System and its integrity during the 1976 campaign and when I became President, the action of the Democratic Congress working with me has been to put Social Security back on a sound financial basis. That is the way it will stay.

MR. SMITH: Governor Reagan?

MR. REAGAN: Well, that just isn't true. It has, as I said, delayed the actuarial imbalance falling on us for just a few years with that increase in taxes, and I don't believe we can go on increasing the tax, because the problem for the young people today is that they are paying in far more than they can ever expect to get out. Now, again this statement that somehow, I wanted to destroy it and I just changed my tune, that I am for voluntary Social Security, which would mean the ruin of it. Mr. President, the voluntary thing that I suggested many years ago was that with a young man orphaned and raised by an aunt who died, his aunt was ineligible for Social Security insurance because she was not his mother. And I suggested that if this is an insurance program, certainly the person who is paying in should be able to name his own beneficiary. That is the closest I have ever come to anything voluntary with Social Security. I, too, am pledged to a Social Security program that will reassure these senior citizens of ours that they are going to continue to get their money. There are some changes that I would like to make. I would like to make a change in the regulation that discriminates against a wife who works and finds that she then is faced with a choice between her father's or her husband's benefits, if he dies first, or what she has paid in; but it does not recognize that she has also been paying in herself, and she is entitled to more than she presently can get. I'd like to change that.

MR. SMITH: President Carter's rebuttal now.

MR. CARTER: These constant suggestions that the basic Social Security System should be changed does call for concern and consternation among the aged of our country. It is obvious that we should have a commitment to them, that Social Security benefits should not be taxed and that there would be no peremptory change in the standards by which Social Security payments are made to retired people. We also need to continue to index Social Security payments, so that if inflation rises, the Social Security payments would rise a commensurate degree to let the buying power of a Social Security check continue intact. In the past, the relationship between Social Security and Medicare has been very important to providing some modicum of aid for senior citizens in the retention of health benefits. Governor Reagan, as a matter of fact, began his political career campaigning around this nation against Medicare. Now, we have an opportunity to move toward national health insurance, with an emphasis on the prevention of disease, an emphasis on out-patient care, not in-patient care; an emphasis on hospital cost containment to hold down the cost of hospital care far those who are ill, an emphasis on catastrophic health insurance, so that if a family is threatened with being wiped out economically because of a very high medical bill, then the insurance would help pay for it. These are the kinds of elements of a national health insurance, important to the American people. Governor Reagan, again, typically is against such a proposal.

MR. SMITH: Governor?

MR. REAGAN: There you go again. When I opposed Medicare, there was another piece of legislation meeting the same problem before the Congress. I happened to favor the other piece of legislation and thought that it would be better for the senior citizens and provide better care than the one that was finally passed. I was not opposing the principle of providing care for them. I was opposing one piece of legislation versus another. There is something else about Social Security. Of course, it doesn't come out of the payroll tax. It comes out of a general fund, but something should be done about it. I think it is disgraceful that the Disability Insurance Fund in Social Security finds checks going every month to tens of thousands of people who are locked up in our institutions for crime or for mental illness, and they are receiving disability checks from Social Security every month while a state institution provides for all of their needs and their care.

MR. SMITH: President Carter, you have the last word on this question.

MR. CARTER: I think this debate on Social Security, Medicare, national health insurance typifies, as vividly any other subject tonight, the basic historical differences between the Democratic Party and Republican Party. The allusions to basic changes in the minimum wage is another, and the deleterious comments that Governor Reagan has made about unemployment compensation. These commitments that the Democratic Party has historically made to the working families of this nation have been extremely important to the growth in their stature and in a better quality of life for them. I noticed recently that Governor Reagan frequently quotes Democratic presidents in his acceptance address. I have never heard a candidate for President, who is a Republican, quote a Republican president, but when they get in office, they try to govern like Republicans. So, it is good fo the American people to remember that there is a sharp basic historical difference between Governor Reagan and me on these crucial issues - also, between the two parties that we represent.

MR. SMITH: Thank you Mr. President, Governor Reagan. We now go to another question - a question to President Carter by Barbara Walters.

MS. WALTERS: Thank you. You have addressed some of the major issues tonight, but the biggest issue in the mind of American voters is yourselves - your ability to lead this country. When many voters go into that booth just a week from today, they will be voting their gut instinct about you men. You have already given us your reasons why people should vote for you, now would you please tell us for this your final question, why they should not vote for your opponent, why his Presidency could be harmful to the nation and, having examined both your opponent's record and the man himself, tell us his greatest weakness.

MR. CARTER: Barbara, reluctant as I am to say anything critical about Governor Reagan, I will try to answer your question. First of all, there is the historical perspective that I just described. This is a contest between a Democrat in the mainstream of my party, as exemplified by the actions that I have taken in the Oval Office the last four years, as contrasted with Governor Reagan, who in most cases does typify his party, but in some cases, there is a radical departure by him from the heritage of Eisenhower and others. The most important crucial difference in this election campaign, in my judgment, is the approach to the control of nuclear weaponry and the inclination to control or not to control the spread of atomic weapons to other nations who don't presently have it, particularly terrorist nations. The inclination that Governor Reagan has exemplified in many troubled times since he has been running for President - I think since 1968 - to inject American military forces in places like North Korea, to put a blockade around Cuba this year, or in some instances, to project American forces into a fishing dispute against the small nation of Ecuador on the west coast of South America. This is typical of his long-standing inclination, on the use of American power, not to resolve disputes diplomatically and peacefully, but to show that the exercise of military power is best proven by the actual use of it. Obviously, no President wants war, and I certainly do not believe that Governor Reagan, if he were President, would want war, but a President in the Oval Office has to make a judgment on almost a daily basis about how to exercise the enormous power of our country for peace, through diplomacy, or in a careless way in a belligerent attitude which has exemplified his attitudes in the past.

MR. SMITH: Barbara, would you repeat the question for Governor Reagan?

MS. WALTERS: Yes, thank you. Realizing that you may be equally reluctant to speak ill of your opponent, may I ask why people should not vote for your opponent, why his Presidency could be harmful to the nation, and having examined both your opponent's record and the man himself, could you tell us his greatest weakness?

MR. REAGAN: Well, Barbara, I believe that there is a fundamental difference - and I think it has been evident in most of the answers that Mr. Carter has given tonight - that he seeks the solution to anything as another opportunity for a Federal Government program. I happen to believe that the Federal Government has usurped powers of autonomy and authority that belong back at the state and local level. It has imposed on the individual freedoms of the people, and there are more of these things that could be solved by the people themselves, if they were given a chance, or by the levels of government that were closer to them. Now, as to why I should be and he shouldn't be, when he was a candidate in 1976,

President Carter invented a thing he called the misery index. He added the rate of unemployment and the rate of inflation, and it came, at that time, to 12.5% under President Ford. He said that no man with that size misery index has a right to seek reelection to the Presidency. Today, by his own decision, the misery index is in excess of 20%, and I think this must suggest something. But, when I had quoted a Democratic President, as the President says, I was a Democrat. I said many foolish things back in those days. But the President that I quoted had made a promise, a Democratic promise, and I quoted him because it was never kept. And today, you would find that that promise is at the very heart of what Republicanism represents in this country today. That's why I believe there are going to be millions of Democrats that are going to vote with us this time around, because they too want that promise kept. It was a promise for less government and less taxes and more freedom for the people.

MR. SMITH: President Carter?

MR. CARTER: I mentioned the radical departure of Governor Reagan from the principles or ideals of historical perspective of his own party. I don't think that can be better illustrated than in the case of guaranteeing women equal rights under the Constitution of our nation. For 40 years, the Republican Party platforms called for guaranteeing women equal rights with a constitutional amendment. Six predecessors of mine who served in the Oval Office called for this guarantee of women's rights. Governor Reagan and his new Republican Party have departed from this commitment - a very severe blow to the opportunity for women to finally correct discrimination under which they have suffered. When a man and a women do the same amount of work, a man gets paid $1.00, a women only gets paid 59 cents. And the equal rights amendment only says that equality of rights shall not be abridged for omen b the Federal Government or by he state governments. That is all it says a simple guarantee of equality of opportunity which typifies the Democratic arty, and which is a very important commitment of mine, as contrasted with Governor Reagan's radical departure from the long-standing policy of his own party.

MR. SMITH: Governor Reagan?

MR. REAGAN: Yes. Mr. President, once again, I happen to be against the amendment, because I think the amendment will take this problem out of the hands of elected legislators and put it in the hands f unelected judges. I am for equal rights, and while you have been in office for four ears and not one single state - and most f them have a majority of Democratic legislators - has added to the ratification r voted to ratify the equal rights amendment. While I was Governor, more than eight years ago, I found 14 separate instances where women were discriminated against in the body of California law, and I had passed and signed into law 14 statutes that eliminated those discriminations, including the economic ones that you have just mentioned - equal pay and so forth. I believe that if in all these years that we have spent trying to get the amendment, that we had spent as much time correcting these laws, as we did in California - and we were the first to do it. If I were President, I would also now take a look at the hundreds of Federal regulations which discriminate against women and which go right on while everyone is looking for an amendment. I would have someone ride herd on those regulations, and we would start eliminating those discriminations in the Federal Government against women.

MR. SMITH: President Carter?

MR. CARTER: Howard, I'm a Southerner, and I share the basic beliefs of my region that an excessive government intrusion into the private affairs of American citizens and also into the private affairs of the free enterprise system. One of the commitments that I made was to deregulate the major industries of this country. We've been remarkably successful, with the help of a Democratic Congress. We have deregulated the air industry, the rail industry, the trucking industry, financial institutions. We're now working on the communications industry. In addition to that, I believe that this element of discrimination is something that the South has seen so vividly as a blight on our region of the country which has now been corrected - not only racial discrimination but discrimination against people that have to work for a living - because we have been trying to pick ourselves up by our bootstraps, since the long depression years, and lead a full and useful life in the affairs of this country. We have made remarkable success. It is part of my consciousness and of my commitment to continue this progress. So, my heritage as a Southerner, my experience in the Oval Office, convinces me that what I have just described is a proper course for the future.

MR. SMITH: Governor Reagan, yours is the last word.

MR. REAGAN: Well, my last word is again to say this: We were talking about this very simple amendment and women's rights. And I make it plain again: I am for women's rights. But I would like to call the attention of the people to the fact that that so-called simple amendment would be used by mischievous men to destroy discriminations that properly belong, by law, to women respecting the physical differences between the two sexes, labor laws that protect them against things that would be physically harmful to them. Those would all, could all be challenged by men. And the same would be true with regard to combat service in the military and so forth. I thought that was the subject we were supposed to be on. But, if we're talking about how much we think about the working people and so forth, I'm the only fellow who ever ran for this job who was six times President of his own union and still has a lifetime membership in that union.

MR. SMITH: Gentlemen, each of you now has three minutes for a closing statement. President Carter, you're first.

MR. CARTER: First of all, I'd like to thank the League of Women Voters for making this debate possible. I think it's been a very constructive debate and I hope it's helped to acquaint the American people with the sharp differences between myself and Governor Reagan. Also, I want to thank the people of Cleveland and Ohio for being such hospitable hosts during these last few hours in my life. I've been President now for almost four years. I've had to make thousands of decisions, and each one of those decisions has been a learning process. I've seen the strength of my nation, and I've seen the crises it approached in a tentative way. And I've had to deal with those crises as best I could. As I've studied the record between myself and Governor Reagan, I've been impressed with the stark differences that exist between us. I think the result of this debate indicates that that fact is true. I consider myself in the mainstream of my party. I consider myself in the mainstream even of the bipartisan list of Presidents who served before me. The United States must be a nation strong; the United States must be a nation secure. We must have a society that's just and fair. And we must extend the benefits of our own commitment to peace, to create a peaceful world. I believe that since I've been in office, there have been six or eight areas of combat evolved in other parts of the world. In each case, I alone have had to determine the interests of my country and the degree of involvement of my country. I've done that with moderation, with care, with thoughtfulness; sometimes consulting experts. But, I've learned in this last three and a half years that when an issue is extremely difficult, when the call is very close, the chances are the experts will be divided almost 50-50. And the final judgment about the future of the nation - war, peace, involvement, reticence, thoughtfulness, care, consideration, concern - has to be made by the man in the Oval Office. It's a lonely job, but with the involvement of the American people in the process, with an open Government, the job is a very gratifying one. The American people now are facing, next Tuesday, a lonely decision. Those listening to my voice will have to make a judgment about the future of this country. And I think they ought to remember that one vote can make a lot of difference. If one vote per precinct had changed in 1960, John Kennedy would never have been President of this nation. And if a few more people had gone to the polls and voted in 1968, Hubert Humphrey would have been President; Richard Nixon would not. There is a partnership involved in our nation. To stay strong, to stay at peace, to raise high the banner of human rights, to set an example for the rest of the world, to let our deep beliefs and commitments be felt by others in other nations, is my plan for the future. I ask the American people to join me in this partnership.

MR. SMITH: Governor Reagan?

MR. REAGAN: Yes, I would like to add my words of thanks, too, to the ladies of the League of Women Voters for making these debates possible. I'm sorry that we couldn't persuade the bringing in of the third candidate, so that he could have been seen also in these debates. But still, it's good that at least once, all three of us were heard by the people of this country. Next Tuesday is Election Day. Next Tuesday all of you will go to the polls, will stand there in the polling place and make a decision. I think when you make that decision, it might be well if you would ask yourself, are you better off than you were four years ago? Is it easier for you to go and buy things in the stores than it was four years ago? Is there more or less unemployment in the country than there was four years ago? Is America as respected throughout the world as it was? Do you feel that our security is as safe, that we're as strong as we were four years ago? And if you answer all of those questions yes, why then, I think your choice is very obvious as to whom you will vote for. If you don't agree, if you don't think that this course that we've been on for the last four years is what you would like to see us follow for the next four, then I could suggest another choice that you have. This country doesn't have to be in the shape that it is in. We do not have to go on sharing in scarcity with the country getting worse off, with unemployment growing. We talk about the unemployment lines. If all of the unemployed today were in a single line allowing two feet for each of them, that line would reach from New York City to Los Angeles, California. All of this can be cured and all of it can be solved. I have not had the experience the President has had in holding that office, but I think in being Governor of California, the most populous state in the Union - if it were a nation, it would be the seventh-ranking economic power in the world - I, too, had some lonely moments and decisions to make. I know that the economic program that I have proposed for this nation in the next few years can resolve many of the problems that trouble us today. I know because we did it there. We cut the cost - the increased cost of government - in half over the eight years. We returned $5.7 billion in tax rebates, credits and cuts to our people. We, as I have said earlier, fell below the national average in inflation when we did that. And I know that we did give back authority and autonomy to the people. I would like to have a crusade today, and I would like to lead that crusade with your help. And it would be one to take Government off the backs of the great people of this country, and turn you loose again to do those things that I know you can do so well, because you did them and made this country great. Thank you.

Chapter 4

Presidential Nomination Acceptance Speeches

4.1　Jimmy Carter's First Presidential Nomination Acceptance Speech

My name is Jimmy Carter, and I'm running for President.

It's been a long time since I said those words the first time, and now I've come here after seeing our great country to accept your nomination.

I accept it, in the words of John F. Kennedy, with a full and grateful heart and with only one obligation: to devote every effort of body, mind and spirit to lead our party back to victory and our nation back to greatness.

It's a pleasure to be here with all you Democrats and to see that our Bicentennial celebration and our Bicentennial convention has been one of decorum and order without any fights or free-for-alls. Among Democrats that can only happen once every two hundred years. With this kind of a united Democratic Party, we are ready, and eager, to take on the Republicans—whichever Republican Party they decide to send against us in November.

Nineteen seventy-six will not be a year of politics as usual. It can be a year of inspiration and hope, and it will be a year of concern, of quiet and sober reassessment of our nation's character and purpose. It has already been a year when voters have confounded the experts. And I guarantee you that it will be the year when we give the government of this country back to the people of this country.

There is a new mood in America. We have been shaken by a tragic war abroad and by scandals and broken promises at home. Our people are searching for new voices and new ideas and new leaders.

Although government has its limits and cannot solve all our problems, we Americans reject the view that we must be reconciled to failures and mediocrity, or to an inferior quality of life. For I believe that we can come through this time of trouble stronger than ever. Like troops who have been in combat, we have been tempered in the fire; we have been disciplined, and we have been educated.

Guided by lasting and simple moral values, we have emerged idealists without illusions, realists who still know the old dreams of justice and liberty, of country and of community.

This year we have had thirty state primaries—more than ever before—making it possible to take our campaign directly to the people of America: to homes and shopping centers, to factory shift lines and colleges, to beauty parlors and barbershops, to farmers' markets and union halls.

This has been a long and personal campaign—a humbling experience, reminding us that ultimate political influence rests not with the power brokers but with the people. This has been a time of tough debate on the important issues facing our country. This kind of debate is part of our tradition, and as Democrats we are heirs to a great tradition.

I have never met a Democratic President, but I have always been a Democrat.

Years ago, as a farm boy sitting outdoors with my family on the ground in the middle of the night, gathered close around a battery radio connected to the automobile battery and listening to the Democratic conventions in far-off cities, I was a long way from the selection process. I feel much closer to it tonight.

Ours is the party of the man who was nominated by those distant conventions and who inspired and restored this nation in its darkest hours—Franklin D. Roosevelt.

Ours is the party of a fighting Democrat who showed us that a common man could be an uncommon leader—Harry S. Truman.

Ours is the party of a brave young President who called the young at heart, regardless of age, to seek a "New Frontier" of national greatness—John F. Kennedy.

And ours is also the party of a great-hearted Texan who took office in a tragic hour and who went on to do more than any other President in this century to advance the cause of human rights—Lyndon Johnson.

Our Party was built out of the sweatshops of the old Lower East Side, the dark mills of New Hampshire, the blazing hearths of Illinois, the coal mines of Pennsylvania, the hard-scrabble farms of the southern coastal plains, and the unlimited frontiers of America.

Ours is the party that welcomed generations of immigrants—the Jews, the

Irish, the Italians, the Poles, and all the others, enlisted them in its ranks and fought the political battles that helped bring them into the American mainstream.

And they have shaped the character of our party.

That is our heritage. Our party has not been perfect. We have made mistakes, and we have paid for them. But ours is a tradition of leadership and compassion and progress.

Our leaders have fought for every piece of progressive legislation, from RFD and REA to Social Security and civil rights. In times of need, the Democrats were there.

But in recent years our nation has seen a failure of leadership. We have been hurt, and we have been disillusioned. We have seen a wall go up that separates us from our own government.

We have lost some precious things that historically have bound our people and our government together. We feel that moral decay has weakened our country, that it is crippled by a lack of goals and values, and that our public officials have lost faith in us.

We have been a nation adrift too long. We have been without leadership too long. We have had divided and deadlocked government too long. We have been governed by veto too long. We have suffered enough at the hands of a tired and worn-out administration without new ideas, without youth or vitality, without vision and without the confidence of the American people. There is a fear that our best years are behind us. But I say to you that our nation's best is still ahead.

Our country has lived through a time of torment. It is now a time for healing. We want to have faith again. We want to be proud again. We just want the truth again.

It is time for the people to run the government, and not the other way around.

It is the time to honor and strengthen our families and our neighborhoods and our diverse cultures and customs.

We need a Democratic President and a Congress to work in harmony for a change, with mutual respect for a change. And next year we are going to have that new leadership. You can depend on it!

It is time for America to move and to speak not with boasting and belligerence but with a quiet strength, to depend in world affairs not merely on the size of an arsenal but on the nobility of ideas, and to govern at home not by confusion and crisis but with grace and imagination and common sense.

Too many have had to suffer at the hands of a political economic elite who have shaped decisions and never had to account for mistakes or to suffer from injustice. When unemployment prevails, they never stand in line looking for a job.

When deprivation results from a confused and bewildering welfare system, they never do without food or clothing or a place to sleep. When the public schools are inferior or torn by strife, their children go to exclusive private schools. And when the bureaucracy is bloated and confused, the powerful always manage to discover and occupy niches of special influence and privilege. An unfair tax structure serves their needs. And tight secrecy always seems to prevent reform.

All of us must be careful not to cheat each other. Too often unholy, selfperpetuating alliances have been formed between money and politics, and the average citizen has been held at arm's length.

Each time our nation has made a serious mistake the American people have been excluded from the process. The tragedy of Vietnam and Cambodia, the disgrace of Watergate, and the embarrassment of the CIA revelations could have been avoided if our government had simply reflected the sound judgement and good common sense and the high moral character of the American people.

It is time for us to take a new look at our own government, to strip away the secrecy, to expose the unwarranted pressure of lobbyists, to eliminate waste, to release our civil servants from bureaucratic chaos, to provide tough management, and always to remember that in any town or city the mayor, the governor, and the President represent exactly the same constituents.

As a governor, I had to deal each day with the complicated and confused and overlapping and wasteful federal government bureaucracy. As President, I want you to help me evolve an efficient, economical, purposeful, and manageable government for our nation. Now, I recognize the difficulty, but if I'm elected, it's going to be done. And you can depend on it!

We must strengthen the government closest to the people. Business, labor, agriculture, education, science, and government should not struggle in isolation from one another but should be able to strive toward mutual goals and shared opportunities. We should make major investments in people and not in buildings and weapons. The poor, the aged, the weak, the afflicted must be treated with respect and compassion and with love.

I have spoken a lot of times this year about love. But love must be aggressively translated into simple justice. The test of any government is not how popular it is with the powerful but how honestly and fairly it deals with those who must depend on it.

It is time for a complete overhaul of our income tax system. I still tell you: It is a disgrace to the human race. All my life I have heard promises about tax reform, but it never quite happens. With your help, we are finally going to make it happen. And you can depend on it.

Here is something that can really help our country: It is time for universal voter registration.

It is time for a nationwide comprehensive health program for all our people.

It is time to guarantee an end to discrimination because of race or sex by full involvement in the decision making process of government by those who know what it is to suffer from discrimination. And they'll be in the government if I am elected.

It is time for the law to be enforced. We cannot educate children, we cannot create harmony among our people, we cannot preserve basic human freedom unless we have an orderly society.

Crime and lack of justice are especially cruel to those who are least able to protect themselves. Swift arrest and trial, fair and uniform punishment, should be expected by anyone who would break our laws.

It is time for our government leaders to respect the law no less than the humblest citizen, so that we can end once and for all a double standard of justice.

I see no reason why big-shot crooks should go free and the poor ones go to jail.

A simple and a proper function of government is just to make it easy for us to do good and difficult for us to do wrong.

As an engineer, a planner, a businessman, I see clearly the value to our nation of a strong system of free enterprise based on increase productivity and adequate wages. We Democrats believe that competition is better than regulation, and we intend to combine strong safeguards for consumers with minimal intrusion of government in our free economic system.

I believe that anyone who is able to work ought to work—and ought to have a chance to work. We will never have an end to the inflationary spiral, we will never have a balanced budget—which I am determined to see—as long as we have eight or nine million Americans out of work who cannot find a job. Any system of economics is bankrupt if it sees either value or virtue in unemployment. We simply cannot check inflation by keeping people out of work.

The foremost responsibility of any President, above all else, is to guarantee the security of our nation—a guarantee of freedom from the threat of successful attack or blackmail, and the ability with our allies to maintain peace.

But peace is not the mere absence of war. Peace is action to stamp out international terrorism. Peace is the unceasing effort to preserve human rights.

Peace is a combined demonstration of strength and good will. We will pray for peace and we will work for peace, until we have removed from all nations for all time the threat of nuclear destruction.

America's birth opened a new chapter in mankind's history. Ours was the first nation to dedicate itself clearly to basic moral and philosophical principles: that all people are created equal and endowed with inalienable rights to life, liberty, and the pursuit of happiness, and that the power of government is derived from the consent of the governed.

This national commitment was a singular act of wisdom and courage, and it brought the best and the bravest from other nations to our shores. It was a revolutionary development that captured the imagination of mankind. It created a basis for a unique role of America—that of a pioneer in shaping more decent and just relations among people and among societies.

Today, two hundred years later, we must address ourselves to that role, both in what we do at home and how we act abroad—among people everywhere who have become politically more alert, socially more congested, and increasingly impatient with global inequities, and who are now organized, as you know, into some one hundred and fifty different nations. This calls for nothing less than a sustained architectural effort to shape an international framework of peace within which our own ideals gradually can become a global reality.

Our nation should always derive its character directly from the people and let this be the strength and the image to be presented to the world—the character of the American people.

To our friends and allies I say that what unites us through our common dedication to democracy is much more important than that which occasionally divides us on economics or politics. To the nations that seek to lift themselves from poverty I say that America shares your aspirations and extends its hand to you. To those nation-states that wish to compete with us I say that we neither fear competition nor see it as an obstacle to wider cooperation. To all people I say that after two hundred years America still remains confident and youthful in its commitment to freedom and equality, and we always will be.

During this election year we candidates will ask you for your votes, and from us will be demanded our vision.

My vision of this nation and its future has been deepened and matured during the nineteen months that I have campaigned among you for President. I have never had more faith in America than I do today. We have an America that, in Bob Dylan's phrase, is busy being born, not busy dying.

We can have an America that has reconciled its economic needs with its desire for an environment that we can pass on with pride to the next generation.

We can have an America that provides excellence in education to my child and your child and every child.

We can have an America that encourages and takes pride in our ethnic diversity, our religious diversity, our cultural diversity—knowing that out of this pluralistic heritage has come the strength and the vitality and the creativity that has made us great and will keep us great.

We can have an American government that does not oppress or spy on its own people but respects our dignity and our privacy and our right to be let alone.

We can have an America where freedom, on the one hand, and equality, on the other hand, are mutually supportive and not in conflict, and where the dreams of our nation's first leaders are fully realized in our own day and age.

And we can have an America which harnesses the idealism of the student, the compassion of a nurse or the social worker, the determination of a farmer, the wisdom of a teacher, the practicality of the business leader, the experience of the senior citizen, and the hope of a laborer to build a better life for us all. And we can have it, and we're going to have it!

As I've said many times before, we can have an American President who does not govern with negativism and fear of the future, but with vigor and vision and aggressive leadership—a President who's not isolated from the people, but who feels your pain and shares your dreams and takes his strength and his wisdom and his courage from you.

I see an America on the move again, united, a diverse and vital and tolerant nation, entering our third century with pride and confidence, an America that lives up to the majesty of our Constitution and the simple decency of our people.

This is the America we want. This is the America that we will have.

We will go forward from this convention with some differences of opinion perhaps, but nevertheless united in a calm determination to make our country large and driving and generous in spirit once again, ready to embark on great national deeds. And once again, as brothers and sisters, our hearts will swell with pride to call ourselves Americans.

4.2 Jimmy Carter's Second Presidential Nomination Acceptance Speech

Fellow Democrats, fellow citizens:

I thank you for the nomination you've offered me, and I especially thank you for choosing as my running mate the best partner any President ever had, Fritz Mondale.

With gratitude and with determination I accept your nomination, and I am proud to run on the progressive and sound platform that you have hammered out at this convention.

Fritz and I will mount a campaign that defines the real issues, a campaign that responds to the intelligence of the American people, a campaign that talks sense. And we're going to beat the Republicans in November.

We'll win because we are the party of a great President who knew how to get reelected—Franklin Delano Roosevelt. And we are the party of a courageous fighter who knew how to give 'em hell—Harry Truman. And as Truman said, he just told the truth and they thought it was hell. And we're the party of a gallant man of spirit—John Fitzgerald Kennedy. And we're the party of a great leader of compassion—Lyndon Baines Johnson, and the party of a great man who should have been President, who would have been one of the greatest Presidents in history—Hubert Horatio Hornblower—Humphrey. I have appreciated what this convention has said about Senator Humphrey, a great man who epitomized the spirit of the Democratic Party. And I would like to say that we are also the party of Governor Jerry Brown and Senator Edward Kennedy.

I'd like to say a personal word to Senator Kennedy. Ted, you're a tough competitor and a superb campaigner, and I can attest to that. Your speech before this convention was a magnificent statement of what the Democratic Party is and what it means to the people of this country and why a Democratic victory is so important this year. I reach out to you tonight, and I reach out to all those who supported you in your valiant and passionate campaign. Ted, your party needs and I need you. And I need your idealism and your dedication working for us. There is no doubt that even greater service lies ahead of you, and we are grateful to you and to have your strong partnership now in a larger cause to which your own life has been dedicated.

I thank you for your support; we'll make great partners this fall in whipping the Republicans. We are Democrats and we've had our differences, but we share a bright vision of America's future—a vision of a good life for all our people, a vision of a secure nation, a just society, a peaceful world, a strong America—confident and proud and united. And we have a memory of Franklin Roosevelt, 40 years ago, when he said that there are times in our history when concerns over our personal lives are overshadowed by our concern over "what will happen to the county we have known." This is such a time, and I can tell you that the choice to be made this year can transform our own personal lives and the life of our country as well.

During the last Presidential campaign, I crisscrossed this country and I listened to thousands and thousands of people-housewives and farmers, teachers and small business leaders, workers and students, the elderly and the poor, people of every race and every background and every walk of life. It was a powerful experience—a total immersion in the human reality of America.

And I have now had another kind of total immersion—being President of the United States of America. Let me talk for a moment about what that job is like and what I've learned from it.

I've learned that only the most complex and difficult task comes before me in the Oval Office. No easy answers are found there, because no easy questions come there.

I've learned that for a President, experience is the best guide to the right decisions. I'm wiser tonight than I was 4 years ago.

And I have learned that the Presidency is a place of compassion. My own heart is burdened for the troubled Americans. The poor and the jobless and the afflicted-they've become part of me. My thoughts and my prayers for our hostages in Iran are as though they were my own sons and daughters.

The life of every human being on Earth can depend on the experience and judgment and vigilance of the person in the Oval Office. The President's power for building and his power for destruction are awesome. And the power's greatest exactly where the stakes are highest—in matters of war and peace.

And I've learned something else, something that I have come to see with extraordinary clarity: Above all, I must look ahead, because the President of the United States is the steward of the Nation's destiny. He must protect our children and the children they will have and the children of generations to follow. He must speak and act for them. That is his burden and his glory.

And that is why a President cannot yield to the shortsighted demands, no matter how rich or powerful the special interests might be that make those demands. And that's why the President cannot bend to the passions of the moment, however popular they might be. That's why the President must sometimes ask for sacrifice when his listeners would rather hear the promise of comfort.

The President is a servant of today, but his true constituency is the future. That's why the election of 1980 is so important.

Some have said it makes no difference who wins this election. They are wrong. This election is a stark choice between two men, two parties, two sharply different pictures of what America is and what the world is, but it's more than that—it's a choice between two futures.

The year 2000 is just less than 20 years away, just four Presidential elections after this one. Children born this year will come of age in the 21st century. The time to shape the world of the year 2000 is now. The decisions of the next few years will set our course, perhaps an irreversible course, and the most important of all choices will be made by the American people at the polls less than 3 months from tonight.

The choice could not be more clear nor the consequences more crucial. In one of the futures we can choose, the future that you and I have been building together, I see security and justice and peace.

I see a future of economic security-security that will come from tapping our own great resources of oil and gas, coal and sunlight, and from building the tools and technology and factories for a revitalized economy based on jobs and stable prices for everyone.

I see a future of justice—the justice of good jobs, decent health care, quality education, a full opportunity for all people regardless of color or language or religion; the simple human justice of equal rights for all men and for all women, guaranteed equal rights at last under the Constitution of the United States of America.

And I see a future of peace—a peace born of wisdom and based on a fairness toward all countries of the world, a peace guaranteed both by American military strength and by American moral strength as well.

That is the future I want for all people, a future of confidence and hope and a good life. It's the future America must choose, and with your help and with your commitment, it is the future America will choose.

But there is another possible future. In that other future I see despair—despair of millions who would struggle for equal opportunity and a better life and struggle alone. And I see surrender—the surrender of our energy future to the merchants of oil, the surrender of our economic future to a bizarre program of massive tax cuts for the rich, service cuts for the poor, and massive inflation for everyone. And I see risk—the risk of international confrontation, the risk of an uncontrollable, unaffordable, and unwinnable nuclear arms race.

No one, Democrat or Republican either, consciously seeks such a future, and I do not claim that my opponent does. But I do question the disturbing commitments and policies already made by him and by those with him who have now captured control of the Republican Party. The consequences of those commitments and policies would drive us down the wrong road. It's up to all of us to make sure America rejects this alarming and even perilous destiny.

The only way to build a better future is to start with the realities of the present. But while we Democrats grapple with the real challenges of a real world, others talk about a world of tinsel and make-believe.

Let's look for a moment at their make-believe world.

In their fantasy America, inner-city people and farm workers and laborers do not exist. Women, like children, are to be seen but not heard. The problems of working women are simply ignored. The elderly do not need Medicare. The young do not need more help in getting a better education. Workers do not require the guarantee of a healthy and a safe place to work. In their fantasy world, all the complex global changes of the world since World War II have never happened. In their fantasy America, all problems have simple solutions—simple and wrong.

It's a make-believe world, a world of good guys and bad guys, where some politicians shoot first and ask questions later. No hard choices, no sacrifice, no tough decisions—it sounds too good to be true, and it is.

The path of fantasy leads to irresponsibility. The path of reality leads to hope and peace. The two paths could not be more different, nor could the futures to which they lead. Let's take a hard look at the consequences of our choice.

You and I have been working toward a more secure future by rebuilding our military strength—steadily, carefully, and responsibly. The Republicans talk about military strength, but they were in office for 8 out of the last 11 years, and in the face of a growing Soviet threat they steadily cut real defense spending by more than a third.

We've reversed the Republican decline in defense. Every year since I've been President we've had real increases in our commitment to a stronger Nation, increases which are prudent and rational. There is no doubt that the United States of America can meet a threat from the Soviet Union. Our modernized strategic forces, a revitalized NATO, the Trident submarine, the Cruise missile, the Rapid Deployment Force—all these guarantee that we will never be second to any nation. Deeds, not words; fact, not fiction. We must and we will continue to build our own defenses. We must and we will continue to seek balanced reductions in nuclear arms.

The new leaders of the Republican Party, in order to close the gap between their rhetoric and their record, have now promised to launch an all-out nuclear arms race. This would negate any further effort to negotiate a strategic arms limitation agreement. There can be no winners in such an arms race, and all the people of the Earth can be the losers.

The Republican nominee advocates abandoning arms control policies which have been important and supported by every Democratic President since Harry, Truman, and also by every Republican President since Dwight D. Eisenhower. This radical and irresponsible course would threaten our security and could put the whole world in peril. You and I must never let this come to pass.

It's simple to call for a new arms race, but when armed aggression threatens world peace, tough-sounding talk like that is not enough. A President must act responsibly.

When Soviet troops invaded Afghanistan, we moved quickly to take action. I suspended some grain sales to the Soviet Union; I called for draft registration; and I joined wholeheartedly with the Congress and with the U.S. Olympic Committee and led more than 60 other nations in boycotting the big propaganda show in Russia—the Moscow Olympics.

The Republican leader opposed two of these forceful but peaceful actions, and he waffled on the third. But when we asked him what he would do about aggression in Southwest Asia, he suggested blockading Cuba. [Laughter] Even his running mate wouldn't go along with that. He doesn't seem to know what to do with the Russians. He's not sure if he wants to feed them or play with them or fight with them.

As I look back at my first term, I'm grateful that we've had a country for the full 4 years of peace. And that's what we're going to have for the next 4 years-peace.

It's only common sense that if America is to stay secure and at peace, we must encourage others to be peaceful as well.

As you know, we've helped in Zimbabwe-Rhodesia where we've stood firm for racial justice and democracy. And we have also helped in the Middle East.

Some have criticized the Camp David accords and they've criticized some delays in the implementation of the Middle East peace treaty. Well, before I became President there was no Camp David accords and there was no Middle East peace treaty. Before Camp David, Israel and Egypt were poised across barbed wire, confronting each other with guns and tanks and planes. But afterward, they talked face-to-face with each other across a peace table, and they also communicated through their own Ambassadors in Cairo and Tel Aviv.

Now that's the kind of future we're offering—of peace to the Middle East if the Democrats are reelected in the fall.

I am very proud that nearly half the aid that our country has ever given to Israel in the 32 years of her existence has come during my administration. Unlike our Republican predecessors, we have never stopped nor slowed that aid to Israel. And as long as I am President, we will never do so. Our commitment is clear: security and peace for Israel; peace for all the peoples of the Middle East.

But if the world is to have a future of freedom as well as peace, America must continue to defend human rights.

Now listen to this: The new Republican leaders oppose our human rights policy. They want to scrap it. They seem to think it's naive for America to stand up for freedom and democracy. Just what do they think we should stand up for?

Ask the former political prisoners who now live in freedom if we should abandon our stand on human rights. Ask the dissidents in the Soviet Union about our commitment to human rights. Ask the Hungarian Americans, ask the Polish Americans, listen to Pope John Paul II. Ask those who are suffering for the sake of justice and liberty around the world. Ask the millions who've fled tyranny if America should stop speaking out for human principles. Ask the American people. I tell you that as long as I am President, we will hold high the banner of human rights, and you can depend on it.

Here at home the choice between the two futures is equally important.

In the long run, nothing is more crucial to the future of America than energy; nothing was so disastrously neglected in the past. Long after the 1973 Arab oil embargo, the Republicans in the White House had still done nothing to meet the threat to the national security of our Nation. Then, as now, their policy was dictated by the big oil companies.

We Democrats fought hard to rally our Nation behind a comprehensive energy policy and a good program, a new foundation for challenging and exciting progress. Now, after 3 years of struggle, we have that program. The battle to secure America's energy future has been fully and finally joined. Americans 'have cooperated with dramatic results. We've reversed decades of dangerous and growing dependence on foreign oil. We are now importing 20 percent less oil—that is 1 1/2 million barrels of oil every day less than the day I took office.

And with our new energy policy now in place, we can discover more, produce more, create more, and conserve more energy, and we will use American resources, American technology, and millions of American workers to do it with.

Now, what do the Republicans propose? Basically, their energy program has two parts. The first part is to get rid of almost everything that we've done for the American public in the last 3 years. They want to reduce or abolish the synthetic fuels program. They want to slash the solar energy incentives, the conservation programs, aid to mass transit, aid to elderly Americans to help pay their fuel bills. They want to eliminate the 55-mile speed limit. And while they are at it, the Republicans would like to gut the Clean Air Act. They never liked it to begin with.

That's one part of their program; the other part is worse. To replace what we have built, this is what they propose: to destroy the windfall profits tax and to "unleash" the oil companies and let them solve the energy problem for us. That's it. That is it. That's their whole program. There is no more. Can this Nation accept such an outrageous program?

AUDIENCE. No !

THE PRESIDENT. No! We Democrats will fight it every step of the way, and we'll begin tomorrow morning with a campaign for reelection in November.

When I took office, I inherited a heavy load of serious economic problems besides energy, and we've met them all head-on. We've slashed Government regulations and put free enterprise back into the airlines, the trucking and the financial systems of our country, and we're now doing the same thing for the railroads. This is the greatest change in the relationship between Government and business since the New Deal. We've increased our exports dramatically. We've reversed the decline in the basic research and development, and we have created more than 8 million new jobs—the biggest increase in the history of our country.

But the road is bumpy, and last year's skyrocketing OPEC price increases have helped to trigger a worldwide inflation crisis. We took forceful action, and interest rates have now fallen, the dollar is stable and, although we still have a battle on our hands, we're struggling to bring inflation under control.

We are now at the critical point, a turning point in our economic history of our country. But because we made the hard decisions, because we have guided our Nation and its economy through a rough but essential period of transition, we've laid the groundwork for a new economic age.

Our economic renewal program for the 1980's will meet our immediate need for jobs and attack the very same, long-range problem that caused unemployment and inflation in the first place. It'll move America simultaneously towards our five great economic goals—lower inflation, better productivity, revitalization of American industry, energy security, and jobs.

It's time to put all America back to work—but not in make-work, in real work. And there is real work in modernizing American industries and creating new industries for America as well. Here are just a few things we'll rebuild together and build together:

—new industries to turn our own coal and shale and farm products into fuel for our cars and trucks and to turn the light of the sun into heat and electricity for our homes;

—a modern transportation system of railbeds and ports to make American coal into a powerful rival of OPEC oil;

—industries that will provide the convenience of futuristic computer technology and communications to serve millions of American homes and offices and factories;

—job training for workers displaced by economic changes;

—new investment pinpointed in regions and communities where jobs are needed most;

—better mass transit in our cities and in between cities;

—and a whole new generation of American jobs to make homes and vehicles and buildings that will house us and move us in comfort with a lot less energy.

This is important, too: I have no doubt that the ingenuity, and dedication of the American people can make every single one of these things happen. We are talking about the United States of America, and those who count this country out as an economic superpower are going to find out just how wrong they are. We're going to share in the exciting enterprise of making the 1980's a time of growth for America.

The Republican alternative is the biggest tax giveaway in history. They call it Reagan-Kemp-Roth; I call it a free lunch that Americans cannot afford. The Republican tax program offers rebates to the rich, deprivation for the poor, and fierce inflation for all of us. Their party's own Vice Presidential nominee said that Reagan-Kemp-Roth would result in an inflation rate of more than 30 percent. He called it "voodoo economics". He suddenly changed his mind toward the end of the Republican Convention, but he was right the first time.

Along with this gigantic tax cut, the new Republican leaders promise to protect retirement and health programs and to have massive increases in defense spending-and they claim they can balance the budget. If they are serious about these promises, and they say they are, then a close analysis shows that the entire rest of the Government would have to be abolished, everything from education to farm programs, from the G.I. bill to the night watchman at the Lincoln Memorial—and their budget would still be in the red. The only alternative would be to build more printing presses to print cheap money. Either way, the American people lose. But the American people will not stand for it.

The Democratic Party has always embodied the hope of our people for justice, opportunity, and a better life, and we've worked in every way possible to strengthen the American family, to encourage self-reliance, and to follow the Old Testament admonition: "Defend the poor and the fatherless; give justice to the afflicted and needy." We've struggled to assure that no child in America ever goes to bed hungry, that no elderly couple in America has to live in a substandard home, and that no young person in America is excluded from college because the family is poor.

But what have the Republicans proposed?--just an attack on everything that we've done in the achievement of social justice and decency that we've won in the last 50 years, ever since Franklin Delano Roosevelt's first term. They would make social security voluntary. They would reverse our progress on the minimum wage, full employment laws, safety in the work place, and a healthy environment.

Lately, as you know, the Republicans have been quoting Democratic Presidents. But who can blame them? Would you rather quote Herbert Hoover or Franklin Delano Roosevelt? Would you rather quote Richard Nixon or John Fitzgerald Kennedy?

The Republicans have always been the party of privilege, but this year their leaders have gone even further. In their platform, they have repudiated the best traditions of their own party. Where is the conscience of Lincoln in the party of Lincoln? What's become of their traditional Republican commitment to fiscal responsibility? What's happened to their commitment to a safe and sane arms control?

Now, I don't claim perfection for the Democratic Party. I don't claim that every decision that we have made has been right or popular; certainly, they've not all been easy. But I will say this: We've been tested under fire. We've neither ducked nor hidden, and we've tackled the great central issues of our time, the historic challenges of peace and energy, which have been ignored for years. We've made tough decisions, and we've taken the heat for them. We've made mistakes, and we've learned from them. But we have built the foundation now for a better future.

We've done something else, perhaps even more important. In good times and bad, in the valleys and on the peaks, we've told people the truth, the hard truth, the truth that sometimes hurts.

One truth that we Americans have learned is that our dream has been earned for progress and for peace. Look what our land has been through within our own memory—a great depression, a world war, a technological explosion, the civil rights revolution, the bitterness of Vietnam, the shame of Watergate, the twilight peace of nuclear terror.

Through each of these momentous experiences we've learned the hard way about the world and about ourselves. But we've matured and we've grown as a nation and we've grown stronger.

We've learned the uses and the limitations of power. We've learned the beauty and responsibility of freedom. We've learned the value and the obligation of justice. And we have learned the necessity of peace.

Some would argue that to master these lessons is somehow to limit our potential. That is not so. A nation which knows its true strengths, which sees its true challenges, which understands legitimate constraints, that nation—our nation—is far stronger than one which takes refuge in wishful thinking or nostalgia. The Democratic Party—the American people-have understood these fundamental truths.

All of us can sympathize with the desire for easy answers. There's often the temptation to substitute idle dreams for hard reality. The new Republican leaders are hoping that our Nation will succumb to that temptation this year, but they profoundly misunderstand and underestimate the character of the American people.

Three weeks after Pearl Harbor, Winston Churchill came to North America and he said, "We have not journeyed all this way across the centuries, across the oceans, across the mountains, across the prairies, because we are made of sugar candy." We Americans have courage. Americans have always been on the cutting edge of change. We've always looked forward with anticipation and confidence.

I still want the same thing that all of you want—a self-reliant neighborhood, strong families, work for the able-bodied and good medical care for the sick, opportunity for our youth and dignity for our old, equal rights and justice for all people.

I want teachers eager to explain what a civilization really is, and I want students to understand their own needs and their own aims, but also the needs and yearnings of their neighbors.

I want women free to pursue without limit the full life of what they want for themselves.

I want our farmers growing crops to feed our Nation and the world, secure in the knowledge that the family farm will thrive and with a fair return on the good work they do for all of us.

I want workers to see meaning in the labor they perform and work enough to guarantee a job for every worker in this country.

And I want the people in business free to pursue with boldness and freedom new ideas.

And I want minority citizens fully to join the mainstream of American life. And I want from the bottom of my heart to remove the blight of racial and other discrimination from the face of our Nation, and I'm determined to do it.

I need for all of you to join me in fulfilling that vision. The choice, the choice between the two futures, could not be more clear. If we succumb to a dream world then we'll wake up to a nightmare. But if we start with reality and fight to make our dreams a reality, then Americans will have a good life, a life of meaning and purpose in a nation that's strong and secure.

Above all, I want us to be what the Founders of our Nation meant us to become—the land of freedom, the land of peace, and the land of hope.

Thank you very much.

Chapter 5

Other Notable Works

5.1 President Carter's Address to the Nation on Proposed National Energy Policy

Good evening.

Tonight I want to have an unpleasant talk with you about a problem unprecedented in our history. With the exception of preventing war, this is the greatest challenge our country will face during our lifetimes. The energy crisis has not yet overwhelmed us, but it will if we do not act quickly.

It is a problem we will not solve in the next few years, and it is likely to get progressively worse through the rest of this century.

We must not be selfish or timid if we hope to have a decent world for our children and grandchildren.

We simply must balance our demand for energy with our rapidly shrinking resources. By acting now, we can control our future instead of letting the future control us.

Two days from now, I will present my energy proposals to the Congress. Its members will be my partners and they have already given me a great deal of valuable advice. Many of these proposals will be unpopular. Some will cause you to put up with inconveniences and to make sacrifices.

The most important thing about these proposals is that the alternative may be a national catastrophe. Further delay can affect our strength and our power as a nation.

Our decision about energy will test the character of the American people and the ability of the President and the Congress to govern. This difficult effort will be the "moral equivalent of war" — except that we will be uniting our efforts to build and not destroy.

I know that some of you may doubt that we face real energy shortages. The 1973 gasoline lines are gone, and our homes are warm again. But our energy problem is worse tonight than it was in 1973 or a few weeks ago in the dead of winter. It is worse because more waste has occurred, and more time has passed by without our planning for the future. And it will get worse every day until we act.

The oil and natural gas we rely on for 75 percent of our energy are running out. In spite of increased effort, domestic production has been dropping steadily at about six percent a year. Imports have doubled in the last five years. Our nation's independence of economic and political action is becoming increasingly constrained. Unless profound changes are made to lower oil consumption, we now believe that early in the 1980s the world will be demanding more oil that it can produce.

The world now uses about 60 million barrels of oil a day and demand increases each year about 5 percent. This means that just to stay even we need the production of a new Texas every year, an Alaskan North Slope every nine months, or a new Saudi Arabia every three years. Obviously, this cannot continue.

We must look back in history to understand our energy problem. Twice in the last several hundred years there has been

133

a transition in the way people use energy.

The first was about 200 years ago, away from wood — which had provided about 90 percent of all fuel — to coal, which was more efficient. This change became the basis of the Industrial Revolution.

The second change took place in this century, with the growing use of oil and natural gas. They were more convenient and cheaper than coal, and the supply seemed to be almost without limit. They made possible the age of automobile and airplane travel. Nearly everyone who is alive today grew up during this age and we have never known anything different.

Because we are now running out of gas and oil, we must prepare quickly for a third change, to strict conservation and to the use of coal and permanent renewable energy sources, like solar power.

The world has not prepared for the future. During the 1950s, people used twice as much oil as during the 1940s. During the 1960s, we used twice as much as during the 1950s. And in each of those decades, more oil was consumed than in all of mankind's previous history.

World consumption of oil is still going up. If it were possible to keep it rising during the 1970s and 1980s by 5 percent a year as it has in the past, we could use up all the proven reserves of oil in the entire world by the end of the next decade.

I know that many of you have suspected that some supplies of oil and gas are being withheld. You may be right, but suspicions about oil companies cannot change the fact that we are running out of petroleum.

All of us have heard about the large oil fields on Alaska's North Slope. In a few years when the North Slope is producing fully, its total output will be just about equal to two years' increase in our nation's energy demand.

Each new inventory of world oil reserves has been more disturbing than the last. World oil production can probably keep going up for another six or eight years. But some time in the 1980s it can't go up much more. Demand will overtake production. We have no choice about that.

But we do have a choice about how we will spend the next few years. Each American uses the energy equivalent of 60 barrels of oil per person each year. Ours is the most wasteful nation on earth. We waste more energy than we import. With about the same standard of living, we use twice as much energy per person as do other countries like Germany, Japan and Sweden.

One choice is to continue doing what we have been doing before. We can drift along for a few more years.

Our consumption of oil would keep going up every year. Our cars would continue to be too large and inefficient. Three-quarters of them would continue to carry only one person — the driver — while our public transportation system continues to decline. We can delay insulating our houses, and they will continue to lose about 50 percent of their heat in waste.

We can continue using scarce oil and natural to generate electricity, and continue wasting two-thirds of their fuel value in the process.

If we do not act, then by 1985 we will be using 33 percent more energy than we do today.

We can't substantially increase our domestic production, so we would need to import twice as much oil as we do now. Supplies will be uncertain. The cost will keep going up. Six years ago, we paid $3.7 billion for imported oil. Last year we spent $37 billion — nearly ten times as much — and this year we may spend over $45 billion.

Unless we act, we will spend more than $550 billion for imported oil by 1985 — more than $2,500 a year for every man, woman, and child in America. Along with that money we will continue losing American jobs and becoming increasingly vulnerable to supply interruptions.

Now we have a choice. But if we wait, we will live in fear of embargoes. We could endanger our freedom as a sovereign nation to act in foreign affairs. Within ten years we would not be able to import enough oil — from any country, at any acceptable price.

If we wait, and do not act, then our factories will not be able to keep our people on the job with reduced supplies of fuel. Too few of our utilities will have switched to coal, our most abundant energy source.

We will not be ready to keep our transportation system running with smaller, more efficient cars and a better network of buses, trains and public transportation.

We will feel mounting pressure to plunder the environment. We will have a crash program to build more nuclear plants, strip-mine and burn more coal, and drill more offshore wells than we will need if we begin to conserve now. Inflation will soar, production will go down, people will lose their jobs. Intense competition will build up among nations and among the different regions within our own country.

If we fail to act soon, we will face an economic, social and political crisis that will threaten our free institutions.

But we still have another choice. We can begin to prepare right now. We can decide to act while there is time.

That is the concept of the energy policy we will present on Wednesday. Our national energy plan is based on ten fundamental principles.

The first principle is that we can have an effective and comprehensive energy policy only if the government takes responsibility for it and if the people understand the seriousness of the challenge and are willing to make sacrifices.

The second principle is that healthy economic growth must continue. Only by saving energy can we maintain our standard of living and keep our people at work. An effective conservation program will create hundreds of thousands of new jobs.

The third principle is that we must protect the environment. Our energy problems have the same cause as our environmental problems — wasteful use of resources. Conservation helps us solve both at once.

The fourth principle is that we must reduce our vulnerability to potentially devastating embargoes. We can protect ourselves from uncertain supplies by reducing our demand for oil, making the most of our abundant resources such as coal, and developing a strategic petroleum reserve.

The fifth principle is that we must be fair. Our solutions must ask equal sacrifices from every region, every class of people, every interest group. Industry will have to do its part to conserve, just as the consumers will. The energy producers deserve fair treatment, but we will not let the oil companies profiteer.

The sixth principle, and the cornerstone of our policy, is to reduce the demand through conservation. Our emphasis on conservation is a clear difference between this plan and others which merely encouraged crash production efforts. Conservation is the quickest, cheapest, most practical source of energy. Conservation is the only way we can buy a barrel of oil for a few dollars. It costs about $13.00 to waste it.

The seventh principle is that prices should generally reflect the true replacement costs of energy. We are only cheating ourselves if we make energy artificially cheap and use more than we can really afford.

The eighth principle is that government policies must be predictable and certain. Both consumers and producers need policies they can count on so they can plan ahead. This is one reason I am working with the Congress to create a new Department of Energy, to replace more than 50 different agencies that now have some control over energy.

The ninth principle is that we must conserve the fuels that are scarcest and make the most of those that are more plentiful. We can't continue to use oil and gas for 75 percent of our consumption when they make up seven percent of our domestic reserves. We need to shift to plentiful coal while taking care to protect the environment, and to apply stricter safety standards to nuclear energy.

The tenth principle is that we must start now to develop the new, unconventional sources of energy we will rely on in the next century.

These ten principles have guided the development of the policy I would describe to you and the Congress on Wednesday.

Our energy plan will also include a number of specific goals, to measure our progress toward a stable energy system.

These are the goals we set for 1985:

—Reduce the annual growth rate in our energy demand to less than two percent.

—Reduce gasoline consumption by ten percent below its current level.

—Cut in half the portion of United States oil which is imported, from a potential level of sixteen million barrels to six million barrels a day.

—Establish a strategic petroleum reserve of one billion barrels, more than six months' supply.

—Increase our coal production by about two thirds to more than one billion tons a year.

—Insulate 90 percent of American homes and all new buildings.

—Use solar energy in more than two and one-half million houses.

We will monitor our progress toward these goals year by year. Our plan will call for stricter conservation measures if we fall behind.

I cant tell you that these measures will be easy, nor will they be popular. But I think most of you realize that a policy which does not ask for changes or sacrifices would not be an effective policy.

This plan is essential to protect our jobs, our environment, our standard of living, and our future.

Whether this plan truly makes a difference will be decided not here in Washington, but in every town and every factory, in every home an don every highway and every farm.

I believe this can be a positive challenge. There is something especially American in the kinds of changes we have to make. We have been proud, through our history of being efficient people.

We have been proud of our leadership in the world. Now we have a chance again to give the world a positive example.

And we have been proud of our vision of the future. We have always wanted to give our children and grandchildren a world richer in possibilities than we've had. They are the ones we must provide for now. They are the ones who will suffer most if we don't act.

I've given you some of the principles of the plan.

I am sure each of you will find something you don't like about the specifics of our proposal. It will demand that we make sacrifices and changes in our lives. To some degree, the sacrifices will be painful — but so is any meaningful sacrifice. It will lead to some higher costs, and to some greater inconveniences for everyone.

But the sacrifices will be gradual, realistic and necessary. Above all, they will be fair. No one will gain an unfair advantage through this plan. No one will be asked to bear an unfair burden. We will monitor the accuracy of data from the oil and natural gas companies, so that we will know their true production, supplies, reserves, and profits.

The citizens who insist on driving large, unnecessarily powerful cars must expect to pay more for that luxury.

We can be sure that all the special interest groups in the country will attack the part of this plan that affects them directly. They will say that sacrifice is fine, as long as other people do it, but that their sacrifice is unreasonable, or unfair, or harmful to the country. If they succeed, then the burden on the ordinary citizen, who is not organized into an interest group, would be crushing.

There should be only one test for this program: whether it will help our country.

Other generation of Americans have faced and mastered great challenges. I have faith that meeting this challenge will make our own lives even richer. If you will join me so that we can work together with patriotism and courage, we will again prove that our great nation can lead the world into an age of peace, independence and freedom.

Thank you very much, and good night.

5.2 The Crisis of Confidence

Good evening.—This is a special night for me. Exactly 3 years ago, on July 15, 1976, I accepted the nomination of my party to run for President of the United States.

I promised you a President who is not isolated from the people, who feels your pain, and who shares your dreams and who draws his strength and his wisdom from you.

During the past 3 years I've spoken to you on many occasions about national concerns, the energy crisis, reorganizing the Government, our Nation's economy, and issues of war and especially peace. But over those years the subjects of the speeches, the talks, and the press conferences have become increasingly narrow focused more and more on what the isolated world of Washington thinks is important. Gradually, you've heard more and more about what the Government thinks or what the Government should be doing and less and less about our Nation's hopes, our dreams, and our vision of the future.

Ten days ago I had planned to speak to you again about a very important subject—energy. For the fifth time I would have described the urgency of the problem and laid out a series of legislative recommendations to the Congress. But as I was preparing to speak, I began to ask myself the same question that I now know has been troubling many of you. Why have we not been able to get together as a nation to resolve our serious energy problem?

It's clear that the true problems of our Nation are much deeper—deeper than gasoline lines or energy shortages, deeper even than inflation or recession. And I realize more than ever that as President I need your help. So, I decided to reach out and listen to the voices of America.

I invited to Camp David people from almost every segment of our society—business and labor, teachers and preachers, Governors, mayors, and private citizens. And then I left Camp David to listen to other Americans, men and women like you.

It has been an extraordinary 10 days, and I want to share with you what I've heard. First of all, I got a lot of personal advice. Let me quote a few of the typical comments that I wrote down.

This from a southern Governor: "Mr. President, you are not leading this Nation—you're just managing the Government."

"You don't see the people enough any more."

"Some of your Cabinet members don't seem loyal. There is not enough discipline among your disciples."

"Don't talk to us about politics or the mechanics of government, but about an understanding of our common good."

"Mr. President, we're in trouble. Talk to us about blood and sweat and tears."

"If you lead, Mr. President, we will follow."

Many people talked about themselves and about the condition of our Nation.

This from a young woman in Pennsylvania: "I feel so far from government. I feel like ordinary people are excluded from political power."

And this from a young Chicano: "Some of us have suffered from recession all our lives."

"Some people have wasted energy, but others haven't had anything to waste."

And this from a religious leader: "No material shortage can touch the important things like God's love for us or our love for one another."

And I like this one particularly from a black woman who happens to be the mayor of a small Mississippi town: "The big-shots are not the only ones who are important. Remember, you can't sell anything on Wall Street unless someone digs it up somewhere else first."

This kind of summarized a lot of other statements: "Mr. President, we are confronted with a moral and a spiritual crisis."

Several of our discussions were on energy, and I have a notebook full of comments and advice. I'll read just a few.

"We can't go on consuming 40 percent more energy than we produce. When we import oil we are also importing inflation plus unemployment"

"We've got to use what we have. The Middle East has only 5 percent of the world's energy, but the United States has 24 percent."

And this is one of the most vivid statements: "Our neck is stretched over the fence and OPEC has a knife."

"There will be other cartels and other shortages. American wisdom and courage right now can set a path to follow in the future."

This was a good one: "Be bold, Mr. President. We may make mistakes, but we are ready to experiment."

And this one from a labor leader got to the heart of it: "The real issue is freedom. We must deal with the energy problem on a war footing."

And the last that I'll read: "When we enter the moral equivalent of war, Mr. President, don't issue us BB guns."

These 10 days confirmed my belief in the decency and the strength and the wisdom of the American people, but it also bore out some of my long-standing concerns about our Nation's underlying problems.

I know, of course, being President, that government actions and legislation can be very important. That's why I've worked hard to put my campaign promises into law - and I have to admit, with just mixed success. But after listening to the American people I have been reminded again that all the legislation in the world can't fix what's wrong with America. So, I want to speak to you first tonight about a subject even more serious than energy or inflation. I want to talk to you right now about a fundamental threat to American democracy.

I do not mean our political and civil liberties. They will endure. And I do not refer to the outward strength of America, a nation that is at peace tonight everywhere in the world, with unmatched economic power and military might.

The threat is nearly invisible in ordinary ways. It is a crisis of confidence. It is a crisis that strikes at the very heart and soul and spirit of our national will. We can see this crisis in the growing doubt about the meaning of our own lives and in the loss of a unity of purpose for our Nation.

The erosion of our confidence in the future is threatening to destroy the social and the political fabric of America.

The confidence that we have always had as a people is not simply some romantic dream or a proverb in a dusty book that we read just on the Fourth of July.

It is the idea which founded our Nation and has guided our development as a people. Confidence in the future has supported everything else—public institutions and private enterprise, our own families, and the very Constitution of the United States. Confidence has defined our course and has served as a link between generations. We've always believed in something called progress. We've always had a faith that the days of our children would be better than our own.

Our people are losing that faith, not only in government itself but in the ability as citizens to serve as the ultimate rulers and shapers of our democracy. As a people we know our past and we are proud of it. Our progress has been part of the living history of America, even the world. We always believed that we were part of a great movement of humanity itself called democracy, involved in the search for freedom, and that belief has always strengthened us in our purpose. But just as we are losing our confidence in the future, we are also beginning to close the door on our past.

In a nation that was proud of hard work, strong families, close-knit communities, and our faith in God, too many of us now tend to worship self-indulgence and consumption. Human identity is no longer defined by what one does, but by what one owns. But we've discovered that owning things and consuming things does not satisfy our longing for meaning. We've learned that piling up material goods cannot fill the emptiness of lives which have no confidence or purpose.

The symptoms of this crisis of the American spirit are all around us. For the first time in the history of our country a majority of our people believe that the next 5 years will be worse than the past 5 years. Two-thirds of our people do not even vote. The productivity of American workers is actually dropping, and the willingness of Americans to save for the future has fallen below that of all other people in the Western world.

As you know, there is a growing disrespect for government and for churches and for schools, the news media, and other institutions. This is not a message of happiness or reassurance, but it is the truth and it is a warning.

These changes did not happen overnight. They've come upon us gradually over the last generation, years that were filled with shocks and tragedy.

We were sure that ours was a nation of the ballot, not the bullet, until the murders of John Kennedy and Robert Kennedy and Martin Luther King, Jr. We were taught that our armies were always invincible and our causes were always just, only to suffer the agony of Vietnam. We respected the Presidency as a place of honor until the shock of Watergate.

We remember when the phrase "sound as a dollar" was an expression of absolute dependability, until 10 years of inflation began to shrink our dollar and our savings. We believed that our Nation's resources were limitless until 1973, when we had to face a growing dependence on foreign oil.

These wounds are still very deep. They have never been healed. Looking for a way out of this crisis, our people have turned to the Federal Government and found it isolated from the mainstream of our Nation's life. Washington, D.C., has become an island. The gap between our citizens and our Government has never been so wide. The people are looking for honest answers, not easy answers; clear leadership, not false claims and evasiveness and politics as usual.

What you see too often in Washington and elsewhere around the country is a system of government that seems incapable of action. You see a Congress twisted and pulled in every direction by hundreds of well-financed and powerful special interests. You see every extreme position defended to the last vote, almost to the last breath by one unyielding group or another. You often see a balanced and a fair approach that demands sacrifice, a little sacrifice from everyone, abandoned like an orphan without support and without friends.

Often you see paralysis and stagnation and drift. You don't like it, and neither do I. What can we do?

First of all, we must face the truth, and then we can change our course. We simply must have faith in each other, faith in our ability to govern ourselves, and faith in the future of this Nation. Restoring that faith and that confidence to America is now the most important task we face. It is a true challenge of this generation of Americans.

One of the visitors to Camp David last week put it this way: "We've got to stop crying and start sweating, stop talking and start walking, stop cursing and start praying. The strength we need will not come from the White House, but from every house in America."

We know the strength of America. We are strong. We can regain our unity. We can regain our confidence. We are the heirs of generations who survived threats much more powerful and awesome than those that challenge us now. Our fathers and mothers were strong men and women who shaped a new society during the Great Depression, who fought world wars, and who carved out a new charter of peace for the world.

We ourselves are the same Americans who just 10 years ago put a man on the Moon. We are the generation that dedicated our society to the pursuit of human rights and equality. And we are the generation that will win the war on the energy problem and in that process rebuild the unity and confidence of America.

We are at a turning point in our history. There are two paths to choose. One is a path I've warned about tonight, the path that leads to fragmentation and self- interest. Down that road lies a mistaken idea of freedom, the right to grasp for ourselves some advantage over others. That path would be one of constant conflict between narrow interests ending in chaos and immobility. It is a certain route to failure.

All the traditions of our past, all the lessons of our heritage, all the promises of our future point to another path, the path of common purpose and the restoration of American values. That path leads to true freedom for our Nation and ourselves. We can take the first steps down that path as we begin to solve our energy problem.

Energy will be the immediate test of our ability to unite this Nation, and it can also be the standard around which we rally. On the battlefield of energy we can win for our Nation a new confidence, and we can seize control again of our common destiny.

In little more than two decades we've gone from a position of energy independence to one in which almost half the oil we use comes from foreign countries, at prices that are going through the roof. Our excessive dependence on OPEC has already taken a tremendous toll on our economy and our people. This is the direct cause of the long lines which have made millions of you spend aggravating hours waiting for gasoline. It's a cause of the increased inflation and unemployment that we now face. This intolerable dependence on foreign oil threatens our economic independence and the very security of our Nation. The energy crisis is real. It is worldwide. It is a clear and present danger to our Nation. These are facts and we simply must face them.

What I have to say to you now about energy is simple and vitally important Point one: I am tonight setting a clear goal for the energy policy of the United States. Beginning this moment, this Nation will never use more foreign oil than we did in 1977 - never. From now on, every new addition to our demand for energy will be met from our own production and our own conservation. The generation - long growth in our dependence on foreign oil will be stopped dead in its tracks right now and then reversed as we move through the 1980s, for I am tonight setting the further goal of cutting our dependence on foreign oil by one-half by the end of the next decade—a saving of over 4 1/2 million barrels of imported oil per day. Point two: To ensure that we meet these targets, I will use my Presidential authority to set import quotas. I'm announcing tonight that for 1979 and 1980, I will forbid the entry into this country of one drop of foreign oil more than these goals allow. These quotas will ensure a reduction in imports even below the ambitious levels we set at the recent Tokyo summit.

Point three: To give us energy security, I am asking for the most massive peacetime commitment of funds and resources in our Nation's history to develop America's own alternative sources of fuel-from coal, from oil shale, from plant products for gasohol, from unconventional gas, from the Sun.

I propose the creation of an energy security corporation to lead this effort to replace 2 1/2 million barrels of imported oil per day by 1990. The corporation I will issue up to $5 billion in energy bonds, and I especially want them to be in small denominations so that average Americans can invest directly in America's energy security.

Just as a similar synthetic rubber corporation helped us win World War II, so will we mobilize American determination and ability to win the energy war. Moreover, I will soon submit legislation to Congress calling for the creation of this Nation's first solar bank, which will help us achieve the crucial goal of 20 percent of our energy coming from solar power by the year 2000.

These efforts will cost money, a lot of money, and that is why Congress must enact the windfall profits tax without delay. It will be money well spent. Unlike the billions of dollars that we ship to foreign countries to pay for foreign oil, these funds will be paid by Americans to Americans. These funds will go to fight, not to increase, inflation and unemployment.

Point four: I'm asking Congress to mandate, to require as a matter of law, that our Nation's utility companies cut their massive use of oil by 50 percent within the next decade and switch to other fuels, especially coal, our most abundant energy source.

Point five: To make absolutely certain that nothing stands in the way of achieving these goals, I will urge Congress to create an energy mobilization board which, like the War Production Board in World War II, will have the responsibility and authority to cut through the red tape, the delays, and the endless roadblocks to completing key energy projects.

We will protect our environment. But when this Nation critically needs a refinery or a pipeline, we will build it.

Point six: I'm proposing a bold conservation program to involve every State, county, and city and every average American in our energy battle. This effort will permit you to build conservation into your homes and your lives at a cost you can afford.

I ask Congress to give me authority for mandatory conservation and for standby gasoline rationing. To further conserve energy, I'm proposing tonight an extra $10 billion over the next decade to strengthen our public transportation systems. And I'm asking you for your good and for your Nation's security to take no unnecessary trips, to use carpools or public transportation whenever you can, to park your car one extra day per week, to obey the speed limit, and to set your thermostats to save fuel. Every act of energy conservation like this is more than just common sense - I tell you it is an act of patriotism.

Our Nation must be fair to the poorest among us, so we will increase aid to needy Americans to cope with rising energy prices. We often think of conservation only in terms of sacrifice. In fact, it is the most painless and immediate way of rebuilding our Nation's strength. Every gallon of oil each one of us saves is a new form of production. It gives us more freedom, more confidence, that much more control over our own lives.

So, the solution of our energy crisis can also help us to conquer the crisis of the spirit in our country. It can rekindle our sense of unity, our confidence in the future, and give our Nation and all of us individually a new sense of purpose.

You know we can do it. We have the natural resources. We have more oil in our shale alone than several Saudi Arabias. We have more coal than any nation on Earth. We have the world's highest level of technology. We have the most skilled work force, with innovative genius, and I firmly believe that we have the national will to win this war.

I do not promise you that this struggle for freedom will be easy. I do not promise a quick way out of our Nation's problems, when the truth is that the only way out is an all-out effort. What I do promise you is that I will lead our fight, and I will enforce fairness in our struggle, and I will ensure honesty. And above all, I will act. We can manage the short-term shortages more effectively and we will, but there are no short-term solutions to our long-range problems. There is simply no way to avoid sacrifice.

Twelve hours from now I will speak again in Kansas City, to expand and to explain further our energy program. Just as the search for solutions to our energy shortages has now led us to a new awareness of our Nation's deeper problems, so our willingness to work for those solutions in energy can strengthen us to attack those deeper problems.

I will continue to travel this country, to hear the people of America. You can help me to develop a national agenda for the 1980s. I will listen and I will act. We will act together. These were the promises I made 3 years ago, and I intend to keep them.

Little by little we can and we must rebuild our confidence. We can spend until we empty our treasuries, and we may summon all the wonders of science. But we can succeed only if we tap our greatest resources-America's people, America's values, and America's confidence.

I have seen the strength of America in the inexhaustible resources of our people. In the days to come, let us renew that strength in the struggle for an energy secure nation.

In closing, let me say this: I will do my best, but I will not do it alone. Let your voice be heard. Whenever you have a chance, say something good about our country. With God's help and for the sake of our Nation, it is time for us to join hands in America. Let us commit ourselves together to a rebirth of the American spirit Working together with our common faith we cannot fail.

Thank you and good night.

5.3 Jimmy Carter's Farewell Address

Good evening. In a few days, I will lay down my official responsibilities in this office — to take up once more the only title in our democracy superior to that of president, the title of citizen.

Of Vice President Mondale, my Cabinet and the hundreds of others who have served with me during the last four years, I wish to say publicly what I have said in private: I thank them for the dedication and competence they have brought to the service of our country.

But I owe my deepest thanks to you, the American people, because you gave me this extraordinary opportunity to serve. We have faced great challenges together. We know that future problems will also be difficult, but I am now more convinced than ever that the United States — better than any other nation — can meet successfully whatever the future might bring.

These last four years have made me more certain than ever of the inner strength of our country — the unchanging value of our principles and ideals, the stability of our political system, the ingenuity and the decency of our people.

Tonight I would like first to say a few words about this most special office, the presidency of the United States.

This is at once the most powerful office in the world — and among the most severely constrained by law and custom. The president is given a broad responsibility to lead — but cannot do so without the support and consent of the people, expressed informally through the Congress and informally in many ways through a whole range of public and private institutions.

This is as it should be. Within our system of government every American has a right and duty to help shape the future course of the United States.

Thoughtful criticism and close scrutiny of all government officials by the press and the public are an important part of our democratic society. Now as in our past, only the understanding and involvement of the people through full and open debate can help to avoid serious mistakes and assure the continued dignity and safety of the nation.

Today we are asking our political system to do things of which the founding fathers never dreamed. The government they designed for a few hundred thousand people now serves a nation of almost 230 million people. Their small coastal republic now spans beyond a continent, and we now have the responsibility to help lead much of the world through difficult times to a secure and prosperous future.

Today, as people have become ever more doubtful of the ability of the government to deal with our problems, we are increasingly drawn to single-issue groups and special interest organizations to ensure that whatever else happens our own personal views and our own private interests are protected.

This is a disturbing factor in American political life. It tends to distort our purposes because the national interest is not always the sum of all our single or special interests. We are all Americans together — and we must not forget that the common good is our common interest and our individual responsibility.

Because of the fragmented pressures of special interests, it's very important that the office of the president be a strong one, and that its constitutional authority be preserved. The president is the only elected official charged with the primary responsibility of representing all the people. In the moments of decision, after the different and conflicting views have been aired, it is the president who then must speak to the nation and for the nation.

I understand after four years in office, as few others can, how formidable is the task the president-elect is about to undertake. To the very limits of conscience and conviction, I pledge to support him in that task. I wish him success, and Godspeed.

I know from experience that presidents have to face major issues that are controversial, broad in scope, and which do not arouse the natural support of a political majority.

For a few minutes now, I want to lay aside my role as leader of one nation, and speak to you as a fellow citizen of the world about three issues, three difficult issues: The threat of nuclear destruction, our stewardship of the physical resources of our planet, and the pre-eminence of the basic rights of human beings.

It's now been 35 years since the first atomic bomb fell on Hiroshima. The great majority of the world's people cannot remember a time when the nuclear shadow did not hang over the earth. Our minds have adjusted to it, as after a time our eyes adjust to the dark.

Yet the risk of a nuclear conflagration has not lessened. It has not happened yet, thank God, but that can give us little comfort — for it only has to happen once.

The danger is becoming greater. As the arsenals of the superpowers grow in size and sophistication and as other governments acquire these weapons, it may only be a matter of time before madness, desperation, greed or miscalculation lets lose this terrible force.

In an all-out nuclear war, more destructive power than in all of World War II would be unleashed every second during the long afternoon it would take for all the missiles and bombs to fall. A World War II every second — more people killed in the first few hours than all the wars of history put together. The survivors, if any, would live in despair amid the poisoned ruins of a civilization that had committed suicide.

National weakness — real or perceived — can tempt aggression and thus cause war. That's why the United States cannot neglect its military strength. We must and we will remain strong. But with equal determination, the United States and all countries must find ways to control and reduce the horrifying danger that is posed by the world's enormous stockpiles of nuclear arms.

This has been a concern of every American president since the moment we first saw what these weapons could do. Our leaders will require our understanding and our support as they grapple with this difficult but crucial challenge. There is no disagreement on the goals or the basic approach to controlling this enormous destructive force. The answer lies not just in the attitudes or actions of world leaders, but in the concern and demands of all of us as we continue our struggle to preserve the peace.

Nuclear weapons are an expression of one side of our human character. But there is another side. The same rocket technology that delivers nuclear warheads has also taken us peacefully into space. From that perspective, we see our Earth as it really is — a small and fragile and beautiful blue globe, the only home we have. We see no barriers of race or religion or country. We see the essential unity of our species and our planet; and with faith and common sense, that bright vision will ultimately prevail.

Another major challenge, therefore, is to protect the quality of this world within which we live. The shadows that fail across the future are cast not only by the kinds of weapons we have built, but by the kind of world we will either nourish or neglect.

There are real and growing dangers to our simple and most precious possessions: the air we breathe; the water we drink; and the land which sustain us. The rapid depletion of irreplaceable minerals, the erosion of topsoil, the destruction of beauty, the blight of pollution, the demands of increasing billions of people, all combine to create problems which are easy to observe and predict but difficult to resolve. If we do not act, the world of the year 2000 will be much less able to sustain life than it is now.

But there is no reason for despair. Acknowledging the physical realities of our planet does not mean a dismal future of endless sacrifice. In fact, acknowledging these realities is the first step in dealing with them. We can meet the resource problems of the world — water, food, minerals, farmlands, forests, overpopulation, pollution — if we tackle them with courage and foresight.

I have just been talking about forces of potential destruction that mankind has developed, and how we might control them. It is equally important that we remember the beneficial forces that we have evolved over the ages, and how to hold fast to them.

One of those constructive forces is enhancement of individual human freedoms through the strengthening of democracy, and the fight against deprivation, torture, terrorism and the persecution of people throughout the world. The struggle for human rights overrides all differences of color, nation or language.

Those who hunger for freedom, who thirst for human dignity, and who suffer for the sake of justice — they are the patriots of this cause.

I believe with all my heart that America must always stand for these basic human rights — at home and abroad. That is both our history and our destiny.

America did not invent human rights. In a very real sense, it is the other way round. Human rights invented America.

Ours was the first nation in the history of the world to be founded explicitly on such an idea. Our social and political progress has been based on one fundamental principle — the value and importance of the individual. The fundamental force that unites us is not kinship or place of origin or religious preference. The love of liberty is a common blood that flows in our American veins.

The battle for human rights — at home and abroad — is far from over. We should never be surprised nor discouraged because the impact of our efforts has had, and will always have, varied results. Rather, we should take pride that the ideals which gave birth to our nation still inspire the hopes of oppressed people around the world. We have no cause for self-righteousness or complacency. But we have every reason to persevere, both within our own country and beyond our borders.

If we are to serve as a beacon for human rights, we must continue to perfect here at home the rights and values which we espouse around the world: A decent education for our children, adequate medical care for all Americans, an end to discrimination against minorities and women, a job for all those able to work, and freedom from injustice and religious intolerance.

We live in a time of transition, an uneasy era which is likely to endure for the rest of this century. It will be a period of tensions both within nations and between nations — of competition for scarce resources, of social political and economic stresses and strains. During this period we may be tempted to abandon some of the time-honored principles and commitments which have been proven during the difficult times of past generations.

We must never yield to this temptation. Our American values are not luxuries but necessities — not the salt in our bread but the bread itself. Our common vision of a free and just society is our greatest source of cohesion at home and strength abroad — greater even than the bounty of our material blessings.

Remember these words:

"We hold these truths to be self-evident, that all men are created equal; that they are endowed by their creator with certain inalienable rights; that among these are life liberty and the pursuit of happiness."

This vision still grips the imagination of the world. But we know that democracy is always an unfinished creation. Each generation must renew its foundations. Each generation must rediscover the meaning of this hallowed vision in the light of its own modern challenges. For this generation, ours, life is nuclear survival; liberty is human rights; the pursuit of happiness is a planet whose resources are devoted to the physical and spiritual nourishment of its inhabitants.

During the next few days I will work hard to make sure that the transition from myself to the next president is a good one so that the American people are served well. And I will continue as I have the last 14 months to work hard and to pray for the lives and the well-being of the American hostages held in Iran. I can't predict yet what will happen, but I hope you will join me in my constant prayer for their freedom.

As I return home to the South where I was born and raised, I am looking forward to the opportunity to reflect and further to assess — I hope with accuracy — the circumstances of our times. I intend to give our new president my support, and I intend to work as a citizen, as I have worked in this office as president, for the values this nation was founded to secure.

Again, from the bottom of my heart, I want to express to you the gratitude I feel.

Thank you, fellow citizens, and farewell.

Chapter 6

Text and image sources, contributors, and licenses

6.1 Text

- **Jimmy Carter's Inaugural Address** *Source:* https://en.wikisource.org/wiki/Jimmy_Carter'{}s_Inaugural_Address?oldid=2848673 *Contributors:* Danny~enwikisource, Politicaljunkie, Pathosbot, JVbot, Kathleen.wright5, Billinghurst, Xxagile, 丸山珠亮, Dromioofephesus, SDrewthbot, The Lloigor and Anonymous: 6

- **Jimmy Carter's First State of the Union Address** *Source:* https://en.wikisource.org/wiki/Jimmy_Carter'{}s_First_State_of_the_Union_Address?oldid=4790997 *Contributors:* Politicaljunkie, Pathosbot, ZSBot, JVbot, Kathleen.wright5, SDrewthbot, Spydyspydy and Anonymous: 4

- **Jimmy Carter's Second State of the Union Address** *Source:* https://en.wikisource.org/wiki/Jimmy_Carter'{}s_Second_State_of_the_Union_Address?oldid=4790998 *Contributors:* Ezhiki, Politicaljunkie, Pathosbot, ZSBot, JVbot, Kathleen.wright5, SDrewthbot, George Orwell III, Spydyspydy and Anonymous: 4

- **Jimmy Carter's Third State of the Union Address** *Source:* https://en.wikisource.org/wiki/Jimmy_Carter'{}s_Third_State_of_the_Union_Address?oldid=4790999 *Contributors:* Politicaljunkie, Pathosbot, ZSBot, JVbot, Kathleen.wright5, SDrewthbot, Spydyspydy and Anonymous: 4

- **Jimmy Carter's Fourth State of the Union Address** *Source:* https://en.wikisource.org/wiki/Jimmy_Carter'{}s_Fourth_State_of_the_Union_Address?oldid=4791000 *Contributors:* Politicaljunkie, Pathosbot, Wikiwriter706, ZSBot, JVbot, Kathleen.wright5, SDrewthbot, George Orwell III, Spydyspydy and Anonymous: 5

- **1976 U.S. Presidential Debate - September 23** *Source:* https://en.wikisource.org/wiki/1976_U.S._Presidential_Debate_-_September_23?oldid=2190608 *Contributors:* Zhaladshar, Politicaljunkie, Pathosbot, Timeshifter, ZSBot, Ingram, Kathleen.wright5, SDrewthbot and Anonymous: 1

- **1976 U.S. Presidential Debate - October 6** *Source:* https://en.wikisource.org/wiki/1976_U.S._Presidential_Debate_-_October_6?oldid=4873240 *Contributors:* Zhaladshar, Politicaljunkie, Pathosbot, ZSBot, ResidentScholar, Kathleen.wright5, SDrewthbot and Anonymous: 1

- **1976 U.S. Presidential Debate - October 22** *Source:* https://en.wikisource.org/wiki/1976_U.S._Presidential_Debate_-_October_22?oldid=2190605 *Contributors:* Zhaladshar, Politicaljunkie, Pathosbot, ZSBot, Kathleen.wright5, SDrewthbot and Anonymous: 1

- **1980 U.S. Presidential Debate - October 28** *Source:* https://en.wikisource.org/wiki/1980_U.S._Presidential_Debate_-_October_28?oldid=4443504 *Contributors:* Zhaladshar, Politicaljunkie, Pathosbot, ZSBot, Phillipedison1891, Kathleen.wright5, SDrewthbot, George Orwell III, Dmartelo and Anonymous: 3

- **Jimmy Carter's First Presidential Nomination Acceptance Speech** *Source:* https://en.wikisource.org/wiki/Jimmy_Carter'{}s_First_Presidential_Nomination_Acceptance_Speech?oldid=2952172 *Contributors:* Politicaljunkie, TalBot, ZSBot, JVbot, Kathleen.wright5, Billinghurst, SDrewthbot and Anonymous: 1

- **Jimmy Carter's Second Presidential Nomination Acceptance Speech** *Source:* https://en.wikisource.org/wiki/Jimmy_Carter'{}s_Second_Presidential_Nomination_Acceptance_Speech?oldid=2952173 *Contributors:* Politicaljunkie, TalBot, ZSBot, JVbot, Kathleen.wright5, Billinghurst, SDrewthbot and Anonymous: 1

- **President Carter's Address to the Nation on Proposed National Energy Policy** *Source:* https://en.wikisource.org/wiki/President_Carter'{}s_Address_to_the_Nation_on_Proposed_National_Energy_Policy?oldid=2797299 *Contributors:* Billinghurst, SDrewthbot and George Orwell III

- **The Crisis of Confidence** *Source:* https://en.wikisource.org/wiki/The_Crisis_of_Confidence?oldid=5752925 *Contributors:* Politicaljunkie, Xenophon (bot), MrDolomite, TalBot, ZSBot, JVbot, Kendrick7, Billinghurst, Dromioofephesus, SDrewthbot, Mattisse, Simon Peter Hughes and Anonymous: 2

- **Jimmy Carter's Farewell Address** *Source:* https://en.wikisource.org/wiki/Jimmy_Carter'{}s_Farewell_Address?oldid=5669863 *Contributors:* Sherurcij, Politicaljunkie, Green Giant, MrDolomite, Az1568, TalBot, ZSBot, JVbot, Billinghurst, SDrewthbot and Anonymous: 4

6.2   Images

- **File:PD-icon.svg** *Source:* https://upload.wikimedia.org/wikipedia/commons/6/62/PD-icon.svg *License:* Public domain *Contributors:* Created by uploader. Based on similar symbols. *Original artist:* Various. See log. (Original SVG was based on File:PD-icon.png by Duesentrieb, which was based on Image:Red copyright.png by Rfl.)

- **File:US-GreatSeal-Obverse.svg** *Source:* https://upload.wikimedia.org/wikipedia/commons/5/5c/Great_Seal_of_the_United_States_%28obverse% 29.svg *License:* Public domain *Contributors:* Extracted from PDF version of *Our Flag*, available here (direct PDF URL here.) *Original artist:* U.S. Government

6.3   Content license